LINGUISTICALLY DIVERSE IMMIGRANT AND RESIDENT WRITERS

Transitions from High School to College

Edited by
Christina Ortmeier-Hooper
and Todd Ruecker

Routledge
Taylor & Francis Group

NEW YORK AND LONDON

First published 2017
by Routledge
711 Third Avenue, New York, NY 10017

and by Routledge
2 Park Square, Milton Park, Abingdon, Oxon, OX14 4RN

Routledge is an imprint of the Taylor & Francis Group, an Informa business

© 2017 Taylor & Francis

Library of Congress Cataloging-in-Publication Data
A catalog record for this title has been requested

ISBN: 978-1-138-12552-0 (hbk)
ISBN: 978-1-138-12553-7 (pbk)
ISBN: 978-1-315-64744-9 (ebk)

Typeset in ApexBembo
by Apex CoVantage, LLC

Printed and bound in the United States of America by Publishers Graphics, LLC on sustainably sourced paper.

CONTENTS

List of Figures   *viii*

List of Tables   *ix*

Preface   *x*

Acknowledgements   *xii*

1 Introduction: Paying Attention to Resident
   Multilingual Students   1
   Todd Ruecker and Christina Ortmeier-Hooper

PART I
Multilingual Writers in High Schools   **17**

2 Opportunity Gaps: Curricular Discontinuities across ESL,
   Mainstream, and College English   21
   Betsy Gilliland

3 The Common Core State Standards and Implications
   for Writing Instruction and Assessment for English
   Language Learners   36
   Luciana C. de Oliveira

4 Resident Multilingual Writers across a Secondary
Curriculum: Toward a Postmethod Approach 49
Sarah Henderson Lee

5 The Role of Social Networks and Social Support in
the Writing and College Planning of Multilingual
Urban Adolescents 63
Jennifer Shade Wilson

6 "I Don't Want to Be Special": English Language Learners
in Rural and Small-Town High Schools 82
Todd Ruecker

PART II
Transition and Disruption: Sponsors,
Programs, Politics, and Policies **95**

7 Promises and Limitations of Literacy Sponsors in
Resident Multilingual Youths' Transitions to
Postsecondary Schooling 99
Amanda Kibler

8 Literacy Sponsorship in Upward Bound: The Impact
of (De)segregation and Peer Dynamics 117
Shauna Wight

9 Digital DREAMS: The Rhetorical Power of Online
Resources for DREAM Act Activists 130
Genevieve García de Müeller

10 Bengali-Speaking Multilingual Writers in Transition
into Community College 143
Ruhma Choudhury and Leigh Garrison-Fletcher

11 Immigrant Mosaics: Advancing Multilingual Education
in Canadian Postsecondary Settings 157
Julia Kiernan

PART III
Resident Multilinguals in First-Year Composition: Reimagining Faculty Development, Curriculum, and Administration

169

12 When the First Language You Use Is Not English:
Challenges of Language Minority College
Composition Students 173
Patti Wojahn, Beth Brunk-Chavez, Kate Mangelsdorf,
Mais Al-Khateeb, Karen Téllez-Trujillo, Laurie Churchill,
and Cathilia Flores

13 Re-Envisioning Faculty Development When
Multilingualism Is the New Norm: Conversations
on First-Year Writing at a Hispanic-Serving University 189
Kimberly Harrison

14 Transitional Access and Integrated Complexity:
Interconnecting People, Research, and Media for
Transitional Writing Students 202
Randall Monty, Karen Holt, and Colin Charlton

15 Teaching Multilingualism, Teaching Identification: Embracing
Resident Multilingualism as a Curricular Paradigm 216
Tarez Samra Graban

16 Internationalization and the Place of Resident ML Students:
Identifying Points of Leverage and Advocacy 229
Christina Ortmeier-Hooper, Dana Ferris, Richard Lizotte,
Patricia Portanova, and Margi Wald

List of Contributors 237
Index 243

FIGURES

2.1   Mr. Richards' Peer Response Sheet   28

3.1   A Developmental Trajectory and Learner Pathway of Genres for the CCSS   45

4.1   Power Relations in the COB Model   52

5.1   Percentages of Network Contacts by Domain   69

5.2   Percentages of Writing Activities ($n = 98$) on Which Participants Reported Interacting with Specific Individuals   70

7.1   Resident Multilingual Writers' Literacy Sponsors in Postsecondary Transitions   103

10.1   Bengali LENS Pre-test and Post-test Results for the Experimental Group   152

TABLES

2.1	Discourses of Writing	24
4.1	Participants	50
5.1	Participants' Demographic Information	66
5.2	Participants' Reading Efficiency Skills	67
5.3	Percentage of Received Social Support by Network Domain	72
7.1	Participant Settings	102
8.1	Demographic Profiles of LM Participants	120
12.1	Rates of Using a Language Other Than English among 197 Students Whose First Language Was Not English	176
12.2	Selection of Best Language for Various Purposes among Those Whose First Language Was Not English	177

PREFACE

The resident multilingual student population in the United States and other countries continues to grow. Resident bilingual and immigrant students in U.S. secondary schools often face difficult challenges as they attempt to transition toward and succeed in higher education; this collection is particularly concerned with the ways that writing and literacy support, writing experiences, and writing instruction impact these students' transitions and educational options. In recent years, the charge led by writing specialists working with resident populations in secondary and college settings has been largely overshadowed by higher education's focus on international students, colleges' moves toward global partnerships and online learning, and college composition's growing interests in internationalization. All the while, resident bilingual and immigrant students, drawn by promises of a better life for themselves and their families, are trying to enter and succeed in higher education in larger numbers.

This collection draws attention to the various contexts and associated experiences of resident bilingual and immigrant student writers in secondary schools, transitional programs, community colleges, and first-year college composition. The chapters include new research from scholars working in a variety of disciplinary contexts (writing and literacy studies, education, and TESOL/applied linguistics). Authors in this volume represent a variety of institutional contexts, including several Hispanic-Serving Institutions, schools of education, and urban community colleges. Chapters provide readers with rich understandings of how high school literacy contexts, policies like the proposed DREAM Act and the Common Core State Standards, bridge programs like Upward Bound, community colleges, and curricula redesign in first-year composition courses designed to recognize increasing linguistic diversity of student populations affect the success of resident multilingual (ML) students transitioning from high school to college. Authors in this

volume write from deep within secondary school settings, examining educational policy, assessment and curricular practices, and student-teacher interactions. These forays into U.S. and Canadian high schools capture portraits of schools and adolescent writers as they consider postsecondary opportunities. For readers from the college setting, this volume provides rich discussion and descriptions of the kinds of secondary school experiences, constraints, and initiatives that shape resident bilingual and immigrant students coming into college composition classrooms.

In Chapter 1, the editors introduce and contextualize the contributions in this collection. The editors discuss the challenges and concerns facing resident bilingual and immigrant student writers that have led to this collection. The chapters that follow are then divided into three thematic sections. *Part I*: Multilingual Writers in High Schools includes chapters focused on educational policy in U.S. secondary schools and students' experiences as writers in these contexts. *Part II*: Transition and Disruption: Sponsors, Programs, Politics, and Policies includes chapters focused on students in the process of making successful transitions to college, some aided by bridge programs like Upward Bound. *Part III*: Resident Multilinguals in First-Year Composition: Reimagining Faculty Development, Curriculum, and Administration includes chapters focused on how program instructors and administrators can undertake curricular and structural changes in order to create stronger opportunities and points of access for resident ML students.

Each section of the book includes a brief introduction to key concepts and discussions that surround the work of the authors in that section and share some of the broader implications of these conversations. These section introductions also aim to bridge the gaps that exist between K–12 and college-level writing studies and to introduce new stakeholders (teachers, graduate students, program administrators) to the larger contexts, constraints, and possibilities made evident in the chapters.

ACKNOWLEDGEMENTS

We'd like to thank the contributors to this collection for their dedication to supporting linguistically diverse students in a variety of contexts. We also thank them for believing in this collection from the beginning and their persistence in revising chapters throughout the process. We would also like to thank Naomi Silverman, our Routledge editor, Eli Hinkel, the ESL & Applied Linguistics Professional Series editor, and Brianna Pennella, our Routledge editorial assistant. Their encouragement, feedback, support, and guidance throughout this process helped us to bring this project to fruition.

Christina would like to thank Todd for saying "yes" to this project, for his talent as a writer and co-editor, and for his passion in furthering the discussion on resident students in his own research and publications. She would also like to thank colleagues that have encouraged her scholarship in second language writing and immigrant adolescent youth, including Kerry Anne Enright, Dana Ferris, Deborah Crusan, Michelle Cox, Paul Kei Matsuda, Linda Harklau, and Yasko Kanno. She also thanks her supportive colleagues at the University of New Hampshire, including Cristy Beemer, Thomas Newkirk, Alecia Magnifico, Soo Hyon Kim, and Marcos del Hierro. Finally, she thanks her husband, Tom, and her sons—Sean, Zachary, and Johnathan—for their patience, love, and continued encouragement.

Todd would like to thank Christina for initially approaching him with the idea of this collection and asking him to be part of this important project. He would also like to thank those who have provided mentorship throughout his early years as an academic, including Kate Mangelsdorf, Beth Brunk-Chavez, and Yasko Kanno. He'd also like to thank family and friends who have supported him in this work, including his partner Brooke Cholka and their schnauzers, who have put up

with him spending lots of time away from home to conduct research on literacy instruction in rural schools.

Finally, we dedicate this book to the resident multilingual students in U.S. and Canadian high schools, bridge programs, and colleges who are the center of this book and who are constantly seeking the best for themselves and their families, despite working in a system that too often ignores and marginalizes them.

1

INTRODUCTION

Paying Attention to Resident Multilingual Students

Todd Ruecker and Christina Ortmeier-Hooper

"How do writing experiences influence the postsecondary pathways of resident multilingual students?" This is the question that guides this collection. In the past two decades, the scholarship on second language writing and multilingual writers has grown exponentially. Yet, the emphasis in much of this work still remains on international students studying English writing in postsecondary colleges and universities. In contrast, then, this edited volume is concerned with the high school experiences and postsecondary transitions of resident bilingual or immigrant youth. To date, there are over 5.1 million students in U.S. schools who are identified as English language learners or limited English proficient (ELL or LEP, i.e., considered eligible for English language support services). In addition, Latino students, who are often bilingual and writing across languages, represent almost 50% of the K–12 student population (Razfar & Simon, 2011). Yet despite these statistics, resident immigrant and multilingual writers are significantly underrepresented in higher education (Kanno & Harklau, 2012; Ornelas & Solorzano, 2004; Razfar & Simon, 2011).

Over the past 30 years, L2 writing scholars like Tony Silva, Ilona Leki, and Paul Kei Matsuda have drawn our attention to growing populations of multilingual writers and led the development of the field of L2 writing, one that has explored a variety of ways to serve these students in both ESL and mainstream writing classrooms while critiquing existing structures. While interested in the needs of all students, we are especially concerned about perhaps one of the most marginalized populations in contemporary U.S. society and schooling systems, resident ML writers. We are continually struck by how many of the resident ML student writers, ages 18 to 21—those not in college, those enrolled in GED programs—remain off the radar screen of writing scholars and researchers. Both L1 and L2 college writing teachers and researchers seldom discuss the fate of resident ML writers

who do not make it onto college campuses. However, it is the ethical responsibility of college writing teachers and scholars to understand this population and how to facilitate their success in postsecondary education, one of the surest ways to a better life for them and their families.

In previous work (e.g., Ortmeier-Hooper & Enright, 2011; Ruecker, 2014), we have argued for the need for L1 and L2 college writing specialists to pay attention to what happens before college, basing this argument in the ethical responsibility to facilitate student success as well as more pragmatic concerns such as knowing the skills students bring to writing classrooms and answering the concerns of external bodies like legislatures and accreditation agencies. With the rise of the Common Core State Standards, U.S. secondary schools are undergoing a rapid change in their curriculum, premised on the idea of "college-readiness." It is vital that postsecondary educators know what changes are taking place, so that they can be prepared to address the needs of differently prepared populations. In knowing more about what happens in secondary schools, college writing specialists might be better prepared to partake in discussions around initiatives like the CCSS among others, potentially having more influence in these conversations. Bilingual resident, immigrant, and refugee students live in towns and cities that often border our college campuses; they attend local high schools and work part-time in local businesses, participate in community events, and play on school sport teams. Yet so many of these young people remain unseen by those in positions of power within higher education and those conducting research in L1 and L2 writing studies. We acknowledge that there are reasons for some of this invisibility—in part, the separation between K–12 and college writing teacher preparation perpetuates a false sense of division between the students and our interests in them. In higher education, resident ML students can remain anonymous, unmarked by the TOEFL exam scores that identify international multilingual students. Resident ML students do not generate the tuition dollars or publicity that are often associated with the growing numbers of international students studying in U.S. higher education. We see a great irony in the fact that as more and more universities and colleges become invested in the linguistic needs of newly recruited international students, the situations and conditions of resident ML student writers are often lost in these growing conversations on multilingualism, transnationalism, internationalization, and second language writing. At the same time, we see more instances of higher education institutions being called upon to raise retention and graduation rate. Resident ML writers reside in *these* discussions and data, and L1 and L2 writing researchers should be prepared to be called upon and respond as these conversations unfold.

In 2012, Kanno and Harklau published a landmark collection, *Linguistic Minority Students Go to College: Preparation, Access, and Persistence*, in which they illustrated the various obstacles—from poverty to testing to financial aid literacy—that impeded U.S. linguistic minority students as they strove to enter higher education. In many ways, our collection follows the pathway forged by Kanno and Harklau

(2012) and others (e.g., Blanton, 2005; Hirano, 2014). Yet, here we consider the role of writing, writing instruction, writing assessment, and college composition programs in the education trajectories of these young adults. It is hardly radical to claim that writing well is a threshold skill that serves a gate-closing and gate-opening function for academic achievement and opportunity. What may, however, prove surprising to readers is how often writing serves as one of the conditions that can impede or facilitate school-age multilingual writers' advancement into college-level academic tracks, guidance, and assistance (Blanton, 2005; Enright, 2006; Fu, 1995; Ortmeier-Hooper, 2013).

Writing instruction, teacher preparation, writing standards, and writing assessments play a significant role in whether immigrant and resident bilingual students are deemed "good enough" and moved toward the pipeline for college and university degrees. The numbers of English language learners and linguistic minority students moving into postsecondary degree programs remains low, despite the fact that the numbers of U.S. high school students attending college continues to grow (U.S. Bureau of Labor, 2014). Only about 18% of English language learners make it to four-year colleges, and "roughly half of English learners never participate in any type of post-secondary education" (Kanno & Harklau, 2012). As Kanno and Cromley (2013) noted, "higher education, especially 4-year college education, is the pinnacle of [a] system of unequal power distribution" (p. 93). We have brought together the authors in this volume to disrupt that "unequal power distribution" and lay open the factors and conditions that surround resident multilingual writers as they strive to "make it" to college and through college composition coursework.

This collection strives to reinvigorate discussion on resident ML students and to bring awareness to the population of ML students as part of our institutional trends and interests in globalization. As L1 and L2 writing teachers, administrators, and researchers, we have a stake in this conversation. From a social justice standpoint, we hope to ignite further research and work that opens doors for the resident students that make it to our campuses and an interest in bettering the educational trajectories of those who do not. The essays in this collection, therefore, provide a careful and rigorous consideration of culturally and linguistically diverse student writers in U.S. high schools and their transitions into college. In this introduction, we begin to map this complex terrain for readers in order to provide a context for the chapters that follow.

Discussing Transitions and Terms

While working on this volume, we noted the intricate juxtaposition between *transition* and *disruption* when it came to the educational trajectories of these students. In short, one cannot be considered without the other. *Transition* reminded us of pathways and movement forward, while *disruption* suggested drastic change or destruction of a process. These two conditions are often intricately linked and intertwined in students' experiences and writing opportunities. A student takes

a few steps forward followed by a few steps backward—for example, a disruptive situation that derails a student's course but then also fuels a student's drive and tenacity to push forward. As the chapters in this book suggest, changes interrupt and sometimes suspend student writers' agency, motivation, and impetus for continuing their education. Disruptions for resident ML writers have personal and academic consequences, but they also have economic ones. For example, a recent comparative study of college and non-college graduates found that "on virtually every measure of economic well-being and career attainment—from personal earnings to job satisfaction to the share employed full time—young college graduates are outperforming their peers with less education" (Pew, 2014). Clearly, there are economic and social costs for individuals, employers, and communities when large numbers of U.S. resident and immigrant multilingual students do not reach higher education.

In L1 and L2 writing studies, scholars and teachers often consider *transition* and *disruption* in dialogue with the concept of transfer, which considers how students develop skills in one context and apply those skills in new contexts (e.g., Yancey, Robertson, & Taczak, 2014). Here, we are concerned about the transfer of writing skills for resident ML writers, but we are also deeply interested in the ecological and social factors that influence the kinds of writing instruction, mentoring, and writing histories that resident immigrants and bilinguals carry with them as they move across social space and time in pursuit of their educational aims. It seems necessary, even crucial, to consider the ways in which ML student writers attempt to navigate their pathways into postsecondary institutions, for the simple reason that so much evidence suggests that these students' experiences are not always transitional—leading successfully across one institutional boundary into the next—but instead, they often are tenuous and disruptive.

Finally, a word about the terms we use to discuss students. Spack (1997), one of the early researchers in second language writing, once wrote: "[Second language] writers are remarkably diverse, and thus no one label can accurately capture their heterogeneity" (p. 765). Like Spack, we recognize that labeling students can be a "hazardous enterprise" and that such labels place us as teachers and authors "in the powerful position of rhetorically constructing their identities" (Spack, 1997, p. 765). As Cox, Jordan, Schwartz, and Ortmeier-Hooper (2010) have argued, in secondary schools, as well as in higher education, the labels and categories used to describe multilingual students can quickly "fall in and out of favor based on a number of factors from political correctness to educational policy" (p. xv). The past two decades have been filled with the comings and goings of various terms (e.g., Generation 1.5, ESOL student) used to describe the students in this book, terms that we have engaged with in other works (Ortmeier-Hooper, 2008; Ruecker, 2011). Recently, many changes in labels have reflected a broader understanding of the gifts and resources that linguistically and culturally diverse students bring to our classrooms. For example, although L2 writing is often used to define a field of study, many scholars in this area now discuss students as bilingual or multilingual (ML)

writers, acknowledging that they may have literacy experiences in two or more languages. In research studies situated in higher education and applied linguistics, these students can also be discussed as "linguistic minorities," which Kanno and Harklau (2012) defined as those students who speak a language other than English at home. In K–12 contexts, we often read about these students as "English language learners (ELLs)" and "limited English proficient (LEP)." When we and authors in this volume have drawn upon sources using these terms, we have kept the original language used by authors and provided definitions for readers.

Readers will find that authors in this collection writing from K–12 perspectives and from the disciplinary perspective of education/literacy studies may use the term *English language learner* (*ELL*) when considering students' experiences in U.S. K–12 schools. Authors writing from the perspectives of college composition and examining these students' experiences at the postsecondary level tend to refer to these students as resident multilingual (ML) writers or linguistic minority students.

We recognize that all terms "mask the complexity" of these students, their language backgrounds, and their identities (Cox, Jordan, Schwartz, & Ortmeier-Hooper, 2010). Similarly, labels inherently obscure and obfuscate the different experiences and circumstances that define and impact U.S. resident multilingual writers. One of the goals of this collection is to move beyond the labels and bring a stronger sense of focus to the inherent complexity that complicates and impedes these student writers as they attempt to move from high school into postsecondary schooling. In the remaining part of this introductory chapter, we lay the groundwork for the chapters that follow by exploring what is known about both the curricular and extracurricular lives of these students.

Students and Their Experiences

It's a total[ly] different environment. If you don't adjust, you're just gonna stay behind.
Bianca, age 18, Texas, on adjusting to college

Bianca, quoted above, is one of millions of resident ML students progressing through the U.S. educational system with aspirations to attend college. Bianca's story, like the stories of many of these students, is one of ups and downs. Although her mother was deported when Bianca was 17, Bianca (a U.S. citizen) continued to be successful in high school and matriculate to college. While she took college classes, she continued to care for three younger siblings. On writing, she noted a clear difference as she struggled to perform to her college instructors' expectations: "In high school, we used to write papers but not like this type of papers, you know? Long and research. Like in high school, we didn't have to research like all, a lot of articles. And cite work, reference page. That's really different. I think high school should start teaching that."

Five and a half million students are identified as English language learners or limited English proficient in U.S. schools. States like California, Texas, Arizona,

and New York have the greatest numbers of multilingual students in K–12 schools, but across the country, the numbers of immigrant and multilingual writers continues to grow, even in rural areas (e.g., Bustamante, Brown, & Irby, 2010; Passel, Cohn, & Hugo Lopez, 2011; see Ruecker, this volume). Similar trends exist in parts of Canada and other English-dominant countries (see Wilson and Kiernan in this volume for discussions on immigrant ML youth in Canada). In Canada, one in five children in the schools in an immigrant, and as in the United States, multilingual immigrant children are the fastest-growing demographic sector in Canadian primary and secondary schools (Milnes & Cheng, 2008; Queen's University, 2010). What seems to be universal for all these students is that entering college or university is a challenge, and even for those who gain access, many struggle to be successful and complete their degree programs.

Bianca is one such case. Bianca's first year in college was, in many ways, quite successful, and she ended the year with a GPA around 3.0. She was supported through the College Assistance Migrant Program (CAMP), which provided financial assistance, a learning community, required tutoring, and other activities throughout her first year. Despite this support and her achievements, Bianca had a difficult first year. She had constant worries of supporting her siblings, attended school full time, and struggled with the limited writing preparation she had received in high school. As her first year ended, the support of the CAMP program largely disappeared and Bianca began to struggle to meet the demands of college, doubting her ambitions. When increasing familial obligations and more challenging coursework came her way, she faltered and dropped out. Her transition into higher education was disrupted. Research suggests that she is not alone in facing these challenges.

Studies on the access and retention of English language learners and ML student writers are often incorporated into larger studies of first-generation college students and minority students. Often such studies focus on socioeconomic backgrounds, race, and ethnicity; rarely do such studies consider linguistic backgrounds and literacy, and ELLs are often not considered as a separate group for analysis. As a result, Kanno and Cromley (2013) reported that little is known about ELLs' college-going patterns. Studies on English learners and language minority students reaching higher education offer some sobering statistics about the plight of these ML writers: only 12% of English language learners and 25% of language minority students completed bachelors' degrees within eight years after high school graduation (Kanno & Harklau, 2012).

Writing and Social Realities of ML Students in U.S. High Schools

How U.S. educational policy defines English language learners illustrates the ways in which this "label" extends rather broadly across a range of multi-language users and the extent to which writing and reading competency are embedded in this definition. In the U.S., federal law requires that all schools provide services to

students who are speakers of languages other than English. According to Title IX (ED, 2015), a person is "limited English proficient,"

(A) who is aged 3 through 21; (B) who is enrolled or preparing to enroll in an elementary school or secondary school; (C) (i) who was not born in the United States or whose native language is a language other than English; (ii) (I) who is a Native American or Alaska Native, or a native resident of the outlying areas; and (II) who comes from an environment where a language other than English has had a significant impact on the individual's level of English language proficiency; or (iii) who is migratory, whose native language is a language other than English, and who comes from an environment where a language other than English is dominant; and (D) whose difficulties in speaking, reading, writing, or understanding the English language may be sufficient to deny the individual—(i) the ability to meet the State's proficient level of achievement on State assessments described in section 1111(b)(3); (ii) the ability to successfully achieve in classrooms where the language of instruction is English; or (iii) the opportunity to participate fully in society.

What No Child Left Behind (NCLB) and other educational policies often fail to acknowledge in their definitions of ELLs are the vast number of factors that impact the level of their writing proficiency and how their secondary writing experiences impact their expectations for college. Their abilities and performances are highly dictated by their experiences in high schools. As Yancey, Robertson, and Taczak (2014) have noted in their work on transfer from high school to college, "students do bring to college what the school culture has emphasized" and "prior knowledge influences new knowledge" (p. 12).

As Leki, Cumming, and Silva (2010) have pointed out, "Of all the settings where L2 writing exists, high school is the most fraught and complex" (p. 17). For one, there is a pronounced level of variability in the kinds of experiences that resident ML students encounter across different U.S. schools, geographic regions, school districts, states, and individual teachers' classrooms. State funding, teacher preparedness, student preparedness, external student support systems, school climate, socioeconomic factors, city/town demographics, class size, school performance/annual yearly progress (AYP), etc. all play a role in the kinds of academic and literacy experiences that ELLs have in the high school contexts (Ortmeier-Hooper & Enright, 2011; Ruecker, 2015). We also know that a single teacher within a given school can shift and inspire the trajectory of a whole set of ML students (Harklau, 1994b). ML students in high schools, like so many adolescents, are also impacted by their own struggles with independence, questions of social identity, and peer relationships (Suárez-Orozco, Suárez-Orozco, & Todorova, 2008). It is these aspects of variability within the U.S. high school setting that makes studies of adolescent multilingual writers so complex.

Of all four language skills (reading, listening, speaking, and writing), writing is often the most difficult for adolescent MLs. Research on second language acquisition

suggests that academic literacy skills, which include academic writing, can take five to seven years to master, if not longer (e.g., Cummins, 1981). Writing in a second language is a highly demanding, cognitive skill, and research suggests that second language writers often need more time to compose, need more time for invention, have fewer opportunities to revise, write shorter texts, and display more errors than those writing in a first language (Silva, 1993). The difficulty of writing in a second language, witnessed by my many teachers, coupled with traditional pedagogical perspectives on English language development, has meant that much of ML students' learning experiences in U.S. classrooms have focused on reading, listening, and speaking over writing (Harklau, 1994a; Larsen, 2013). These pedagogical perspectives have drawn heavily from early research from children's first language acquisition studies, which focused on the acquisition of speaking and listening comprehension, rather than literacy. The rationale for emphasis on speaking, reading, and listening often heard from teachers is that ELL students could not write extensively without extensive foundational knowledge in phonetics, vocabulary, reading, grammar, and sentence structures (Harklau, 1994a). Although current research dispels these myths, this "writing-last" teaching approach continues to be a strong undercurrent in the education of many English language learners and resident bilinguals in U.S. schools. For many ELL writers, the result is that writing practice and instruction is often limited to sentence writing, paragraphs, and grammatical worksheets with the promise that once they master these, they will be allowed to write more (Enright, 2010; Fu, 1995, 2009; Harklau, 1994a; Ortmeier-Hooper, 2013).

Some defining challenges impacting the pathways of resident multilingual students moving through U.S. high schools and into college include the following:

- **A narrowing curriculum for ML students.** Although language acquisition and literacy experts like Snow, Burns, and Griffin (1998) claimed that "being able to read and write in two languages confers numerous intellectual, cultural, economic, and social benefits," educational policies at the federal and local level within the U.S. ended many bilingual and dual language programs by the late 1990s, and even those programs that remained tended to emphasize English proficiency over bilingualism (Fu & Matoush, 2006; Moll, Saez, & Dworin, 2001). Standards movements and national education legislation, like the No Child Left Behind Act, added new complexities (e.g., more state-mandated testing, curricular mandates, and annual yearly progress reports on specific student populations) with far-reaching implications for the education of resident ESL and bilingual students in K–12 schools. Disturbingly, ELLs were largely an afterthought in development of the Common Core, meriting only a brief mention in the Standards (see de Oliveira, this volume, for more on this).
- **Teacher preparedness.** Teacher preparedness also plays a role in the outcomes of resident ML writers in U.S. schools, which may in part stem from disciplinary divisions of labor (see Matsuda, 2006). Few high school teachers

in North America are trained to work with second language writers (Ortmeier-Hooper & Enright, 2011). Most ESL teachers are not required to take a course dedicated to teaching second language writing (Larsen, 2013). Even for those teachers who intuitively sense that ML and ELL writers may need additional support and specific pedagogical interventions, the time and planning required for such adjustments can feel daunting and unsupported. As Roberge, Losey, and Wald (2016) note, teachers need concrete curricular ideas and "seek specific strategies, techniques, practices, and activities that go beyond a generic notion of 'good teaching'" (p. 2).

- **Academic tracking.** Most high schools in the United States have some tiered system that places students into different ability groupings and academic tracks (i.e., Basic, General, Honors, AP, etc.). ELL students are often placed in lower-level academic tracks when they enter U.S. high schools (Fu, 1995, 2009; Harklau, 1994b; Ortmeier-Hooper, 2010). ELL and bilingual students often find themselves "ghetto-ized" into two types of academic tracks in U.S. schools: (1) ESL courses/tracks, and (2) general/mainstream lower-level academic tracks. For some students, the ELL classroom has a trained ELL writing teacher who creates a safe environment for them to experiment with language, writing, peer review, and revision (Harklau, 1994a). But even when ESL classrooms are imbued with these kinds of rich literacy experiences, the separate classrooms also segregate students from the wider monolingual, English-speaking school community. The fallout from segregation is that ELL students are often "invisible" to many mainstream teachers, administrators, guidance counselors, and monolingual students in their schools.

Beyond the academic factors (and the politics surrounding them), there are a number of other challenges that resident ML students face as they pursue a college education.

- **Poverty.** We mentioned earlier in this introduction that there are economic consequences when resident ML students are unable to enter or attain college education. But these economic and educational challenges are often cyclical, stemming from poverty, which is a defining characteristic of many resident ML students' lives. For instance, the Pew Research Center (2014) found, in an analysis of the Census American Community Survey, that 66% of ELLs lived in families that were below 200% of the poverty line, a number that was only 37% among non-ELL youths. In part because of the declining buying power of Pell Grants, resident ML students tend to choose community college, where the funding goes further (Fry, 2011; Hassel & Giordano, 2013; Ruecker, 2015). But the completion and transfer rates to four-year degree programs for many ML students are dismal.
- **Work responsibilities.** Many linguistic minority students from lower-income families are anxious about the costs of college and the procedures

for applying for loans and scholarships, and are unsure about their eligibility. Consequently, they are reluctant to take on loans (Ruecker, 2015), preferring to work additional hours to make up for the cost differential. They may also need to work in order to contribute to their family's income or to help offset the costs of their own college-related expenses. Working, especially in jobs that are off-campus or unrelated to school/university work-study programs, can lead to documented concerns with lower persistence, difficult work-school balances, and poorer academic achievement among lower-income, linguistic minority secondary and college students (Astin, 1997; Marsh & Kleitman, 2005).

• **Family responsibilities.** Resident ML students often have a strong connection to family, which can both support and hinder student success. For example, the largest population of resident ML students in the United States are Latinos, who often place great importance on the cultural and traditional value of *familismo* (Sy & Romero, 2008; Vega, 1990). Sy and Romero (2008) explained this idea: "In contrast to the values of individuality and independence emphasized in dominant U.S. culture, familismo requires an individual family member to put the needs of the family first, even if it means making personal sacrifices" (p. 214). Such sacrifices include attending a less competitive college closer to home, taking care of siblings, and working extra hours to support the family.

Despite these many challenges, it is important to note that ML students possess a variety of strengths, which are unfortunately largely ignored by educational institutions. Yosso (2005) explored the way that students drew on a variety of sources of capital in themselves and their communities (aspirational, familial, social, navigational, resistant, and linguistic) to support their transitions between home and the classroom. Elsewhere, Oropeza, Varghese, and Kanno (2010) and Ruecker (2015) and drawn on Yosso's (2005) model to explore the workings of this capital in particular students' lives. Harklau and McClanahan (2012) did similar work, noting how factors like a student's religiosity, traditionally strong in Latino communities, can contribute to the student's success. This collection aims to give voice to the disruptions, but also to the factors that contribute to the success of student journeys.

Fewer Options for Higher Education

In general, resident ML students are more prevalent at traditionally more affordable public institutions of higher education, a divide exacerbated by the continually declining value of Pell Grants from an all-time high in the 1970s. With cost an important consideration among resident ML students seeking postsecondary education, it is perhaps unsurprising that linguistic minority students are overrepresented at two-year colleges (e.g., Nuñez & Sparks, 2012).

Community colleges offer a variety of advantages for resident ML students. They may meet students' career plans more closely because they typically offer an opportunity to pursue associate degrees in a number of professional areas and, for those students interested, eventually transfer into bachelor's degree programs. Students and families often see community colleges as more affordable and flexible, and they generally allow students to attend college closer to home, which helps students maintain family ties. As Ruecker (2015) reported elsewhere, students may also value community colleges because of their smaller class sizes and the perception of easier classes, making the transition to college smoother for students who may have not received adequate academic preparation in high school. Finally, community colleges have traditionally been more welcoming of underprepared students as four-year institutions have sometimes pushed their entire developmental curriculum to community colleges or have become more selective as they seek to improve their own retention and graduation rates.

However, there are also concerns surrounding resident ML students' inclination to begin at community colleges. Recent studies suggest that the transfer rates from two-year to four-year colleges are low, with Bradburn, Hurst, and Peng (2001) reporting that of the 71% of two-year college students expecting to complete a BA degree or higher, only 36% actually transferred to a four-year institution. Of particular concern for linguistic minority students, Almon (2010), Kanno and Cromley (2015), and Razfar and Simon (2011) have noted that ELL students with intentions to transfer are even less likely than their non-ELL counterparts to transfer from a two-year to a four-year college. For instance, Razfar and Simon (2011) found that "Less than 5% overall and only 7.3% of the anticipating transfer students ever enrolled in transfer-level English composition" (p. 612). Students dreaming of attending medical or law school or becoming engineers may find their dreams cut short if they are unable to move beyond the two-year degree programs; many resident ML students are unaware of these statistics and are counseled, beginning in high school, that community colleges are the same as four-year colleges or even more bluntly told that four-year colleges are out of reach for them.

How the Book Was Developed

Neither of us would be involved with this project if it weren't for our own transitions and encounters with students along the way. As editors we were guided by our own interactions and research on ML writers in U.S. high schools, local communities, and colleges.

As a former secondary school ELL teacher, Christina has worked with resident ML students on reading and writing skills for close to twenty years. Firsthand, she witnessed the aspirations of these youths as they joyously considered the options of college in 8th and 9th grade and the transitions of these same students as they encountered the often more difficult realities of entering college and college composition classrooms. However, she also hears stories from students who

had aspirations of becoming doctors and lawyers but found themselves placed in lower-level academic tracks, where social pressures and anonymity often led them to question those aspirations and their intellectual capacities. Many would amend their dreams. Aspirations of becoming a medical nurse or pharmacist transformed to the completion of a ten-month for-profit program leading to a far lower-paying position as a licensed nursing assistant.

Todd has taught English in a variety of environments, ranging from an elite school for Russian expats in Prague to an underfunded public high school in Chile to three different public universities in the United States. From these experiences as well as work studying the transitions of Latina and Latino students from high school to community college and university on the U.S.-Mexico border, he has learned firsthand how educational institutions vary greatly and how students' lives outside the classroom differ just as much. Like Christina, he has heard positive stories of resident multilingual students achieving success against huge odds; however, he has also heard stories of such students concentrated in high schools where instruction is dominated by test preparation or stories of students with the potential for success held back in remedial programs. Our shared experiences led us to this project.

As editors, we have approached this volume from a sociolinguistic justice (Bucholtz et al., 2014) and activist stance. Chapters in this collection explore writing issues, but these are all social justice issues that are deeply tied to socioeconomic concerns, access and power, and student agency. This collection serves as a call to action to those in the fields of L1 and L2 writing, applied linguistics, and teacher education. We contend that the study of resident and immigrant bilingual student writers is critical for increased social *justice* and social change. These are writing and language issues, but they are also social justice issues that compel us to think and act more resolutely to develop ways to increase the numbers of immigrant and resident bilingual students gaining admissions to our colleges and universities, and the numbers that are successfully completing their writing requirements and degrees at these institutions.

Contributing authors were asked to consider the kinds of programs and interventions that help multilingual writers to succeed, but also to identify transitional moments and factors that lead to disruption in students' educational trajectory as they attempted to move out of secondary schools and into colleges and universities. We were particularly interested in research that described how writing expectations and conditions for instruction, as well as the ways ML students were labeled or tracked, would hinder or facilitate transitions between institutions.

Content in This Volume

The chapters in this collection include contributions from scholars working in a variety of disciplinary contexts (writing and literacy studies, education, and TESOL/applied linguistics) to report on the experiences of students engaging in

successful and unsuccessful transitions as they write themselves across different institutional contexts and into various educational trajectories. Authors in this volume write from deep within secondary school settings, examining educational policy, assessment and curricular practices, and student-teacher interactions. These forays into U.S. and Canadian high schools capture portraits of schools and adolescent writers as they consider postsecondary opportunities. For readers from the college writing setting, our goal is to provide rich discussion and descriptions of the kinds of secondary school experiences, constraints, and initiatives that shape resident bilingual and immigrant students coming into college composition classrooms.

The collection is divided into three thematic sections. *Part I*: Multilingual Writers in High Schools includes chapters focused on educational policy in U.S. secondary schools and students' experiences as writers in these contexts. *Part II*: Transition and Disruption: Sponsors, Programs, Politics, and Policies includes chapters focused on students in the process of making successful transitions to college, some aided by bridge programs like Upward Bound. *Part III*: Resident Multilinguals in First-Year Composition: Reimagining Faculty Development, Curriculum, and Administration includes chapters focused on how program instructors and administrators can undertake curricular and structural changes in order to create stronger opportunities and points of access for resident ML students. Section introductions also aim to bridge the gaps that exist between K–12 and college-level writing studies and to introduce new stakeholders (teachers, graduate students, program administrators) to the larger contexts, constraints, and possibilities made evident in the chapters.

Bibliography

Almon, C. (2010). English language learner engagement and retention in a community college setting. Retrieved from ProQuest. 3408684.

Astin, A. W. (1997). *What matters in college?: Four critical years revisited*. San Francisco: Jossey-Bass.

Blanton, L. L. (2005). Student, interrupted: A tale of two would-be writers. *Journal of Second Language Writing, 14*(2), 105–121.

Bradburn, E. M., Hurst, D. G., & Peng, S. S. (2001). *Community college transfer rates to 4-year institutions using alternative definitions of transfer*. Washington, DC: National Center for Education Statistics. Retrieved from http://nces.ed.gov/pubs2001/2001197.pdf

Bucholtz, M., Lopez, A., Mojarro, A., Skapoulli, E., VanderStouwe, C., & Warner-Garcia, S. (2014). Sociolinguistic justice in the schools: Student researchers as linguistic experts. *Language and Linguistics Compass, 8*(4), 144–157.

Bustamante, R. M., Brown, G., & Irby, B. J. (2010). Advocating for English language learners: U.S. teacher leadership in rural Texas schools. In K. A. Schafft & A. Y. Jackson (Eds.), *Rural education for the twenty-first century* (pp. 232–252). University Park, PA: Penn State Press.

Cox, M., Jordan, J., Schwartz, G. G., & Ortmeier-Hooper, C. (Eds.) (2010). *Reinventing identities in second language writing*. Urbana, IL: NCTE.

Cummins, J. (1981). Age on arrival and immigrant second language learning in Canada: A reassessment. *Applied Linguistics, 2*, 131–149.

Department of Education. (2015). *Title IX-General provisions.* Retrieved from www2. ed.gov/policy/elsec/leg/esea02/pg107.html

Enright, K. A. (2006). Reforming high school writing: Opportunities and constraints for generation 1.5 writers. In P. K. Matsuda, C. Ortmeier-Hooper, & X. You (Eds.), *The politics of second language writing: In search of the promised land* (pp. 30–55). West Lafayette, IN: Parlor Press.

Enright, K. A. (2010). Academic literacies and adolescent learners: English for subject-matter secondary classrooms. *TESOL Quarterly, 44*(4), 804–810.

Fry, Richard. (2011). *Hispanic college enrollment spikes, narrowing gaps with other groups.* Washington, DC: Pew Hispanic Center. Retrieved from www.pewhispanic.org/ files/2011/08/146.pdf

Fu, D. (1995). *My trouble is my English: Asian students and the American dream.* Portsmouth, NH: Boynton/Cook.

Fu, D. (2009). *Writing between languages: How English language learners make the transition to fluency, grades 4–12.* Portsmouth, NH: Heinemann.

Fu, D., & Matoush, M. (2006). Writing development and biliteracy. In P.K. Matsuda, C. Ortmeier-Hooper, & X. You (Eds.), *The politics of second language writing* (pp. 5–29). West Lafayette, IN: Parlor Press.

Harklau, L. (1994a). ESL and mainstream classes: Contrasting second language learning contexts. *TESOL Quarterly, 28*(2), 241–272.

Harklau, L. (1994b). Tracking and linguistic minority students: Consequences of ability grouping for second language learners. *Linguistics and Education, 6,* 221–248.

Harklau, L., & McClanahan, S. (2012). How Paola made it to college: A linguistic minority student's unlikely success story. In Y. Kanno & L. Harklau (Eds.), *Linguistic minority students go to college: Preparation, access, and persistence* (pp. 74–90). New York: Routledge.

Hassel, H., & Giordano, J. B. (2013). Occupy writing studies: Rethinking college composition for the needs of the teaching majority. *College Composition and Communication, 65*(1), 117–139.

Hirano, E. (2014). Refugees in first-year college: Academic writing challenges and resources. *Journal of Second Language Writing, 23,* 37–52.

Kanno, Y., & Cromley, J. G. (2013). English language learners' access to and attainment in postsecondary education. *TESOL Quarterly, 47*(1), 89–121.

Kanno, Y., & Cromley, J. G. (2015). English language learners' pathways to four-year colleges. *Teachers College Record, 117*(12), 1–44.

Kanno, Y., & Harklau, L. (Eds.) (2012). *Linguistic minority students go to college: Preparation, access, and persistence.* New York, NY: Routledge.

Larsen, D. (2013). Focus on pre-service preparation for ESL writing instruction: Secondary teacher perspectives. In L. de Oliveira & T. Silva (Eds.), *L2 writing in the secondary classrooms* (pp. 119–132). New York, NY: Routledge.

Leki, I., Cumming, A., & Silva, T. (2010). *A synthesis of research on second language writing in English.* New York, NY: Routledge.

Marsh, H. W., & Kleitman, S. (2005). Consequences of employment during high school: Character building, subversion of academic goals, or a threshold? *American Educational Research Journal, 42*(2), 331–369.

Matsuda, P. K. (2006). The myth of linguistic homogeneity in US college composition. *College English, 68*(6), 637–651.

Milnes, T., & Cheng, L. (2008). Teachers' assessment of ESL students in mainstream classes: Challenges, strategies, and decision-making. *TESL Canada Journal, 25*(2), 40–65.

Moll, L., Saez, R., & Dworin, J. (2001). Exploring biliteracy: Two student case examples of writing as a social practice. *The Elementary School Journal, 101*(4), 435–449.

Moore, J. (2012). Mapping the questions: The state of writing-related transfer research. *Composition Forum, 26*, Fall 2012. Retrieved from http://compositionforum.com/issue/26/map-questions-transfer-research.php

Nuñez, A. M., & Sparks, P. J. (2012). Who are linguistic minority students in higher education? An analysis of the beginning postsecondary students study 2004. In Y. Kanno & L. Harklau (Eds.), *Linguistic minority students go to college: Preparation, access, and persistence* (pp. 110–129). New York, NY: Routledge.

O'Neil, P., Murphy, S., Huot, B., & Williamson, M. (2005). What teachers say about different kinds of mandated state writing tests. *Journal of Writing Assessment, 2*, 81–108.

Ornelas, A., & Solorzano, D. G. (2004). Transfer conditions of Latina/o community college students: A single institution case study. *Community College Journal of Research and Practice, 28*(3), 233–248.

Oropeza, M. V., Varghese, M. M., & Kanno, Y. (2010). Linguistic minority students in higher education: Using, resisting, and negotiating multiple labels. *Equity & Excellence in Education, 43*(2), 216–231.

Ortmeier-Hooper, C. (2008). English may be my second language, but I'm not 'ESL'. *College Composition and Communication, 59*(3), 389–419.

Ortmeier-Hooper, C. (2010). The shifting nature of identity: Social identity, L2 writers, and high school. In M. Cox, J. Jordan, C. Ortmeier-Hooper, & G. Gray Schwartz (Eds.). *Reinventing identities in second language writing* (pp. 5–28). Urbana, IL: NCTE Press.

Ortmeier-Hooper, C. (2013). *The ELL writer: Moving beyond basics in the secondary classroom.* New York, NY: Teachers College Press.

Ortmeier-Hooper, C., & Enright, K. A. (2011). Mapping new territory: Toward an understanding of adolescent L2 writers and writing in U.S. contexts. *Journal of Second Language Writing, 20*(3), 167–181.

Passel, J., Cohn, D., & Lopez, M. H. (2011, March). *Hispanics account for more than half of nation's growth in past decade.* Washington, DC: Pew Hispanic Center. Retrieved from http://pewhispanic.org/reports/report.php?ReportID=140

Pew Research Center. (2014). *The rising cost of not going to college.* Washington, DC: Pew Research Center. Retrieved from www.pewsocialtrends.org/2014/02/11/the-rising-cost-of-not-going-to-college/

Queen's University. (2010). First-generation immigrants to Canada struggling in education system. *ScienceDaily.* Retrieved from www.sciencedaily.com/releases/2010/01/100113111915.htm

Razfar, A., & Simon, J. (2011). Course-taking patterns of Latino ESL students: Mobility and mainstreaming in urban community colleges in the United States. *TESOL Quarterly, 45*(4), 595–627.

Roberge, M. M., Losey, K. M., & Wald, M. (Eds.) (2016). *Teaching U.S.-educated multilingual writers: Practices from and for the classroom.* Ann Arbor, MI: University of Michigan Press.

Ruecker, T. (2011). Improving the placement of L2 writers: The students' perspective. *WPA: Writing Program Administration, 35*(1), 92–118.

Ruecker, T. (2014). Here they do this, over there they do that: Latinas/os writing across institutions. *College Composition and Communication, 66*(1), 91–119.

Ruecker, T. (2015). *Transiciones: Pathways of Latinas and Latinos writing in high school and college.* Logan, UT: Utah State University Press.

Silva, T. (1993). Toward an understanding of the distinct nature of L2 writing: The ESL research and its implications. *TESOL Quarterly, 27*(4), 657–677.

Snow, C., Burns, S., & Griffin, P. (Eds.) (1998). *Preventing reading difficulties in young children.* Washington, DC: National Academy Press. Retrieved from www.nap.edu/catalog/6023/preventing-reading-difficulties-in-young-children

Spack, R. (1997). The rhetorical construction of multilingual students. *TESOL Quarterly, 31*(4), 765–774.

Suárez-Orozco, C., Suárez-Orozco, M., & Todorova, I. (2008). *Children of immigration.* Cambridge, MA: Harvard University Press.

Sy, S. R., & Romero, J. (2008). Family responsibilities among Latina college students from immigrant families. *Journal of Hispanic Higher Education, 7*(3), 212–227.

U.S. Bureau of Labor. (2014). *College enrollment and work activity of 2013 high school graduates.* Retrieved from www.bls.gov/news.release/hsgec.nr0.htm

Vega, W. A. (1990). Hispanic families in the 1980s: A decade of research. *Journal of Marriage and the Family, 52*, 1015–1024.

Yancey, K., Robertson, L., & Taczak, K. (2014). *Writing across contexts: Transfer, composition, and sites of writing.* Logan, UT: Utah State University Press.

Yosso, T. J. (2005). Whose culture has capital? A critical race theory discussion of community cultural wealth. *Race Ethnicity and Education, 8*(1), 69–91.

PART I

Multilingual Writers in High Schools

Resident bilinguals, immigrant youth, English language learners, English learners, linguistic minorities—there are many labels used to identify multilingual writers in U.S. and Canadian schools. Whatever labels may be employed in various states and provinces throughout North America, the concerns and statistics remain disconcerting. We know that these student writers' trajectories toward higher education can be eased, disrupted, or challenged by a number of social, education, and even political factors (Ortmeier-Hooper & Enright, 2011). But often, we have a hazy understanding of what those factors are or how students encounter them while they are still in high school. To understand the transitions of resident multilingual writers from high school to college, we need a stronger understanding of these students' experiences as writers and literacy learners in secondary schools. Part I helps build that understanding. The chapters in this section call attention to the curriculum, to federal policies, to students' social worlds, to issues of access and power, and to an expanded knowledge of where these students reside and how the material conditions in their lives and in their schools contribute to their motivations, academic preparedness, and college aspirations.

In Chapter 2, Betsy Gilliland adds to emerging research in education and TESOL and highlights how students in ELL tracks are often either reluctant or discouraged from completing coursework for college readiness. Based on research at a high school in California, Gilliland's chapter explores how multilingual students are denied opportunities to learn how to write for academic purposes by the lack of curricular alignment across programs. As Gilliland argues here, the traditional back-to-basics literacy instruction used with many linguistic minority students in secondary schools draws on an autonomous mindset, one that sees literacy as autonomous and skill-based and that "treats writing as neutral and universal." In contrast, instruction in college-readiness composition courses drew

on instructional practices that stressed literacy as socially situated and encouraged students to critically think through and engage with literacy as "a social act imbued with power relations from the outset" (Street, 2012, p. 29, quoted in Gilliland, this volume).

In part, the concerns articulated by Gilliland have been put into place by national educational policies that have often inadvertently worked against the success of linguistic minority students. The recent U.S. Common Core State Standards (CCSS) initiative echoes many of the trends that were put into place by the No Child Left Behind (NCLB) Act of 2001. NCLB pushed high-stakes testing and accountability into public schools throughout the country, but it has not necessarily improved the educational opportunities or conditions for many multilingual students and their schools or teachers. Over a decade after NCLB, the Common Core has promised to create a more level playing field across K–12 schools in the United States; however, concerns about inequities in terms of school funding, curricula, high-stakes testing, and access to teachers and technology persist in this new era (e.g., Zancanella and Moore, 2014). In Chapter 3, Luciana de Oliveira considers how the CCSS are shaping writing instruction for ELLs in high schools with an eye toward certain genres and the mantras of college- and career-readiness. De Oliveira points out that ELL students were largely ignored in the creation of the CCSS, which is problematic since the Standards aim to help ensure that all students in U.S. schools obtain a similar education. De Oliveira also explains how the implementation of CCSS has led to a reductive notion of writing depending in part on a modes-based model (e.g., the argumentative paper, analysis paper, narrative). She also shares concerns that even those schools that take a more genre-based approach to teaching writing do not have teachers who are making the genre-based model (e.g., primary research report, profile piece, community problem report) more prevalent in current practices.

The next two chapters take us deeper into adolescent ML student writers' own words, experiences, and schools. In Chapter 4, Sarah Henderson Lee provides a rich portrait of seven multilingual writers as they navigate across a U.S. secondary curriculum. Her analysis, framed by a language socialization framework and drawing on work by linguists Bonnie Norton and others, illustrates how ML students' learning experiences are shaped in the context of discourses and practices surrounding language learners. Students in the study were in a double bind, marginalized by teachers across the curriculum because of their language background, and then having those same teachers mark the safe and complex educational space of their ELL classroom as a "ghetto."

In Chapter 5, Jennifer Wilson takes us into an urban city in Canada and explores the schooling and support systems that are experienced by immigrant youth. Here, Wilson offers us a way of thinking through the kinds of resources and support systems that students may need to have in place in order to successfully aim for college during their younger years. The study offers critical insight into how such resources can fall short for certain students. She argues for increased

attention to the material conditions that may surround these young people, and how we might need to account for material conditions as we think through new theories of writing and literacy resources. For readers, Wilson's chapter offers an important point of comparison and provides insights into the plight of adolescent immigrant writers in another national context, one that operates within a different educational policy reality but still has many similar concerns as those illustrated by the U.S.-based studies in this volume.

The final chapter in Part I expands our vantage point even further. To date, much of the research on multilingual youth has focused almost exclusively on diverse urban and suburban schools and districts. The experiences of multilingual adolescents—immigrants, migrants, and linguistic minorities—in rural and small-town schools and districts have not been studied sufficiently. In this chapter, Ruecker profiles two immigrant students at a high school in a town of 10,000 people, exploring how the language support they received was limited. While highlighting the growing linguistic minority student populations in rural and small-town high schools, Ruecker provides insights into how federal poverty rates, lack of financial and familial resources, and difficulties with material conditions—teacher turnover, lack of qualified applicants, and so forth—make it difficult for even the most well-intentioned administrators to prepare ELL students in these communities for college.

The five chapters in this section illustrate the wide variability in the K–12 contexts. These contexts are constantly being shaped by new policies like the CCSS that emerge from national policymakers or local decisions, such as the level of financial resources put in place to support language learners by the state or district. It behooves college teachers and administrators to learn more about the different educational experiences their students bring to the classroom and to use them to think about strengths and weaknesses students bring to the college writing classroom in terms of literacy abilities, something that will be dealt with more explicitly in the next section.

Bibliography

Ortmeier-Hooper, C. & Enright, K. A. (2011). Mapping new territory: Toward an understanding of adolescent L2 writers and writing in U.S. contexts. *Journal of Second Language Writing. 20*(3), 167–181.

Zancanella, D. & Moore, M. (2014). The origins of the Common Core: Untold stories. *Language Arts, 91* (4): 273–279.

2

OPPORTUNITY GAPS

Curricular Discontinuities across ESL, Mainstream, and College English

Betsy Gilliland

Introduction

Young writers most in need of consistent language-focused instruction may receive the least consistent support in building their writing proficiency (Menken, 2008). Developing writers need curricular continuity within and across programs and grade levels (Addison & McGee, 2010). While fluent English speakers may progress steadily through a school district's programs, multilingual[1] youth in the same district may experience disruptive discontinuities in their educational trajectories when curricular programs do not bridge language development and mainstream English. This chapter highlights discontinuities of one high school's English as a second language (ESL)[2] and English language arts (ELA) writing curricula from the perspectives of multilingual adolescents transitioning from ESL to ELA and college composition. A lack of alignment across programs denied multilingual students opportunities to learn how to write for academic purposes. After reviewing research that found similar discontinuities, I report findings from a yearlong ethnographic study at one California high school, analyzing the writing curriculum for conflicting conceptions of literacy within and across academic programs.

Limited Opportunities to Learn

Research with multilingual youth in American secondary schools has documented gaps in writing curriculum and instruction between ESL and mainstream classes as well as between high school and college. These gaps limit students' opportunities to learn essential academic literacy practices. For example, writing in classes for English learners may focus on vocabulary memorization over conceptual understanding (Richardson Bruna, Vann, & Perales Escudero, 2007) or controlled writing and copying from models (Hartman & Tarone, 1999; Valdés,

2001). Teacher support of multilingual writers can be similarly reductive, meeting assessment requirements at the expense of supporting learners' long-term writing development (Gilliland, 2014; Ruecker, 2013; Villalva, 2006). Mainstream English classes may also constrain what is taught about writing, focusing on worksheets and mechanical tasks (Allison, 2009), with written work rarely exceeding a single page (Applebee & Langer, 2011). Official curriculum often emphasizes formulaic five-paragraph essays that value structure and correctness over message (Enright & Gilliland, 2011; Ortmeier-Hooper, 2013). Such a focus on "survival genres" can limit multilingual students' opportunities to learn other genres or purposes for writing (Ortmeier-Hooper, 2013; Ruecker, 2013). Research has also observed ESL students transitioning to mainstream classes unprepared for the new academic expectations (Fu, 1995; Harklau, 1994).

In contrast with the limited scholarship on multilingual youths' high school experiences, more research has documented their challenges in college writing (e.g., Kanno & Harklau, 2012; Roberge, Siegal, & Harklau, 2009), though little is still known about their transition between high school and college writing. Many students report being challenged with literacy assignments for which their high school English classes had not prepared them (Crosby, 2009). Ruecker (2013) found that multilingual students' college instructors expected them to already have some previous experience with genres they had not written in high school. Kibler (2013) observed multilingual college students drawing on the limited strategies they had developed in high school, but struggling with writing in ways they had not previously learned.

To identify structural factors that contribute to multilingual high school students' struggles transitioning across programs, this chapter analyzes how a lack of curricular alignment across courses led to differing conceptions of what writing was, and limited multilingual students' opportunities to learn to write for success in mainstream and college courses.

Context and Participants

Data were collected during a yearlong (2009–2010) ethnographic study of three classrooms at Willowdale High School[3] (WHS) in central California, which served 1,503 students in grades 9 to 12. Students were 55% Hispanic[4] and 40% white (non-Hispanic) from diverse socioeconomic backgrounds; 20% were classified as English learners (ELs) and another 20% considered "fluent English proficient."[5]

I observed two sections of *Transition to English* (Transitions), a two-period, yearlong class for advanced proficiency EL students. Writing assignments were designed to prepare students for grade-level academic tasks and the state high school exit exam. Evelyn Chou's section of Transitions had 15 students in 10th to 12th grades. All but three were Spanish speakers. Shawn Brown's section had 32 ninth grade students, all Spanish speakers. In both classes, some students were recent immigrants, while others had lived in the United States for many years or

their entire lives. I also observed Chris Richards' section of *Senior Literature and Composition* (which everyone at the school called Senior Lit), a mainstream English language arts course with 24 twelfth grade students, including some multilingual former ELs.

Methods

As a participant observer, I took field notes and audio-recorded classroom talk on days focused on writing instruction. I collected student writing, course texts, and documents from curricular programs, and I interviewed the three teachers and 12 focal students at the end of each semester. I interviewed six focal students the following year, asking about their experiences transitioning from ESL to mainstream and college writing.

For this chapter, I focused analysis on data where participants called attention to physical (worksheets, textbooks, and other objects) or theoretical (personal beliefs and official messages about writing development) aspects of the curriculum. After inductive open coding, I refined categories to identify patterns related to participants' understanding of and beliefs about curriculum (LeCompte & Schensul, 1999). These patterns, emerging from the data, indexed theoretical perspectives on writing instruction that underlay curricular materials and teachers' implementation thereof. Analyses were triangulated among data sources.

Theoretical Framework

I analyze the data from a New Literacy Studies (NLS) perspective (Street, 2012), focusing on the ideologies of writing instruction in the written and enacted curriculum. NLS argues that all literacy activity is inherently social and situated within specific contexts (Barton & Hamilton, 2000). Literacy instruction designed from an *autonomous* approach treats writing as neutral and universal, assuming that teaching basic skills such as grammar or formulaic writing should automatically generate higher cognitive learning (Street, 2012). In contrast, an *ideological* understanding recognizes that "engaging with literacy is always a social act imbued with power relations" (Street, 2012, p. 29); pedagogy must help students recognize how people use literacy to achieve sociopolitical goals.

Applying NLS specifically to writing instruction, Ivanič (2004) defines *discourses of writing* as "constellations of beliefs about writing, beliefs about learning to write, ways of talking about writing, and the sorts of approaches to teaching and assessment which are likely to be associated with these beliefs" (p. 224). In Ivanič's framework (Table 2.1), the lowest discourse levels (Skills, Creativity, and Process) situate the construct of "writing" within an individual writer who deploys knowledge of patterns to create a text—an autonomous stance on literacy. The fourth level (Genre) recognizes that the text types created by writers are socially situated, but maintains an autonomous image of teachers passing information to students.

TABLE 2.1 Discourses of Writing (Ivanič, 2004; Street, 2012)

Discourse	Role of writer	How writing works	How writing is taught	Belief about literacy
1. Skills 2. Creativity 3. Process	Individual writer acting alone	Writer applies knowledge of structures to create text	Teacher gives students skills (grammar or formulas)	Autonomous
4. Genre	Individual writer follows social norms	Writer includes appropriate characteristics of a particular text type	Teacher gives students genre knowledge, or students identify genre features	Autonomous to ideological, depending on instruction
5. Social Practices 6. Sociopolitical	Writer is an actor in social practices	Writer uses writing to achieve a social purpose	Curriculum fosters critical literacy	Ideological

The highest levels (Social Practices and Sociopolitical) recognize ideological and communicative purposes for writing, the sociopolitical nature of writing, and its role in writers' identities and positioning.

Here, I use Ivanič's (2004) framework to compare the curricular programs at WHS in order to identify students' opportunities to learn writing practices necessary for success moving across grade levels and into college. I analyze the two high school courses (Transitions and Senior Lit) for the discourses of writing in their official curricula, focusing on ideological discontinuities within and across courses. I then examine reports from graduated focal students about their experiences in college writing and discontinuities with their high school learning.

Findings

Transitions: Conflicting Curricular Ideologies

In this section I analyze conflicting discourses of writing present in the official Transitions curriculum. The course covered both advanced English language development and mainstream 9th grade ELA curricula, as the school district considered 9th grade English foundational for college-prep English classes. This dual mandate led the district to include two commercial programs presenting conflicting discourses of writing, which created discontinuities within the course itself.

Almost all writing in the two Transitions classrooms related to the school district's required Benchmark Assignments (BAs). Developed by a team of district English teachers, the BAs were intended "to ensure equal access to rigorous curricula" and to "drive instruction to the extent that it immediately informs the student and teacher what needs to be re-taught."[6] This curriculum laid out grading

and assessment policies, specifying exactly when each of five essays should be taught, minimum scores for passing, and remediation policies for failing students. Each BA rubric assessed six to eight criteria (content and language conventions) on a four-point scale. Transitions teacher Mr. Brown explained that the district considered students passing BA essays more important than any other aspect of the curriculum; teachers whose students passed the BAs without remediation received praise.

The BA essay prompts came from Writing Workshops in the 9th grade Holt textbook (Beers & Odell, 2003b), which portrays writing as a formulaic, linear process. The district explained that the prompts were "selected from the core curriculum that demonstrate student mastery of essential academic standards and curriculum;"[7] these text types were also in the 9th and 10th grade state standards and tested on the high school exit exam. Prioritizing the quality of the final product, the BAs represented a *skills discourse* in which structure, accuracy, and correctness of the final text took prominence in assessment.

In addition to the BAs, the district also expected Transitions teachers to follow a writing curriculum from the WRITE Institute.[8] While the text types in BA and WRITE were similar (including literary analysis and personal narrative), the two programs represented contrasting ideological stances on writing. Explicitly stating that it took a *genre discourse*, the WRITE curriculum provided photocopiable reading and writing activities for each unit, developing students' personal connections to issues, analyzing genre-appropriate or theme-related texts, and writing an essay in that genre. In keeping with the genre discourse, the WRITE curriculum promoted identifying purposes for writing a particular genre and connecting the writing to students' previous experiences. Ms. Chou explained that teachers were told at WRITE trainings to use 80% of the provided materials to fulfill the purpose of the program, which was designed to teach students how to analyze genres and engage in real-world writing practices.

With district requirements to implement two ideologically different writing programs, the Transitions teachers made choices about integrating the materials. The school district officially stated that they should teach both programs fully, but simultaneously implied that the BAs were more valuable because of their immediate connection to high-stakes assessments. Both teachers focused on the skills discourse of the BAs, effectively negating the WRITE program's genre discourse.

New to BAs and WRITE, Ms. Chou initially felt pressure to follow the district's timeline and directives. Not understanding the purpose of many of the WRITE materials, however, she had students complete dozens of worksheets without making the connections to genre or social function as the program's creators intended. She explained her confusion: "I don't quite get it either, but they're supposed to answer those questions in general about the book because that's supposed to help them come up with a sentence or two about the book. . . . The thing is, because this is part of the curriculum, I'm mandated that I need to use 80% of it. Some of these things, I look at them and I have a chart and," she laughed in frustration, "I don't

know." As the school year progressed, Ms. Chou learned from other teachers that the district prioritized her students' final scores on the BAs and would not check their participation in WRITE. In teaching the later BAs, she ignored most of the WRITE materials, using only a few worksheets that fit with her previous teaching.

Having served on the BA revision committee, Mr. Brown understood the district's value on the BAs over WRITE. Aware of the district pressure to complete all the essays within a limited time frame, he dropped any pretense of teaching the WRITE materials and designed graphic organizers and other materials to expedite students' completion of the BA writing tasks. He explained his decision: "Not using the actual WRITE, but the concepts. But part of it was because the WRITE essays didn't align with the [Benchmark] essays we needed to write for this class."

The Transitions curriculum demonstrated internal discontinuities that limited students' opportunities to learn academic writing. The BA and Holt materials shared an *autonomous* view of literacy as a set of skills that could be mastered in isolation from any real-world purpose. WRITE's *genre discourse* and recognition of students as members of social communities conflicted with the literacy perspectives in the rest of the Transitions curriculum. By using the WRITE materials selectively, the teachers lost WRITE's larger goal of engaging students in connecting writing assignments to their funds of knowledge and broader applications. The reduction of WRITE to a set of worksheets represents the teachers' awareness of the school district's prioritizing the final product of the BAs and their ideological misalignment with the underlying philosophy of WRITE. While these decisions reduced the curricular discontinuities within the Transitions curriculum, they created greater misalignment with the curriculum of the mainstream English language arts classes into which the Transitions students progressed.

Senior Lit: Independent Writing Processes

Although the internal discontinuities of the Transitions curriculum were absent from the mainstream Senior Lit class, discontinuities between Transitions and Senior Lit meant that multilingual students crossing from one class to the next were faced with unfamiliar messages about what counted as academic writing. In teaching Senior Lit, Mr. Richards balanced district expectations to address the California standards using the 12th grade Holt textbook (Beers & Odell, 2003a) with his own beliefs about what students should learn about writing as they progress from high school to college. He maintained a consistent *process* discourse in his class, focusing on text creation but rarely connecting those texts to purposes beyond the classroom.

The 12th grade Holt textbook (Beers & Odell, 2003a) was laid out similarly to its 9th grade counterpart, with excerpts from longer literary works grouped in units, each piece followed by comprehension and analysis questions. Unlike in Transitions, however, the school district allowed Senior Lit teachers to select readings and decide how to integrate writing into their classes. As a result, each section of Senior Lit had different writing assignments, taught and evaluated according to the teacher's perspectives. Mr. Richards used the Holt book as prompts for brief writing

he assigned as homework. To accompany the textbook excerpts from *Beowulf,* for example, he assigned three choices of topics, each in a different rhetorical mode:

Short Essay Topics

Descriptive—p. 40—Description of the Mom

Analysis—p. 40—Analyzing the Monster Grendel (use quotations)

Compare/Contrast—Write an essay in which you compare/contrast a modern day hero with Beowulf. You must establish a definition for "epic hero" as well as what we, as a society, currently view as a hero. Don't forget the differences!

These prompts, two from the textbook and the third created by the teacher, maintain an *autonomous* view of literacy. While Mr. Richards provided class time for students to talk with each other about how they defined the concept *hero*, they wrote individually for the teacher as reader. Taking a *process discourse* not present in the textbook prompts, Mr. Richards asked students to bring drafts for peer review and revise based on peer feedback. These sessions nevertheless reinforced an ideology of writing as politically neutral, where textual patterns and grammatical accuracy were central. Figure 2.1 is the Peer Response Sheet Mr. Richards gave students for this assignment.

Mr. Richards further developed a process discourse in Senior Lit through the Senior Project, a research-based expository paper he had developed in response to a state standard ("Write historical investigation reports."). He set due dates for students to write a proposal, document notes and sources, and then outline, write, revise, and orally present the eight-page paper. Assignment guidelines focused on topic recommendations, due dates, and source requirements. This project, like other writing in Senior Lit, emphasized content, structure, and procedure over students' purposes for writing or the text's social functions. Mr. Richards dedicated many class days to this project, including time for students to do online research and instruction in outlining, but throughout the assignment, he treated students' projects as isolated assessments written for him as the sole reader, rather than as texts serving communicative purposes. Without connections to either the text's functions beyond this particular class or the social role of research-based writing, Mr. Richards' students missed an opportunity to learn how these literacy skills might be transferred to their post–high school activities.

Espousing a *process discourse*, Mr. Richards showed students that he valued both final products and writing processes. More problematic for multilingual students in his class, however, was his belief that the seniors already understood writing from this perspective and were able to employ processes independently. He enumerated criteria he considered essential to good writing: "They need to know how to cite, and paragraph development. They're going to need the usual, the topic sentences, the evidence, the data, kind of the explanation, the warrants—any sense of that's how you're developing a paragraph." These factors reflect foundational writing skills and academic language he thought seniors already had.

Revision/Editing Groups

1. Exchange papers with a partner—I will select your partner today.

2. Read through the essay once. Put questions marks where you don't understand.

3. Re-read the introduction. Find and underline the thesis. If descriptive, does it have a controlling or dominant impression or mood? Is it specific enough for the content of the essay? If not, can you make a suggestion on how to improve it?
   WRITE IT HERE OR ON THE PAPER.

4. If it's a compare/contrast, is the writer using a point-by-point method or the block style? Write down which one.

5. Do the topic sentences address the thesis? If compare/contrast and also point-by-point, do the topic sentences name the quality being discussed? If not, what can the writer do to improve the topic sentences? If descriptive, does each paragraph address a different aspect of Grendel's mom?

6. Body paragraphs—Are there examples? Does the writer need to include more? If the writer did the analysis of Grendel, are there direct quotations with line numbers in parentheses? If descriptive, does the writer use concrete sensory details, imagery, figurative language, specific nouns, and strong verbs? Answer all that apply.

7. Does the writer explain or provide commentary on how the examples make the point of the topic sentence? If not, write down some suggestions on how to do it.

8. Does the conclusion wrap up the essay with a sense of resolution or insight? (The essay may or may not restate the thesis or summarize the main points and still be effective.) How can the conclusion be improved?

9. Correct for spelling, punctuation, correct verbs, and style (word choice). Suggest more varied sentence structure if the paper has few simple and complex sentences.

FIGURE 2.1 Mr. Richards' Peer Response Sheet

Mr. Richards' instruction, therefore, emphasized new skills students needed for college. As he told his class, this included a focus on accuracy of citations and language:

> You guys have done some research papers in the past, but, it looks like works cited was, you didn't quite get it yet. And it's something that when you go to college, they're gonna expect that you know how to do this.

To be prepared for unknown college writing instructors, he suggested, the students needed to develop more advanced skills than their high school teachers had required. Mr. Richards positioned Senior Lit as their last chance to learn before entering this critical and unforgiving new world. This stance reflects a greater awareness of the ideological nature of writing than the written curriculum suggested, acknowledging that student writers would face power imbalances based on their ability to create texts to meet various readers' expectations.

Discontinuities from Transitions to Senior Lit

The official WHS curriculum assumed a coherent development of writing skills from the 9th grade BAs (used in Transitions) to Senior Lit, preparing all graduates for college writing. In reality, Transitions and Senior Lit served different purposes in the overall curriculum. Transitions was both a capstone of the ESL program for students who were still learning English, and entry to the accountability routines of mainstream English language arts classes and the high school exit exam. Senior Lit, in contrast, specifically intended to "prepare students for college English courses."[9] As the above analyses show, the classes do reflect their course descriptions. The problem lies in the gap between the two, specifically in students' opportunities to learn the writing practices needed for success at higher levels.

The academic writing practices emphasized in Senior Lit diverged widely from those of Transitions, particularly with respect to expectations of students' independence as writers. In Senior Lit, students still wrote for purposes determined by the teacher, but some assignments could also serve as college or scholarship application essays. In keeping with a *process* discourse, students had choice of both form and topic for their writing. More significantly, they wrote independently, writing and revising their texts with limited feedback from the teacher. Through a *skills* discourse curriculum, Transitions students, in contrast, learned that what mattered was the correctness of the final product; they had little opportunity to learn the processes of creating that product. This gap between discourses of writing in Transitions and Senior Lit interfered with students' movement into mainstream classes.

Mr. Richards was not the only WHS English teacher to assume multilingual students were familiar with writing processes. After Ms. Chou's Transitions class his junior year, focal student Ivan explained his experience in Senior English with another teacher:

> . . . the teacher just gave us topics and walk us through. You know she just assumed that everybody was at the same level and I was not, so I have to went to the learning center to get [help], and I didn't want to say nothing because, it seemed like I was the only one, so for some reason, I didn't want to.

Here, Ivan commented on his Senior English teacher's expectations about students' equal preparation for writing at the level of the curriculum. Ivan also named

another pattern I noted in Mr. Richards' classroom with respect to multilingual seniors: in the teacher's assumption of students' readiness, those who did not feel capable were isolated and ashamed to ask for help.

Ivan's classmate Orlando reported a similar experience moving from Transitions to mainstream classes with other teachers. His Senior Lit teacher told the class he was holding them to college standards. Orlando said that he and his classmates were shocked by how much this teacher expected the seniors to do independently, including submitting written assignments online mere hours after class, and by how much proficiency with academic language the teacher believed students already possessed.

College Composition: Different Emphases

I followed up with the graduated focal students after their first semester of college for their perspectives on whether WHS English classes had prepared them for college writing. They perceived discontinuities between their high school classes and the expectations of their college writing classes.

Placing into developmental writing courses at community college gave two students from Ms. Chou's Transitions class opportunities to learn academic writing practices they had not seen earlier. While the instruction they described still reflects lower-level discourses of writing, the students also felt that their high school instruction was misaligned with what they needed to succeed in college. For example, Ivan reflected on two semesters of developmental college writing, listing aspects such as transition words, outlining, and capitalization, using specialized terminology to label the various topics he now knew he had not previously learned:

> Some vocabulary, sentence structure. I learned a lot of that, see Miss Chou never teaches that. It has like independent and dependent. They never, that's the funny thing, how come I never seen. Or I never put attention, it was me, or something, cause, I never saw that in high school!

Ivan felt he should have learned more foundational writing skills during his junior and senior years. His college writing instructor had given him the language to talk *about* writing, an essential move toward making connections between texts and their social purposes.

Ivan's classmate Javier had fewer concerns about how Transitions had prepared him for college writing. He noted that in high school ESL classes, he had learned how to "write much, show in details," particularly through summaries and vocabulary development. Nevertheless, Javier felt that extensive writing in his high school Advanced Placement Spanish classes had helped him improve his writing more than English class assignments had and thought that WHS's English teachers should assign more essays. From the students' descriptions, it seems that

their developmental writing courses followed a *skills* discourse. Ivan's list of grammatical structures and Javier's comment about vocabulary suggest these young men had not seen a connection between their college writing classes and greater social purposes for writing.

Fatima, a focal student from Mr. Richards' Senior Lit class, placed in a multilingual section of first-year composition (FYC) with an additional one-unit support class at a local public university campus. She appreciated the additional feedback she received from her support class, where students had time to write and receive frequent responses to their FYC assignments. Fatima felt that she had learned much in high school that had prepared her for college writing, including outlining ideas before writing, a strategy Mr. Richards had reinforced in Senior Lit. She wished, however, that she had learned in high school to think about more sophisticated readers while writing: "In college, they want sort of academic audience, and it's kind of different in high school. It's just a high school audience, so like your word choice and stuff, it changes." In this way she called out one of the ideological differences between the WHS writing curriculum and the expectations of college writing: the intended audience.

Discontinuities from High School to College

The text types emphasized in the BAs and Holt textbooks included genres typical of college writing assignments, but the formulaic nature of the BA and the standardized high school exit exam fostered different writing processes and expectations. Ivan and Javier placed into much lower-level writing courses in college than the high school's course sequencing would have suggested: they went from writing full-length essays in high school to focusing on paragraphs in their college classes. As both young men noted, however, they were learning language and writing skills they had not covered at WHS. Compared to the Transitions and Senior English tasks, Mr. Richards' Senior Lit assignments were closer to the expectations for writing process and quality that his students experienced when they got to college. As Fatima pointed out, however, college writing also required students to engage with different audiences, a move toward a *social practices* discourse of writing.

Discussion

This chapter has examined ideological discontinuities in how writing was viewed and taught for multilingual learners at Willowdale High School. Students in the Transitions course experienced an internally misaligned curriculum, where the skills discourse BAs took precedence over the genre discourse of WRITE because of school district emphasis on the BAs. Moving into mainstream English language arts courses, including Senior Lit, students encountered teachers who assumed they had mastered basic skills and could engage with a process discourse curriculum

independently. Progressing to college, students discovered further discontinuities, placing into developmental courses that addressed skills they had not learned in high school and first-year composition courses that asked them to consider writing as communication with new audiences.

These curricular misalignments at each step of students' trajectories indicate that they missed opportunities to learn essential writing practices as they moved across programs. A New Literacies Studies perspective allows consideration of the messages that each curricular program sends about what counts as literacy and identification of fundamental differences that contribute to the discontinuities limiting multilingual writers' opportunities to learn. As the Transitions class illustrated, discontinuities *within* a course meant that the teachers were tasked with finding a balance. In the case documented here, the teachers' options were influenced by the school district's assessment policies prioritizing the *skills* discourse BAs over the *genre* discourse WRITE. Although these decisions smoothed the instructional process within Transitions, they broadened the gap between this course and subsequent mainstream courses. Senior Lit, like other upper-grade English classes at WHS, had fewer institutional requirements, allowing individual teachers like Mr. Richards to establish what counted as writing. The *process* discourse of these classes challenged multilingual students who had previously not been expected to engage independently with writing. Neither Transitions nor Senior Lit, however, gave multilingual writers opportunities to learn all they needed for college writing.

While many WHS students likely struggled with these same discontinuities, they posed an even greater challenge for the multilingual students in this study. Because they were newer to the discourses of high school English language arts, having spent much of their academic careers in ESL courses, multilingual students had to learn new ways of participating in writing class as they crossed boundaries (from Transitions to Senior Lit and from high school to college). At each transition, what their teachers shared about writing and reasons for writing changed. Students recognized these gaps and felt their teachers at earlier levels should have taught what they needed to know for the higher-level classes. The focal students interviewed in this chapter, however, are those who succeeded at making these transitions; Mr. Richards told me that many multilingual students at WHS dropped out before their senior year. These curricular discontinuities may have posed even greater barriers to multilingual students with academic ambition but without the persistence that allowed students like Ivan to succeed.

Implications of this study highlight a need for coherence in writing curriculum across programs both within a school and beyond. When ideologies behind curricular programs conflict with each other, approaches to teaching writing do not align. Large-scale curricular decisions must happen at the district level, where textbook packages are selected and supplemental programs purchased. Decision makers need to recognize that not all students in their schools move in a clear progression across mainstream classes—multilingual learners in particular

may jump tracks from ESL to mainstream, and like some of my focal students, from an ESL class using the 9th grade textbook to a mainstream class using the 12th grade textbook. Thus even a textbook series with a clear progression from one grade to the next is not enough. Ideally, district curriculum planners will also be able to communicate with college faculty, sharing knowledge and planning "a vertical curriculum that begins in high school, continues through college, and specifically fosters transfer across contexts" (Addison & McGee, 2010, p. 170).

Most importantly, teachers are essential to developing and maintaining curricular coherence for multilingual learners. They need time and institutional encouragement to communicate with each other across curricular tracks about both what is taught and how it is taught, including what discourses of writing are behind the curriculum. As Mr. Richards did to some extent, teachers can individually give their students access to social and ideological perspectives on writing. Teachers need to get to know their students' linguistic and academic trajectories, recognizing that while they may have "covered" a set of text types in one course, they may not have learned how those text types are connected to writing beyond the classroom or how they can apply their knowledge of those text types in later writing assignments. As the people closest to the application of curriculum into practice, teachers should play a role in the redesign of curricular articulation. Multilingual students can only benefit when their schools and their teachers invest in smoothing their transitions across grade levels and programs.

Notes

1. *Multilingual students* refers to participants in my study and others like them, young people who use more than one language in their lives. Multilingual students may be classified by the school as English language learners, but others are officially redesignated as fluent English users or were never classified as such.
2. California uses ELD (English language development), not ESL (English as a second language), for school-level classes. I use ESL here to keep with terminology in the research literature.
3. All names of people and places are pseudonyms.
4. California uses "Hispanic" in reporting demographics to include students of any race who report being "Hispanic" or "Latino" as ethnicity. It does not imply anything about language.
5. In California "fluent English proficient" refers to students "whose primary language is other than English and who have met the district criteria for determining proficiency in English" (www.cde.ca.gov/ds/sd/cb/glossary.asp#f, accessed September 10, 2014).
6. WHS accreditation report, 2010.
7. WHS accreditation report, 2010.
8. The WRITE Institute (Writing Reform and Innovation for Teaching Excellence: https://writeinstitute.sdcoe.net/) curriculum promotes teacher professional development to support English language learners' academic writing and language learning.
9. WHS Course Catalog, 2009–2010.

Bibliography

Addison, J., & McGee, S. J. (2010). Writing in high school/writing in college. *College Composition and Communication, 62*(1), 147–179.

Allison, H. (2009). High school academic literacy instruction and the transition to college writing. In M. M. Roberge, M. Siegal, & L. Harklau (Eds.), *Generation 1.5 in college composition* (pp. 75–90). New York: Routledge.

Applebee, A. N., & Langer, J. A. (2011). A snapshot of writing instruction in middle schools and high schools. *English Journal, 100*(6), 14–27.

Barton, D., & Hamilton, M. (2000). Literacy practices. In D. Barton, M. Hamilton, & R. Ivanič (Eds.), *Situated literacies: Reading and writing in context* (pp. 7–15). London: Routledge.

Beers, K., & Odell, L. (2003a). *Literature and language arts: Essentials of British and world literature (Annotated teacher's edition)* (Vol. Sixth Course). Austin: Holt, Rinehart, and Winston.

Beers, K., & Odell, L. (2003b). *Literature and language arts: Mastering the California standards (Annotated teacher's edition)* (Vol. Third Course). Austin: Holt, Rinehart and Winston.

Crosby, C. (2009). Academic reading and writing difficulties and strategic knowledge of generation 1.5 learners. In M. M. Roberge, M. Siegal, & L. Harklau (Eds.), *Generation 1.5 in college composition* (pp. 105–119). New York: Routledge.

Enright, K. A., & Gilliland, B. (2011). Multilingual writing in an age of accountability: From policy to practice in U.S. high school classrooms. *Journal of Second Language Writing, 20*(3), 182–195. doi: 10.1016/j.jslw.2011.05.006

Fu, D. (1995). *"My trouble is my English": Asian students and the American dream.* Portsmouth, NH: Boynton/Cook Heinemann.

Gilliland, B. (2014). Academic language socialization in high school writing conferences. *Canadian Modern Language Review, 70*(3), 303–330. doi: 10.3138/cmlr.1753

Harklau, L. (1994). ESL versus mainstream classes: Contrasting L2 learning environments. *TESOL Quarterly, 28*(2), 241–272. doi: 10.2307/3587433

Hartman, B., & Tarone, E. (1999). Preparation for college writing: Teachers talk about writing instruction for Southeast Asian American students in secondary school. In L. Harklau, K. M. Losey, & M. Siegal (Eds.), *Generation 1.5 meets college composition* (pp. 99–118). Mahwah, New Jersey: Lawrence Erlbaum Associates.

Ivanič, R. (2004). Discourses of writing and learning to write. *Language and Education, 18*(3), 220–245. doi: 10.1080/09500780408666877

Kanno, Y., & Harklau, L. A. (Eds.) (2012). *Linguistic minority students go to college: Preparation, access, and persistence.* New York: Routledge.

Kibler, A. (2013). "Doing like almost everything wrong": An adolescent multilingual writer's transition from high school to college. In L. C. de Oliveira & T. Silva (Eds.), *L2 writing in secondary classrooms* (pp. 44–63). New York: Routledge.

LeCompte, M. D., & Schensul, J. J. (1999). *Analyzing and interpreting ethnographic data.* Walnut Creek, CA: Altamira Press.

Menken, K. (2008). *English learners left behind: Standardized testing as language policy.* Clevedon, England: Multilingual Matters.

Ortmeier-Hooper, C. (2013). *The ELL writer: Moving beyond basics in the secondary classroom.* New York: Teachers College Press.

Richardson Bruna, K., Vann, R., & Perales Escudero, M. (2007). What's language got to do with it?: A case study of academic language instruction in a high school "English Learner Science" class. *Journal of English for Academic Purposes, 6*(1), 36–54. doi: 10.1016/j.jeap.2006.11.006

Roberge, M. M., Siegal, M., & Harklau, L. (Eds.) (2009). *Generation 1.5 in college composition.* New York: Routledge.

Ruecker, T. (2013). High-stakes testing and Latina/o students: Creating a hierarchy of college readiness. *Journal of Hispanic Higher Education, 12*(4), 303–320. doi: 10.1177/1538192713493011

Street, B. (2012). New literacy studies. In M. Grenfell, D. Bloome, C. Hardy, K. Pahl, J. Rowsell, & B. Street (Eds.), *Language, ethnography, and education: Bridging new literacy studies and Bourdieu* (pp. 27–49). New York: Routledge.

Valdés, G. (2001). *Learning and not learning English: Latino students in American schools.* New York: Teachers College Press.

Villalva, K. E. (2006). Reforming high school writing: Opportunities and constraints for generation 1.5 writers. In P. K. Matsuda, C. Ortmeier-Hooper, & X. You (Eds.), *The politics of second language writing* (pp. 30–55). West Lafayette, IN: Parlor Press.

3

THE COMMON CORE STATE STANDARDS AND IMPLICATIONS FOR WRITING INSTRUCTION AND ASSESSMENT FOR ENGLISH LANGUAGE LEARNERS

Luciana C. de Oliveira

The Common Core State Standards (CCSS) set high expectations for the learning of all students, including English language learners (ELLs). The CCSS were developed by the National Governors Association Center for Best Practices (NGA) and the Council of Chief State School Officers (CCSSO), in response to a perceived need by members of these associations for a set of consistent learning goals that would be common for all students across states. They claim that schools have gradually lowered standards for grade-level expectations over the last half century (NGA & CCSSO, 2010a). The NGA and CCSSO identified the need to increase the difficulty of what students are expected to know and be able to do at each grade level in order to prepare students to be college and career ready.

The CCSS are divided into two sets of standards: English language arts (ELA) and mathematics. These standards were developed for a general student population and did not take into consideration the demands they would present for specific populations, including special education students and English language learners (ELLs). These standards are meant to serve as the target for student performance skills at each grade level and have their roots in the standards movement in the United States.

The goal of this chapter is to contextualize the development of the Common Core State Standards in the United States in the context of the standards movement and its implications for the teaching of writing to English language learners (ELLs). The chapter describes how the CCSS addresses English language learners, and then explores how the development of habits of mind in the context of a developmental trajectory for writing and a learner pathway could address the shortfalls of the CCSS focus on text types.

Standards in the United States

The development of standards in the United States has a long history, dating back to the late 1800s (Kusch, 2009), although standards reform began to take shape after the watershed *Nation at Risk* (1983) report declared "all children can learn" (as cited in Rothman, 2011, p. 15). In his history of the CCSS, Rothman explains that the rise of standards was intended to help fulfill this belief in universal achievement: "By making clear what good performances are, schools can signal to students what they need to do to succeed" (p. 16). Rothman also cites Smith and O'Day (1991) as influential in standards reform, arguing for the uniqueness of their holistic approach of creating curriculum materials, assessments, and professional development to align to a set framework of what students should know and be able to do. Without this coordinated effort, Rothman argues, standards as educational reform are not as effective. The problem of alignment in standards reform was demonstrated later, after the landmark No Child Left Behind legislation institutionalized standards in American education.

A new era in the history of U.S. public education, an era defined by the rapid progression of the high-stakes testing movement, started with the passage of No Child Left Behind (NCLB) in 2001. NCLB requires states to test all students in grades 3 through 8 (approximately ages 8–13) and in high school annually using standardized tests. Test scores are used to gauge student performance on content standards in Reading/English Language Arts, Mathematics, Science, and Social Studies. No federal education policy has greatly impacted English language learners more than NCLB since the passage of the Bilingual Education Act in 1968 (Menken, 2008).

As stated in NCLB, the purpose of Title I is to "ensure that all children have a fair, equal, and significant opportunity to obtain a high-quality education and reach, at a minimum, proficiency on challenging State academic achievement standards and state academic assessments" (NCLB, 2002, Sec. 1001). Title I seeks to meet these goals primarily through assessments, curriculum aligned with state standards, teacher preparation, and targeting resources to educational agencies at the local level. Therefore, NCLB requires each state to test students for proficiency in subjects—and to define what *proficiency* means. As a result, all states developed a set of standards for subject areas tested. But implementation of these standards became a cause for concern. Discrepancies arose between student performance on state proficiency tests and the National Assessment of Educational Progress (NAEP), which might have suggested standards varied widely from state to state or that some states' standards were inadequate (Rothman, 2011). But the picture became murkier after Whitehurst (2009) found that even states with high-quality standards were doing poorly on NAEP. Whitehurst argued that standards were a "leaky bucket" (Whitehurst, 2009, p. 7)—because even if states set high and explicit standards for students, implementation of those standards varied so widely from school district to

school district that the effectiveness of the standards on student achievement was greatly diminished on student assessments. The need for a national set of unified standards and a solution to Whitehurst's "leaky bucket" motivated the formation of the CCSS in the late 2000s.

The development of the CCSS was based on three criteria that aimed to address the issues of "leaky bucket" and variation. These criteria included: "academic knowledge and skills all students need to be ready for college and careers," "research on college and career readiness," and "international benchmarking" (NGA & CCSSO, 2010c, p. 66). The variation problem was addressed namely through international benchmarking, but the "leaky bucket" remained an issue. Even if the standards were more focused on college and career readiness and were based on a variety of kinds of research, implementation could dissipate that focus if teachers interpreted differently what the standards meant. In the case of the ELA standards, student writing models with annotation as well as exemplar reading texts (NGA & CCSSO, 2010b) help stop the holes in the "leaky bucket." The development of common assessments by the Smarter Balance and Partnership for Assessment of Readiness for College and Careers (PARCC) consortia also aims to ensure that implementation is aligned to the standards in all participating states.

The CCSS are not intended to establish a national curriculum that prescribes a certain teaching pedagogy or forces teachers to teach according to the standards. States, districts, schools, and teachers are left to determine how to support their students in achieving the standards. However, as assessments designed for the CCSS are implemented, this may lead school districts to develop and implement accountability measures, benchmarks, structured curriculum, and other processes in order to streamline teaching in their schools. If, as under NCLB, student assessment will continue to be tethered to school funding and teacher pay, then the accountability measures will continue to be high stakes, stripping away more and more teacher autonomy and professional judgment, leading to the prevalence of prepackaged curriculum and routine student assessments. Often, these measures are designed to keep pace with established educational standards and how students should be performing according to the expectations of the current standards, which do a disservice to students who may need additional support in certain areas. If structured curricula are mandated along with assessments, teachers will not have the freedom to use their professional judgment to focus more time on trouble areas or to take advantage of teachable moments but will have to follow the regimented curriculum despite how well students understand the material (Zacher Pandya, 2011). Teachers who fail to implement these standards-based curricula or rearrange them according to what they feel is more appropriate for their students may face assessments designed to be taken in a predetermined order. Teachers may face poor performance reviews and their jobs may be in jeopardy because of these actions (Zacher Pandya, 2011).

The CCSS in English Language Arts

In this context of the standards movement in the United States, the CCSS call for all students to address reading, writing, language, and speaking in "Anchor Standards" that are designed to prepare students to be college and career ready (NGA & CCSSO, 2010b). These standards are designed for a general student population. They do not refer to English language learners (ELLs) nor explain how they expect them to fulfill the standards. The standards specifically say that it is beyond the scope of the CCSS to address the needs of ELLs (and special education students), and offers a short three-page document about the CCSS and ELLs titled "Application of Common Core State Standards for English Language Learners" (NGA & CCSSO, 2010a). This lack of attention to ELLs in the CCSS has led scholars to focus on the needs of ELLs in explicit ways, and several publications have addressed the language and content demands of the CCSS for ELLs by providing specific pedagogical practices for this student population (see Bright, Hansen-Thomas, & de Oliveira, 2015; Civil & Turner, 2014; de Oliveira, in press; de Oliveira, Klassen, & Maune, 2015b; Spycher, 2014).

The CCSS for ELA (NGA & CCSSO, 2010b), in particular, present challenges for teachers who have ELLs in their classrooms due to the CCSS demands for engaging in discussions, expressing ideas clearly and fluently, reading and writing complex texts, and using language at an advanced level. An emphasis is placed on writing as the primary means of demonstrating knowledge and communicating knowledge clearly to an audience based on real and imagined experiences (NGA & CCSSO, 2010b). For ELLs, the means to realize these expectations are not made clear within the standards, and effective practices and pedagogical practices regarding ELLs are not mentioned explicitly. The fulfillment of the secondary writing standards are contingent on the comprehension and execution of the reading and language standards, which present particular challenges for ELLs, even at advanced levels of language proficiency.

The CCSS for Writing: Some Specifics

Text Types

The CCSS for Writing describe the kinds of writing that are unique to certain situations and purposes. The CCSS organize these different kinds of writing into three "text types": *narrative*, *informational/explanatory*, and *argument* (NGA & CCSO, 2010b). The purpose of each text type is written explicitly in the standards. This is true at the most basic level, as well as at the higher levels. As the standards progress from K through 11th–12th grade, more detail is added to each of the standards, which are expanded into substandards. The substandards from 3rd grade correspond to individual elements of the text type, such as introducing topics or

situations, providing reasons/details/descriptions, and using specific types of language in each, such as linking words, temporal words, and so forth to accomplish the purpose of the text type. While going into explicit detail is beyond the scope of the CCSS, they outline what aspects of the text type are the most critical in making each text type fulfill their purpose, and provide teachers a blueprint to analyze how to make the usage of language in a text type explicit for their students. The CCSS also provide a compilation of student samples (NGA & CCSSO, 2010c) that serve examples of how the language is used to fulfill the purpose of the text types, which the teacher could utilize to conduct a language analysis of the text type with students to determine the type of language that is commonly used to fulfill the purposes of the text type.

The purpose of the narrative text type includes students' ability to "develop real or imagined experiences . . . using effective techniques, well-chosen details, and well-structured event sequences" in grades 6–12 (NGA & CCSSO, 2010b, p. 45). The purpose of this text type is carried out using language that orients the reader and introduces narrator and/or characters, establishing the point of view of the audience. The plot is developed using a progression of events that establish experiences, events, and/or characters, and finally provides a conclusion for the entire story in grades 11–12.

The purpose of the informational/explanatory text type begins with simply supplying "some information about the topic" in kindergarten (NGA & CCSSO, 2010c, p. 19) and evolves to "examine and convey complex ideas, concepts and information" in grades 11–12 (NGA & CCSSO, 2010c, p. 45), while providing explicit substandards for each section of an informative/explanatory text type. The portrayal of information in this text type must be done clearly and accurately by using information and examples, as mentioned in the standards for grades 11–12, as well as using "precise language and domain specific vocabulary" as well as "an objective tone . . . attending to the norms and conventions of the discipline" (NGA & CCSSO, 2010c, p. 45).

The purpose of the argumentative text type begins with "stating an opinion or preference about the topic or book" in kindergarten (NGA & CCSSO, 2010c, p. 19) and evolves into eventually being able to "support claims in an analysis of substantive topics or texts" in 11th–12th grades (NGA & CCSSO, 2010c, p. 45). Students have to provide not only support for their own opinions or arguments but also counter-claims to their arguments, citing evidence for each while addressing audience, noting biases, and maintaining the appropriate register for the situation at hand.

According to the CCSS, the argumentative text type is the most important of the three text types in terms of college preparedness, as university is characterized as an "argument culture" (Graff, 2003, as cited in NGA & CCSSO, 2010d, p. 24), and that up until now, only 20% of students had been adequately prepared for the argumentative writing they would be expected to do. Therefore, the explicit detailing of how to create a plausible or persuasive argument, establishing trust-worthiness and the encouragement of critical thinking, is particularly important

according to the CCSS. Although the argumentative text type is said to be the most critical for academic and career success, students must also be able to apply techniques from all of the text types, and be comfortable with combining different elements from each.

In grades 6–12, students are expected to write more informative and argumentative texts and fewer narrative texts. The emphasis on informational writing raises specific linguistic challenges for ELLs. Many ELLs do not have experiences with informational texts in their home lives and, therefore, may be unfamiliar with the language expectations of informational texts in school. This has the effect of favoring students of certain backgrounds who have access to such writing; on the other hand, it makes it more difficult for ELLs who do not have access to informational texts outside of school to achieve as much success in writing as their more favored classmates. Explicit instruction in the language expectations of writing can help improve ELLs' writing skills and give them access to types of reading and writing that are important in many parts of schooling (de Oliveira, Klassen, & Maune, 2015b).

Student Outcomes

The CCSS expect students to be able to produce "clear and coherent writing" that maintains "development, organization and style" to the appropriate purpose, task, and audience of the target text type (NGA & CCSSO, 2010c, p. 41). The CCSS include details referring to audience, language, culture, and politics throughout the standards, making explicit mention of their importance within the text types: students are expected to "produce . . . writing which . . . (is) appropriate to task, purpose and audience" (p. 18) and "write . . . for a range of tasks, purposes, and audiences" (p. 41) (NGA & CCSSO, 2010b). It makes explicit to teachers that "students must take task, purpose and audience into careful consideration . . . how to combine elements of different kinds of writing . . . to produce complex and nuanced writing" (NGA & CCSSO, 2010c, p. 41) and that students must "learn to appreciate that a key purpose of writing is to communicate clearly to an external, sometimes unfamiliar audience" (NGA & CCSSO, 2010c, p. 18). Students should be able to write routinely for a range of tasks, purposes, and audiences.

The CCSS mention that students are expected to maintain a formal style throughout each text type. They "need to know how to combine different elements of writing . . . to produce complex and nuanced writing" (NGA & CCSSO, 2010a, p. 18) and be able to use technology to produce writing and to interact and collaborate. More details are given in the general "language standards," which apply to spoken language as well as written and require students to "understand how language functions in different contexts, to make effective choices for meaning or style" as well as "demonstrate understanding of figurative language, word relationships and nuances" (NGA & CCSSO, 2010c, p. 51). Under "Conventions of Standard English," students are expected to "demonstrate command of the

conventions of standard English grammar and usage . . . capitalization, punctuation and spelling when writing" (NGA & CCSSO, 2010c, p. 51).

The expectation of the CCSS is that the text types will be taught from grades K through 12; the first time students write an *argument* piece is in kindergarten—although, at that grade level, the text type is labeled *opinion*. As the authors note, "Each year in their writing, students should demonstrate increasing sophistication in all aspects of language use, from vocabulary and syntax to the development and organization of ideas, and they should address increasingly demanding content and sources" (NGA & CCSSO, 2010b, p. 19). I conceive of this "increasing sophistication" as a continuum of expectations, where students are expected to build on their concept of each text type as they advance to each grade level. This continuum is demonstrated in a number of ways through the language choices of the CCSS.

Habits of Mind in a Developmental Trajectory for Writing

The CCSS identified the need to increase the difficulty of what students are expected to know and be able to do at each grade level in order to prepare students to be "college and career ready." Determination of whether students are indeed "college and career ready" come in the form of large-scale assessments. But being college-and-career ready involves more than what writers should know and be able to do. The *Framework for Success in Postsecondary Writing*, for example, jointly developed by the Council of Writing Program Administrators, the National Council of Teachers of English, and the National Writing Project, describes "*habits of mind and experiences with writing, reading, and critical analysis* that serve as foundations for writing in college-level" (2011, p. 2). This framework, then, moves beyond a discussion of what student writers should know and be able to do to also include how students write and think as well as how they may experience writing (Johnson, 2013). The introduction of the notion of habits of mind—or intellectual behaviors—helps us to move beyond standards and focus us on attitudes and intellectual processes (Johnson, 2013) and can start in earlier years such as at the elementary grades into high school so students are better prepared for the kinds of tasks that they will be required to perform in postsecondary settings. With the attitudes and intellectual processes necessary at the postsecondary levels, students may be more able to think critically, develop a love for continuous learning, and experience writing in positive ways.

The language expectations described above show that students are expected to develop more abstract and increasingly complex conceptual understandings of writing as they advance through school. However, the current conceptualization of the text types into three general categories ignores many years of research on a developmental trajectory of learning to write across the years of schooling and a variety of genres (e.g., Christie & Derewianka, 2008; Derewianka & Jones, 2013; Schleppegrell, 2004).

The text types of the CCSS can be seen as "modes of discourse" that include Narration, Description, Exposition, and Argument. Dating back to 1827

(Newman, 1827), this classification system in composition studies was very influential and became the "norm" for teaching composition in the nineteenth and twentieth centuries. As the field of composition became more specialized and focused on writers' purposes, the importance of the modes classification scheme diminished, especially after 1950 (Connors, 1981). With the focus on the main text types as narrative, informational/explanatory, and argument, the CCSS seem to be going back to the nineteenth and twentieth century system of classification, as there clearly is little understanding about a much more useful concept—genre and genre families. There is, therefore, a modes/genres disconnect between the CCSS and composition teaching in college because there is little conversation and collaboration between secondary and postsecondary instructors.

The text types of the CCSS can be considered "macrogenres" or "genre families." Genre families can be subdivided even further into specific genres to facilitate writing instruction across grades K–12. Without an understanding of specific genres, their purposes and stages, and specific language features, the CCSS provide a cursory view of writing. According to systemic-functional linguistics, genres are "recurrent configurations of meanings . . . that . . . enact the social practices of a given culture," or "staged, goal oriented social processes. Staged, because it usually takes us more than one step to reach our goals; goal oriented because we feel frustrated if we don't accomplish the final steps . . .; social because writers shape their texts for readers of particular kinds" (Martin & Rose, 2008, p. 6). Different stages within a particular genre are identifiable by their linguistic and grammatical patterns to achieve a social purpose in a particular context. Similar genres can be connected to form genre families. In the U.S. context, very little has been taught in teacher education programs in terms of genre instruction (de Oliveira & Iddings, 2014). An understanding of genre would be extremely beneficial to teachers to address writing expectations and moves that go beyond an introduction, body, and conclusion. A more nuanced view of writing as having a purpose, audience, specific goals and stages, and patterns that construct these expectations is a critical need for teachers.

In addition, the CCSS focus on informational/explanatory and argument text types from the elementary grades ignores the notion that there is a developmental trajectory in learning to write from the elementary grades on to middle and high school. This developmental trajectory includes the major shifts in using language across four phases of development that students go through as they learn to write:

1. Early childhood: 6–8 years (Grades K–2)
2. Late childhood to early adolescence: 9–12 years (Grades 3–7)
3. Mid-adolescence: 13–15 years (Grades 8–10)
4. Late adolescence: 16–18 years (Grades 11–12).

Along this developmental trajectory, a learner pathway that moves students from narrative to expository to argument that builds on linguistic development across these phases has been well established in the literature, though ignored or not

understood by the developers of the CCSS. This learner pathway includes the major shifts in using language across these phases and demonstrates how narrative genres in earlier years arranged through time move to expositions and arguments arranged through cause in later years (Christie & Derewianka, 2008). This learner pathway is valuable for understanding a progression from the more everyday, commonsense narrative genres to the more academic, uncommon sense of expositions and arguments. This would involve a reconceptualization of the CCSS with a focus on narrative genres in grades K–4 with a move toward exposition in grades 5–8 and arguments in grades 9–12. Even though this kind of understanding was not highly recognized in the U.S. context, now it would be even more challenging to bring these ideas to the forefront because of the CCSS. Figure 3.1 provides an overview of a learner pathway that includes the different genres that could be taught within each one of the CCSS text types (genre families) along a developmental trajectory.

Figure 3.1 provides an overview of various genres that could be the focus of attention across the years of schooling. The ladder shape of the figure highlights the foundational nature of narratives for the more complex informational/explanatory and argument genres. Though we know ELLs may enter schools at various grade levels, it is important to provide a foundational knowledge of narrative genres as they move to informational/explanatory and argument genres. It is beyond the scope of this chapter to provide further attention to which genres could be the focus of each grade level, but years of research have provided ideas for this kind of attention (see, for example, Brisk, 2015; de Oliveira, 2011). It is important, therefore, to develop students' habits of mind in earlier years, and continue to reiterate them as they move to secondary and postsecondary settings. All of this is a tall order, but one that is a necessary step toward instilling in students a love for writing that so many of us share, along with preparing them for their future in postsecondary settings.

Conclusion

The Common Core State Standards set high expectations for the learning of all students, including English language learners (ELLs). Although addressing the needs of ELLs in the documentation of the CCSS is "beyond (its) scope," the CCSS claim that "all students must have the opportunity to learn and meet the same . . . standards" of native English-speaking students (NGA & CCSSO, 2010c, p. 6). They go on to say that "it is possible to meet the standards . . . without displaying native-like control," which seems to place the responsibility of addressing ELLs' language development solely on the shoulders of teachers. The "Application of Common Core State Standards for English Language Learners" document notes general advice for the CCSS implementation, noting that these students will "require additional time, . . . support and aligned assessments . . . adjusting instruction . . ." and mentions that ELLs have access to various support facilities (NGA & CCSSO, 2010a, p. 3).

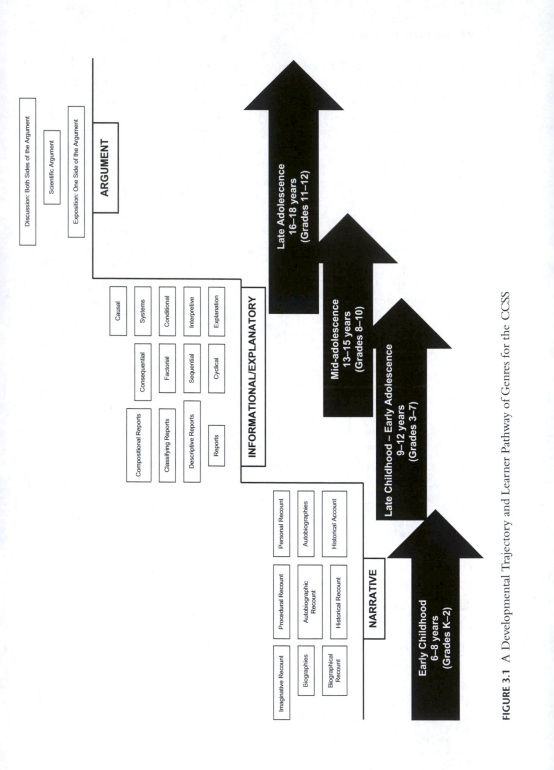

FIGURE 3.1 A Developmental Trajectory and Learner Pathway of Genres for the CCSS

As more and more ELLs are integrated into mainstream English classrooms, all teachers will be expected to teach these students along with their mainstream students. This student population is consistently ignored when content standards are conceptualized, but should not be an afterthought. The CCSS ultimately are designed to provide students and teachers with consistency and stability across all grade levels, schools, and states in order to establish an overall "standard" of performance across the nation. Although the prescription of teacher pedagogy is not outlined in the CCSS, past research (e.g., Enright & Gilliland, 2011; Zacher Pandya, 2011) has shown that as assessments are created based on standards, the professional practice of teachers will be affected. ELLs may find themselves having to meet standards regardless of their needs and backgrounds. Teachers of ELLs may find themselves struggling to meet the needs of this population unless more is done to specifically prepare them to teach writing in ways that would provide more of a learner pathway and consider the developmental trajectory for writing.

English teachers striving to address the CCSS will need a conceptual understanding of the full continuum of expectations for writing in order to understand the continuum of experiences their ELLs bring to the classroom. Teachers need to be able to adapt their instruction to the ELLs' experiences, being reflexive to the needs of the students rather than following the grade-level standards too strictly. A better understanding of text types as "genre families" may help teachers to focus on specific genres that are more precise in their purposes and language choices. Because of the lack of attention to a developmental trajectory and learner pathway in the CCSS, my prediction is that teachers will realize that students will struggle with expository and argument genres in earlier years. This hopefully will lead to a focus on narratives in earlier years and exposition and arguments in later years. We should expect a lot of confusion on the part of teachers as well as students as implementation continues to take hold across the country. As I explain in this chapter, there also needs to be greater knowledge about a developmental trajectory and learner pathway for these genre families. Making connections between what students are learning at the secondary levels through the CCSS and what they will be learning in college is paramount for teachers and students in both these levels.

Acknowledgements

The author wishes to thank her collaborators, Marshall Klassen and Michael Maune, for their work on the CCSS for ELA, which has led to several publications and presentations.

Bibliography

Bright, A., Hansen-Thomas, H., & de Oliveira, L. C. (Eds.) (2015). *The common core state standards in mathematics and English language learners: High school.* Alexandria, VA: TESOL Press.

Brisk, M. E. (2015). *Engaging students in academic literacies: Genre-based pedagogy for K–5 classrooms*. New York: Routledge.

Christie, F., & Derewianka, B. (2008). *School discourse: Learning to write across the years of schooling*. New York: Continuum.

Civil, M., & Turner, E. (Eds.) (2014). *The common core state standards in mathematics for English language learners: Grades K–8*. Alexandria, VA: TESOL Press.

Connors, R. J. (1981). The rise and fall of the modes of discourse. *College Composition and Communication, 32*(4), 444–455.

Council of Writing Program Administrators, National Council of Teachers of English, and National Writing Project. (2011). *Framework for success in postsecondary writing*. Retrieved from http://wpacouncil.org/files/framework-for-success-postsecondary-writing.pdf

de Oliveira, L. C. (2011). *Knowing and writing school history: The language of students' expository writing and teachers' expectations*. Charlotte, NC: Information Age Publishing.

de Oliveira, L. C. (Ed.) (2016). *The common core state standards in literacy in History/Social studies, science, and technical subjects for English language learners: Grades 6–12*. Alexandria, VA: TESOL Press.

de Oliveira, L. C., & Iddings, J. (Eds.) (2014). *Genre pedagogy across the curriculum: Theory and application in U.S. classrooms and contexts*. London, England: Equinox.

de Oliveira, L. C., Klassen, M., & Maune, M. (Eds.) (2015a). *The common core state standards in English language arts and English language learners: Grades 6–12*. Alexandria, VA: TESOL Press.

de Oliveira, L. C., Klassen, M., & Maune, M. (2015b). From detailed reading to independent writing: Scaffolding instruction for ELLs through knowledge about language. In L. C. de Oliveira, M. Klassen, & M. Maune (Eds.), *The common core state standards in English language arts for English language learners: Grades 6–12* (pp. 65–77). Alexandria, VA: TESOL Press.

de Oliveira, L. C., & Lan, S-W. (2014). Writing science in an upper elementary classroom: A genre-based approach to teaching English language learners. *Journal of Second Language Writing, 25*(1), 23–39.

Derewianka, B., & Jones, P. (2013). *Teaching language in context*. Oxford: Oxford University Press.

Enright, K. A., & Gilliland, B. (2011). Multilingual writing in an age of accountability: From policy to practice in US high school classrooms. *Journal of Second Language Writing, 20*(3), 182–195.

Johnson, K. (2013). Beyond standards: Disciplinary and national perspectives on habits of mind. *College Composition and Communication, 64*(3), 517–541.

Kusch, J. (2009). The chicken that wins: The history of assessment. In T. A. Price & E. Peterson (Eds.), *The myth and reality of no child left behind* (pp. 13–26). Lanham: University Press of America.

Martin, J. R., & Rose, D. (2008). *Genre relations: Mapping culture*. London: Equinox Publishing.

Menken, K. (2008). *English learners left behind: Standardized testing as language policy*. Clevedon, England: Multilingual Matters Ltd.

National Governors Association Center for Best Practices & Council of Chief State School Officers. (2010a). *Application of common core state standards for English language learners*. Washington, DC: National Governors Association Center for Best Practices & Council of Chief State School Officers. Retrieved from www.corestandards.org/assets/application-for-english-learners.pdf

National Governors Association Center for Best Practices & Council of Chief State School Officers. (2010b). *Common core state standards for English language arts & literacy in History/ Social studies, science, and technical subjects appendix c: Samples of student writing.* Washington, DC: National Governors Association Center for Best Practices & Council of Chief State School Officers. Retrieved from www.corestandards.org/assets/Appendix_C.pdf

National Governors Association Center for Best Practices & Council of Chief State School Officers. (2010c). *Common core state standards for English language arts & literacy in History/ Social studies, science, and technical subjects.* Washington, DC: National Governors Association Center for Best Practices & Council of Chief State School Officers. Retrieved from www.corestandards.org/assets/CCSSI_ELA%20Standards.pdf

National Governors Association Center for Best Practices & Council of Chief State School Officers. (2010d). *Common core state standards for English language arts & literacy in History/ Social studies, science, and technical subjects appendix a: Research supporting key elements of the standards & glossary of key terms.* Washington, DC: National Governors Association Center for Best Practices & Council of Chief State School Officers. Retrieved from www. corestandards.org/assets/CCSSI_ELA%20Standards.pdf

Newman, S. P. (1827). *A practical system of rhetoric.* New York: Mark H. Newman.

No Child Left Behind Act of 2001, P.L. 107–110, 20 U.S.C. § 6319 (2002).

Rothman, R. (2011). *Something in common: The common core standards and the next chapter in American education.* Cambridge, MA: Harvard Education Press.

Schleppegrell, M. J. (2004). *The language of schooling: A functional linguistics perspective.* Mahwah, NJ: Erlbaum.

Smith, M. S., & O'Day, J. (1991). *Putting the pieces together: Systemic school reform* (CPRE Policy Brief, RB-06–4/91). New Brunswick, NJ: Consortium for Policy Research in Education.

Spycher, P. (Ed.) (2014). *The common core state standards in English language arts for English language learners: Grades K–5.* Alexandria, VA: TESOL Press.

Whitehurst, G. (2009). *Don't forget curriculum* (Brown Center Letters on Education). Washington, DC: Brookings Institution.

Zacher Pandya, J. (2011). *Overtested: How high-stakes accountability fails English language learners.* New York, NY: Teachers College Press.

4

RESIDENT MULTILINGUAL WRITERS ACROSS A SECONDARY CURRICULUM

Toward a Postmethod Approach

Sarah Henderson Lee

I spent my first year as a high school ELL teacher not only trying to survive as a new teacher in public education, but also trying to figure out exactly what Vincent,[1] a student of mine, had meant by the following statement: "You want to hear me when I write in English; they want to hear a white student." He was, after all, one of my strongest writers. How could he be failing the writing assignments in his other courses, especially courses led by well-liked, highly qualified teachers? My interest in the complexities of multilingual writing was born out of the conversations surrounding Vincent's comments and my desire to help resident multilingual writers who share his frustration.

Even though writing is often viewed as one of the most important language skills for academic competence, research on the writing of resident multilingual learners in the secondary context is still somewhat sparse. This is, in part, due to the complex nature of the secondary educational environment, where the writing of these students is often overshadowed by "the more dramatic, threatening, and far-reaching issues learners face and the seriousness of the other language, identity, and agency issues their cases present" (Leki, Cumming, & Silva, 2008, p. 26). In order to contribute to multilingual writing research and, moreover, better meet the needs of resident multilingual writers transitioning into higher education and/or the workforce, issues of language, identity, and agency can no longer be separated from the students' writing and their writing experiences. Using findings from a semester-long study of seven resident multilingual high school seniors, this chapter explores four disruptive themes, including forced representations of resident multilingual writers and an unequal trade between language acquisition and subtractive bilingualism, and suggests a postmethod approach to writing programs.

Conceptual Framework

While there have been several calls for the incorporation of social and contextual issues into language acquisition research, Roberts (1998) points out that merely identifying those elements plays "a marginal role in language development" (p. 31). Rather, she encourages the use of a language socialization framework to investigate how learners are introduced to, produce, and understand discourses and how such learning is influenced by assumptions about multilingual learners. According to Bayley and Schecter (2003), multilingual contexts offer a more accurate picture of language socialization, where the process is lifelong and those being socialized often exhibit agency by choosing among identities offered to them or constructing new identities in situations where they find no desirable choice. Here, I adopt Norton's (2000) definition of identity, which references "how a person understands his or her relationship to the world, how that relationship is constructed across time and space, and how the person understands possibilities for the future" (p. 5). Because multilingual learners are "socialized by and through language into new domains of knowledge and cultural practice" (Bayley & Schecter, 2003, p. 2) and "it is through language that a person negotiates a sense of self within and across different sites at different points in time" (Norton, 2000, p. 5), a convergence of language socialization and learner identity provided an appropriate framework for this across-curriculum study.

Contextualizing the Study

The research site was Crestwood High School (CHS), one of five high schools in a midwestern state's largest district. CHS houses the district's only ELL program for grades 9 though 12, which at the time of this study consisted of 78 students representing 19 primary languages.

The participants included seven resident multilingual learners: Tina, Tim, Tony, Marlene, Jack, Andi, and Elise. During this study, each student was enrolled as a senior and shared a minimum of one of the following classes: ELL, English IV, World History, and Earth Science. Further details of the participants, including gender, age, primary language, and time in U.S. schools, are included in Table 4.1.

TABLE 4.1 Participants

Name	Gender	Age	Primary language	Time in U.S. schools
Tina	F	20	Vietnamese	3 years
Tim	M	19	Vietnamese	3 years
Tony	M	18	Spanish	3 years, 3 months
Marlene	F	17	Spanish	3 years, 7 months
Jack	M	18	Burmese (Chin)	3 years, 7 months
Andi	M	18	Mandarin	4 years
Elise	F	18	Romanian (Moldovan)	7 years

Data Collection and Analysis

A critical case study methodology was employed to represent the transformative purpose underlying the social constructivism practices of qualitative research. The single-case design (Yin, 2009) allowed for multiple data sources, including in-depth interviews, nonparticipant observations, and written artifacts, to capture the specifics of a commonplace situation (i.e., resident multilingual writers across a secondary curriculum). To understand the lived experience of others and the meaning they make of that experience, in-depth interviewing, specifically Rubin and Rubin's (2005) responsive interviewing model, was employed in a three-interview (pre, during, post) series for participants. All interviews were digitally recorded and transcribed verbatim. Participants were given an opportunity to review each of their interview transcripts prior to data analysis. To gain an additional layer of understanding and insight into the instructional and interactional patterns of participants, I conducted nonparticipant observations in the four across-curriculum classes. During the data collection period, I observed each class six times and used Merriam's (2009) checklist of observable elements, including the physical setting, the participants, activities and interactions, conversation, subtle factors, and my behavior as the researcher. Finally, participants' written texts from both in and out of school were collected on a voluntary basis during the data collection period. Prepared independently from the study, such written artifacts provided a data source unaffected by the research process.

Recursive content analysis was used in this study to ensure constant alignment between the research questions and the data collection methods. Hornberger's (2003) continua of biliteracy model, which represents the multiple and complex interrelationships between bilingualism and literacy, was used to help categorize and contextualize the data sources and "make explicit the power relationships which define bi(multi)literacies" (Hornberger & Skilton-Sylvester, 2000, p. 96). The specific continua, across which biliteracy is represented, are categorized by context, development, content, and media (Figure 4.1). The context of biliteracy continua highlight the interrelatedness of oracy and literacy, with differences occurring contextually; the development of biliteracy continua emphasize the more collective nature of language acquisition; the content of biliteracy continua focus on meaning types expressed in regards to the other continua; and the media of biliteracy continua stress the multiple languages of resident multilingual students. To employ the dual process of immersion and crystallization, I read the collected data sources multiple times and reflected on their relationships to the study's conceptual framework and analytic lens in an attempt to identify and articulate emerging themes (Janesick, 2000).

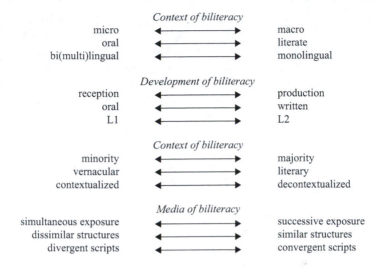

Traditionally less powerful   **Traditionally more powerful**

Context of biliteracy

micro   macro
oral   literate
bi(multi)lingual   monolingual

Development of biliteracy

reception   production
oral   written
L1   L2

Context of biliteracy

minority   majority
vernacular   literary
contextualized   decontextualized

Media of biliteracy

simultaneous exposure   successive exposure
dissimilar structures   similar structures
divergent scripts   convergent scripts

FIGURE 4.1 Power Relations in the COB Model (Hornberger & Skilton-Sylvester, 2000, p. 99)

Findings and Discussion

Emerging from the data analysis were four across-participant themes influenced by the traditionally more powerful and often disruptive ends of Hornberger's continua of biliteracy: (1) writing instruction, practices, and feedback inconsistencies; (2) forced representations of resident multilingual writers; (3) the ELL classroom as both a safe space and a ghetto; and (4) an unequal trade between language acquisition and subtractive bilingualism.

Writing Instruction, Practices, and Feedback Inconsistencies

For many of the participants, writing instruction, practices, and feedback were associated solely with their English and ELL classes. While the division between these two contexts is noteworthy, a greater divide existed between them and other general education classes, mirroring Valdés' (1999) two-world distinction for resident multilingual learners in U.S. high schools. Moreover, the writing-across-the-curriculum divide reinforced the power relation extremes of all continua of biliteracy.

All participants struggled to identify writing instruction in non-English-related general education classes, where the written L2 product was valued over the learner-specific process. This, in turn, resulted in the privileging of power-influenced meaning (i.e., the majority, literary, and decontextualized ends of the content of biliteracy continua), which further disadvantaged resident multilingual

students whose writing did not relay similar meaning. In classes where note taking was the dominant writing practice, including World History and Earth Science, strategies specific to this type of writing were not directly taught. This supports the traditionally more powerful side of the development of biliteracy continua, where learners are responsible for specific L2 written products regardless of their background. Here, students like Tina, Tim, Jack, and Tony were expected to independently recognize and summarize key information during lectures (World History) and/or complete a provided template with missing words from lecture slides (Earth Science). In both instances, the power-weighted ends of the biliterate content continua restricted students' access to content by not reflecting their prior knowledge, experiences, and languages. Additionally, students were not engaged in subject and thought through writing, de-emphasizing the writing-across-the-curriculum component of writing to learn, where all forms of writing are seen as vehicles to increase students' content area understanding. From the two experienced approaches to writing notes, participants responded with frustration and boredom. Tina, for example, was upset that the effort she put into her World History notes benefited her very little when it came to tests because what she viewed as important to write down did not address the teacher's questions. Tim and Tony both questioned what little effort was required of them for their Earth Science notes and linked this approach to their struggle to remember the content material. Because of the complete lack of writing instruction specific to note taking, all participants believed they were expected to already know how to take effective notes in a given subject area and/or note taking was not an equally valuable writing practice across the curriculum.

Also contributing to the participants' consensus that writing was never taught in non-English-related general education courses was the fact that reading texts were rarely investigated as writing texts. Writing samples of scientific observations, lab reports, and historical research, for example, were not analyzed as genres with unique discourses, styles, and formats in the classes where students were expected to complete such writing tasks. This absence of intertextuality, or "juxtaposition of texts" (Bloome & Egan-Robertson, 2004, p. 16), represents the power-weighted ends of both the biliterate development and content continua and prevented the fulfillment of the writing-across-the-curriculum component "rhetoric of inquiry," where features of discipline-specific texts are explored (Bazerman et al., 2005). The intertextuality emphasis in English and ELL classes, on the other hand, introduced various writing genres through reading samples. For example, in the English IV class, the writing genre of satire was introduced first as a reading genre, where students read to understand both the text and its writing components. Such incorporation of intertextuality, according to Bazerman et al. (2005), is essential for successful writing-across-the-curriculum programs and curriculums. It cannot, however, be limited to the ELL and English classroom contexts.

To distinguish the writing practices of English and ELL classes, participants focused on genre differences. Andi described the writing practices of his English

classes, especially his English IV class, as involving advanced genres. These included a college application letter, satire, and comparative research paper. Participants described the writing practices of their ELL classes as involving mostly personal experience writing. For some, this writing genre seemed too simple and monotonous. Tim laughed when he thought about how many times he had written about his most influential life event. Realizing the success of his immigrant story, Tim reworked it for a variety of personal experience writing assignments, favoring the traditionally more powerful sides of the context and content of biliteracy. Here, the macro power-weighted end of the biliterate context continua speaks to the societal attitude of the "forever immigrant" while the majority power-weighted end of the biliterate content continua privileges the American dream perspective where immigrant struggles are only associated with individuals' home countries.

For other participants, like Andi and Marlene, such personal experience assignments served as writing vehicles through which they could represent their true identities and, ultimately, move to the traditionally less powerful sides of the biliterate context and content continua, where their resident multilingual status is valued. In fact, they questioned why this genre was, for the most part, limited to the ELL classroom. Both Marlene and Andi suspected that this genre of writing would be even less incorporated in the college classroom. This was especially bothersome to Marlene, who appreciated being able to use her existing words and knowledge, from both of her languages and cultures, to compose personal experience essays. This she contrasted to the extra work of translating between Spanish and English to simply meet the requirements of informative and analytical writing, which she associated more with college-level writing. In addition to the extra time needed, this process proved to be particularly difficult for Marlene due to her lack of simultaneous language exposure at CHS, supporting the power-weighted successive exposure end of the biliterate media continua.

A writing challenge imbalance existed across the curriculum for the participants. Tony, for example, felt challenged by the writing requirements of his English IV class, where he manipulated language to achieve a genre's specific purpose. This was not the case for the writing practices of his other classes, which were limited to summarizing and reporting. For Tony, consistent and high expectations were needed to build confidence in resident multilingual writers, like himself, who were planning to attend college. Tim, on the other hand, represented the challenge imbalance by contrasting the personal experience writing most prevalent in the ELL classroom with a Civil War writing assignment in American History. The content specificity of the Civil War writing assignment proved extremely difficult for Tim, who had no prior knowledge of the American war and felt overwhelmed by the related vocabulary. Such an assignment privileged the traditionally more powerful ends of the content of biliteracy continua and ignored the balanced point of intersection, where subject and thought is supported through the incorporation of students' background knowledge, experiences, and languages. Here, the lack of contextualized texts, acknowledging the position of readers/writers, was absent,

limiting valued meaning on the topic. The incorporation of Civil War texts from minority perspectives, for example, might have provided Tim with a contextualized starting point from which to create meaning.

All of the participants noted a significant difference in the grading criteria and feedback of their writing across the curriculum. In classes other than English and ELL, the grading focus was primarily on content, supporting the traditionally more powerful ends of the biliterate content continua where meaning is limited, and little to no verbal or written feedback was received. Here, students were not given the opportunity to perform, read, or discuss their texts. As a result, language components were divorced from whole texts, and the teacher's meaning was the valued meaning. For a few participants, including Andi, Elise, and Tony, the experience of writing not being directly taught in non-English classes was equated with the "real" world, where they would be expected to know how to write. The consistent lack of writing feedback was, however, classified by most participants as a missed opportunity to improve their overall English writing ability and, furthermore, better prepare them for college and professional writing. In fact, several participants recalled their written drafts never being returned at all. While Andi believed that his teachers knew about writing in their discipline, he questioned why fellow students only felt comfortable conversing about writing with English and ELL teachers. These teachers consistently encouraged student engagement in content through writing, favoring the traditionally less powerful micro and oral ends of the biliterate context continua. Here, writing instruction was embedded in content instruction. Moreover, the ELL teacher consistently invited resident multilingual students into conversations about their writing, an act that was significantly less prevalent in the general education classes where access to academic discourse intricacies, as Delpit (1995) notes, is often limited for minority students because they are not familiar with the "codes or rules for participating in power" (p. 24).

In both English and ELL classes, students recalled receiving a grading rubric when the writing assignment was first introduced. These rubrics presented a balance between content and grammar, often including categories for mechanics/conventions, idea development, and organization. Such a balance favors the contextualized end of the biliterate content continua by not separating language parts from whole texts and presents an opportunity for students to study the relationship between language and content. Some participants, like Marlene, appreciated this balance and found it surprising that her attention to language in her writing was not equally evaluated across the curriculum. According to her, such a writing evaluation imbalance was a writing-across-the-curriculum inconsistency that, if changed, could positively impact writers like her. Participants like Andi, on the other hand, questioned why grammar was evaluated in classes where grammar was not directly taught. In fact, he complained that he was consistently graded down for grammar on his English IV essays even though grammar was not part of the classroom instruction. This was especially surprising to him since he always took advantage of the teacher's offer to proofread resident multilingual students' papers

prior to the due date. Similarly, Tim expressed dislike for such unidirectional feedback and suggested writing feedback be presented as a conversation between student/teacher and student/student, emphasizing process writing over product writing and supporting the traditionally less powerful oral end of the context of biliteracy continua where resident multilingual writers find voice and agency in discussing their texts.

Forced Representations of Resident Multilingual Writers

Tina, Tim, and Andi viewed their resident multilingual status negatively in terms of both their classroom and writing experiences across the curriculum. In World History, for example, Tina spent the majority of class time working independently because she was certain neither her teacher nor her classmates would directly call on her. This, she felt, was mostly due to the fact that she was a resident multilingual student. Additionally, she thought her older age contributed to this divide. Mostly on the periphery of classroom conversations (Duff, 2002), Tina felt that her teacher and classmates viewed her as less interested or competent even though she consistently performed well on assignments and tests, and this minimized her investment, interest, and motivation. Movement toward the traditionally less powerful sides of all continua of biliteracy would place value on Tina's age, languages, and cultures and, in turn, help maximize her investment, interest, and motivation.

Both Tina and Tim could only recall instances of classroom discourse invites when the topic revolved around their home country, Vietnam. Likewise, Andi remembered only discourse invites in his math and science classes. In many of his other classes, Andi described being purposefully skipped, which resulted in, according to him, many of his teachers and classmates knowing little about him. This would have required them to acknowledge his racial and ethnic differences, which according to Harklau's (2003) "colorblind" representation is discriminatory.

The limited discourse invites also perpetuated a lack of confidence, which for Jack led to hiding his work from both his teacher and classmates in Earth Science. Marlene, however, thought being ignored was better than always being viewed as needing help, which had been her experience. This representation mirrored Harklau's (2003) "linguistically deficient" representation, where lack of standard English production is viewed as either a linguistic or cognitive deficit. Such forced representations were most frequently experienced by participants in their general education classes, where the monolingual, L2, and majority ends of the biliterate context, development, and content continua respectively were privileged. Tony was the only participant to view these representations positively. Concerned about losing his primary language, Tony viewed speaking and writing about his country as an opportunity to connect to his primary language and culture, which rarely happened in his experiences across a U.S. high school curriculum.

Harklau's (2003) "Ellis Island" representation was most frequently observed in ELL classes where participants recalled writing about their immigrant experience

for a number of personal experience assignments. Here, students' ethnolinguistic identity was privileged over their individual identity, indicative of a power-weighted context (macro) and content (majority) influence. While not all of these assignments required students to retell their story of coming to America, many required them to make connections to previous experiences in their home countries. For some, like Jack, these were often painful memories, ones he wanted to replace with his current preferred life. For others, who had been in the U.S. for a longer period of time, it was sometimes difficult to even make such connections. Similar to receiving classroom praise for being hard workers, many of these students received high marks on these writing tasks with comments linked to them overcoming great obstacles.

Regardless of the continually expanding body of literature calling for a bridge between in- and out-of-school literacy practices (Barton & Hamilton, 1998; Gee, 1996; Heath, 1983; Hull & Schultz, 2002), a significant divide existed between home and school literacies for the participants of this study. Here, they assumed their teachers saw them as non-writers outside of the classroom because no reference to out-of-school writing practices was made during in-school writing instruction, practices, and feedback. This was, however, not the case. Proficient vernacular writers, such as Jack and Marlene, expressed that they wrote outside of school just as much or more than they did in school. Such out-of-school writings included letters, journal entries, songs, and stories for friends and family. Neither Jack nor Marlene, however, recalled an opportunity to bring these writings into the classroom, privileging the power-weighted ends of the content of biliteracy continua and identifying a much needed area of improvement for writing-across-the-curriculum programs and curriculums. For them and other participants, the message here was that in-school writing was more important than out-of-school writing. The representations of these resident multilingual writers across a secondary curriculum resulted in no participants considering themselves to be "good" writers, an obvious consequence for students' language investment (Harklau, 2003; Norton Pierce, 1995). In fact, to avoid such consequences, Elise freed herself from such representations by exiting herself from ELL classroom services after her first year of high school.

The ELL Classroom as Both a Safe Space and a Ghetto

Even though several participants viewed the writing practices of the ELL classroom as "easier" because of the preferred personal experience genre and the level of teacher involvement throughout the entire writing process, they also expressed feeling most comfortable in this context, which acknowledged the micro, oral, and bilingual ends of the biliterate context continua. Here, students were valued for their linguistically and culturally unique voices. This, according to Jack, was because of the ELL teacher's eagerness to help resident multilingual students with their writing, no matter which class it was for, by starting a conversation about

their work and providing comprehensive feedback. For some resident multilingual students, this level of attention created a dependency on the ELL classroom, which was often reinforced by general education teachers' willingness to let resident multilingual students go to the ELL classroom to receive help with assignments and tests instead of helping them within the discipline-specific context. In spite of the fact that they allowed students to frequent the ELL classroom, both the Earth Science and the World History teacher were suspicious of the happenings in the ELL classroom. They, for example, wondered how a resident multilingual student who clearly struggled in their class could return from the ELL classroom with "A" work. Further strengthening the divide between ELL and general education classes and teachers is that neither of the teachers addressed their concerns by starting a related dialogue with the student and/or the ELL teacher.

This existing disconnect between the *safe house*, or ELL classroom, and the *contact zone*, or general education classrooms (Canagarajah, 1997), is representative of the power relation extremes of the context of biliteracy continua. From the participants' perspective, the ELL classroom was a safe space for intercultural and linguistic interaction, favoring the traditionally less powerful micro, oral, and bi(multi)lingual ends of the continua. Here, their unique lived experiences, communicative abilities, and vernaculars were valued. The general education teachers, on the other hand, perpetuated the idea of the ELL classroom as a "ghetto" (Valdés, 1998) because it contradicted their familiarity with the power-weighted macro, literate, and monolingual ends of the continua. Here, students are often isolated from general education classes because teachers are uncomfortable with students' resident multilingual status and view them solely as the responsibility of the language specialist. To heal such a divide, Canagarajah (1997) argues that *safe houses* are essential to *contact zones*, supporting a balanced position on the biliterate context continua.

For most of the participants, the idea of not having a resident multilingual-specific student space in college was worrisome, reiterating Stegemoller's (2009) call for university safe spaces for immigrant students. In fact, Tina and Tim, who planned to attend the local community college, envisioned themselves still using the neighboring high school ELL teacher as a resource. Andi and Marlene, on the other hand, saw their college selves as individually responsible for improving their writing. Such responsibility to them included practicing college-level writing genres like analysis during the summer months and becoming comfortable with asking any professor for writing help.

An Unequal Trade between Language Acquisition and Subtractive Bilingualism

All participants noted a discrepancy between the acquisition of English and the maintenance of primary languages during their high school career, favoring the successive exposure, similar structures, and convergent scripts ends of the media

of biliteracy continua where no language other than English was incorporated into instruction. For several participants, including Tony, Marlene, Andi, and Elise, this divide was viewed as harmful. The minor improvements made in their English writing, for example, did not offset the significant loss of literacy skills within their first languages. In addition to the academic struggles associated with their English language skills, several participants now worried about inadequacies in their primary language. This was problematic for those working in family businesses, as well as those in communication with family and friends in their home countries. Tim, for example, shared being regularly teased by his friends in Vietnam about the mistakes he made in Vietnamese when they chatted online. Jack was the only participant to see value in the tradeoff between learning English and losing part of his primary language. This was in part due to the distance he wanted to create between his current English writing identity and former refugee self.

Several of the students realized quickly that the preservation of primary language skills, specifically literacy skills, was completely their out-of-school responsibility. Marlene, for example, continued to journal at home in Spanish. Likewise, Tony shared his recent goal of reading and writing song lyrics in Spanish during his free time. Unfortunately, the out-of-school limitation on primary language writing practices resulted in students classifying code-switching as an unacceptable academic writing practice, further supporting the successive exposure end of the biliterate media continua. Even though she felt prepared for postsecondary writing, Elise noted that her writing identity had been compromised by the absence of her primary language. Similar to other participants, Elise thought the one language limitation on writing was a missed empowerment opportunity for, not only her as a writer, but also for teachers and students who could benefit from the inclusion and acceptance of resident multilingual learners and their languages.

The participants' above experiences with acquiring English at the cost of losing their primary languages reinforce the traditionally more powerful side of the media of biliteracy continua, where successive exposure, similar structures, and convergent scripts are valued. While the dissimilar-similar structures and the divergent-convergent scripts continua speak to language form and orthographic differences, the simultaneous-successive exposure continuum notes how schools and educators approach languages. A focus shift from solely English acquisition to biliteracy by both teachers and schools would result in a repositioning of resident multilingual students' experiences toward the traditionally less powerful ends of all continua of biliteracy. To accomplish this, however, Fu and Matoush (2006) argue that writing-across-the-curriculum collaboration must first be built on the understanding of writing development as bilingual thinking. When given the writing freedom to move between their primary language and English, Fu and Matoush (2006) note that resident multilingual students tend to focus less on correct English grammar and more on their content and ideas.

Conclusion

Consisting of parameters of particularity, practicality, and possibility, postmethod pedagogy refutes the one-size-fits-all approach positioned on the traditionally more powerful and often disruptive sides of Hornberger's (2003) continua of biliteracy. Like Kumaravadivelu's (2001) re-visioning of language programs through the parameter of particularity, writing programs "must be sensitive to a particular group of teachers teaching a particular group of learners pursuing a particular set of goals within a particular institutional context embedded in a particular sociocultural milieu" (p. 538). A pedagogical shift to the parameter of particularity would require teachers across the curriculum, not solely ELL teachers, to use local knowledge of the individual writer to identify problems and address them with contextually appropriate solutions. Here, all teachers must recognize writing development as biliterate thought to achieve resident multilingual student engagement in subject and thought through writing. By providing resident multilingual learners with writing opportunities to move between their primary language and English, teachers would be valuing development of discipline-specific content and ideas over strict English usage. Such a focus shift would support a view of bi(multi)literacy as a resource for academic success as opposed to a hindrance, favoring the traditionally less powerful ends of all continua of biliteracy.

Referring to the relationship between theory and practice, Kumaravadivelu's (2001) parameter of practicality moves beyond the dichotomy of theorists as the producers of knowledge/teachers as the consumers of knowledge to reflective teachers as authentic producers of practicing theory. In terms of writing programs, the parameter of practicality must be collaborative. Conversations between teachers across the curriculum should begin with context-specific reflections of writing instruction, practices, and feedback and build toward a collective agreement on the across-curriculum writing goals. To further support effective writing-across-the-curriculum collaboration, teachers as reflective practitioners can begin transforming privileged power issues along with their students through the parameter of possibility. They might, for example, introduce students to critical discourse analysis (Rogers, 2004) to foster conversations about the power relationships between learners' primary and secondary discourses. By evaluating content-specific texts and media for privileged discourses and forced representations, resident multilingual students gain a sense of empowerment, which can result in students challenging representations of themselves and working toward social justice within their own writing, both in and out of school.

When I think back to my high school ELL teaching career, I cannot help but wonder how many students shared Vincent's frustrations but were never provided with an opportunity to voice them. Clearly, he saw what I could not see—the suppression of his linguistic and cultural identities by a dominant discourse. While I associated language use with linguistic development as a new teacher, Vincent and the other resident multilingual writers of my classroom needed me to make the

connection between language use and identity. By shedding light on the power-weighted positions of seven resident multilingual writers' experiences across a secondary curriculum, this chapter calls for all educators to reorient themselves together toward the needs of these students who deserve "our continual reimagining and opening up of educational spaces that foster their ongoing development and creative transformation of their transnational—and biliterate—lives and literacies" (Hornberger, 2007, p. 333). Such reflective and collaborative pedagogical change is critical to providing resident multilingual learners with the agency and voice needed to begin claiming their right to write, where those who write regard those who read as worthy to read, and those who read regard those who write as worthy to write (Norton Pierce, 1995). Awareness of this right by researchers, teachers, and students themselves will help to establish and promote effective learning environments across critical transitions. Here, resident multilingual writers become empowered to impact their own learning outcomes, regardless of context.

Note

1. All names are pseudonyms.

Bibliography

Barton, D., & Hamilton, M. (1998). *Local literacies: Reading and writing in one community.* London, UK: Routledge.

Bayley, R., & Schecter, S. R. (2003). Introduction: Toward a dynamic model of language socialization. In R. Bayley & S. R. Schecter (Eds.), *Language socialization in bilingual and multilingual societies* (pp. 1–6). Clevedon, UK: Multilingual Matters.

Bazerman, C., Bethel, L., Chavkin, T., Fouquette, D., Garufis, J., & Little, J. (2005). *Reference guide to writing across the curriculum.* West Lafayette, IN: Parlor Press.

Bloome, D., & Egan-Robertson, A. (2004). The social construction of intertextuality in classroom reading and writing lessons. In N. Shuart-Faris & D. Bloome (Eds.), *Uses of intertextuality in classroom and educational research* (pp. 15–62). Greenwich, CT: Information Age.

Canagarajah, S. (1997). Safe houses in the contact zone: Coping strategies of African-American students in the academy. *College Composition and Communication, 48*(2), 173–196.

Delpit, L. D. (1995). *Other people's children: Cultural conflict in the classroom.* New York, NY: New Press.

Duff, P. A. (2002). The discursive co-construction of knowledge, identity, and difference: An ethnography of communication in the high school mainstream. *Applied Linguistics, 23*(3), 289–322.

Fu, D., & Matoush, M. (2006). Writing development and biliteracy. In P. K. Matsuda, C. Ortmeier-Hooper, & X. You (Eds.), *The politics of second language writing: In search of the promised land* (pp. 5–29). West Lafayette, IN: Parlor Press.

Gee, J. P. (1996). *Social linguistics and literacies: Ideology in discourses* (3rd ed.). London, UK: Taylor & Francis.

Harklau, L. (2003). Representational practices and multi-modal communication in U.S. high schools: Implications for adolescent immigrants. In R. Bayley & S. R. Schecter (Eds.), *Language socialization in bilingual and multilingual societies* (pp. 83–97). Clevedon, UK: Multilingual Matters.

Heath, S. B. (1983). *Ways with words: Language, life, and work in communities and classrooms.* Cambridge, UK: Cambridge University Press.

Hornberger, N. H. (2003). *Continua of biliteracy: An ecological framework for educational policy, research, and practice in multilingual settings.* Clevedon, UK: Multilingual Matters.

Hornberger, N. H. (2007). Biliteracy, transnationalism, multimodality, and identity: Trajectories across space and time. *Linguistics and Education, 18*, 325–334.

Hornberger, N. H., & Skilton-Sylvester, E. (2000). Revisiting the continua of biliteracy: International and critical perspectives. *Language and Education, 14*(2), 96–122.

Hull, G., & Schultz, K. (Eds.) (2002). *School's out: Bridging out-of-school literacies with classroom practice.* New York, NY: Teachers College Press.

Janesick, V. J. (2000). The choreography of qualitative research design: Minuets, improvisations, and crystallization. In N. K. Denzin & Y. S. Lincoln (Eds.), *The handbook of qualitative research* (pp. 379–400). Thousand Oaks, CA: Sage.

Kumaravadivelu, B. (2001). Towards a postmethod pedagogy. *TESOL Quarterly, 35*(4), 537–560.

Leki, I., Cumming, A., & Silva, T. (2008). *A synthesis of research on second language writing in English.* New York, NY: Routledge.

Merriam, S. B. (2009). *Qualitative research: A guide to design and implementation.* San Francisco, CA: Jossey-Bass.

Norton, B. (2000). *Identity and language learning: Gender, ethnicity and educational change.* Harlow, UK: Pearson Education.

Norton Pierce, B. (1995). Social identity, investment, and language learning. *TESOL Quarterly, 29*, 9–31.

Roberts, C. (1998). Language acquisition or language socialization in and through discourse? Towards a redefinition of the domain of SLA. *Working Papers in Applied Linguistics, 4*, 31–42. London, UK: Thames Valley University.

Rogers, R. (2004). An introduction to critical discourse analysis in education. In R. Rogers (Ed.), *An introduction to critical discourse analysis in education* (pp. 1–18). Mahwah, NJ: Lawrence Erlbaum.

Rubin, H. J., & Rubin, I. S. (2005). *Qualitative interviewing: The art of hearing data.* Thousand Oaks, CA: Sage.

Stegemoller, W. J. (2009). *Latino students and biliteracy at a university: Literacy histories, agency, and writing.* Retrieved from ProQuest Digital Dissertations. (AAT 3392484)

Valdés, G. (1998). The world outside and inside schools: Language and immigrant children. *Educational Research, 27*(6), 4–18.

Valdés, G. (1999). Incipient bilingualism and the development of English language writing abilities in the secondary school. In C. Faltis & P. Wolfe (Eds.), *So much to say: Adolescents, bilingualism, and ESL in the secondary school* (pp. 138–175). New York, NY: Teachers College Press.

Yin, R. K. (2009). *Case study research: Design and methods* (4th ed.). Thousand Oaks, CA: Sage.

5

THE ROLE OF SOCIAL NETWORKS AND SOCIAL SUPPORT IN THE WRITING AND COLLEGE PLANNING OF MULTILINGUAL URBAN ADOLESCENTS

Jennifer Shade Wilson

> *Literacy cannot be described outside of social networks and the relationships that exist among their members.*
>
> (Hayden & Fagan, 1995, p. 260)

A teenaged guy whose older sister suggests that he keep a daily journal to help him improve his writing—and he does it willingly. A high school girl who writes stories for fun and shares them with her best friend. Two college freshmen who take initiative to seek out tutorial help on their academic essays. These four students, plus three others described in this chapter, are multilingual teens who were identified as "at risk for literacy development," yet they were utilizing support from important people in their social networks and, eventually, succeeding in school.

This chapter reports on a study that investigated the ways writing was involved in the social relationships of a group of multilingual adolescents in a major North American city. Using the lenses of social support and social network theory, I address the following questions:

- With whom did these inner-city, multilingual students report interacting on a regular basis?
- What types of texts were these students writing with important people in their lives, and what types of support did these individuals provide the students for writing?
- In what ways did their social relationships influence students' plans for and success in higher education?

Framing the Study

Why "Social Networks" and "Social Support"?

The underlying principle of *social network theory* is that interpersonal relationships—and the patterns formed by these relations—are the building blocks of social life (Marin & Wellman, 2011). This field has its roots in sociological theories from the early 1900s that hypothesized that society is "nothing more than a web of relations" (p. 14); the current social network perspective has been adopted by scholars in fields as disparate as computer science, medicine, and economics in order to investigate the nature and implications of social connections between human beings.

An early proponent of social network analysis in language research was sociolinguist Lesley Milroy, who studied patterns of linguistic variation as related to individuals' ties to their local communities in Belfast, Ireland, in the 1970s and '80s (e.g., Milroy, 1987). However, Milroy applied a whole network approach, in which a researcher takes a "bird's-eye view" (Marin & Wellman, 2011, p. 19) of all members in a network and the connections between them. In contrast, I have used the personal network approach, which focuses only on a single individual and the links between this individual and others.

My approach was also based in *social support* research, which "pursue[s] a wide range of questions concerning the positive (and negative) outcomes that people receive from social relationships" (Morgan, 1990, p. 195). The interdisciplinary field of social support has a long-standing association with research in social networks: In order for social support researchers to gain a perspective on the important relationships that exist in participants' lives, they generally need at least a snapshot of participants' social networks.

Social support as a research field grew out of epidemiological work in the 1970s on the benefits of social interactions in preventing disease. In more recent years, researchers from a variety of fields have studied the effects of social support on depression, delinquency, and academic performance in children (Richman, Rosenfeld, & Bowen, 1998). Over three decades of research, social psychologists have confirmed that the people perceived by students to be supportive fall into five distinct categories: parent, teacher, classmate, close friend, and school personnel (cf. Malecki & Demaray, 2006).

In particular, the study in this chapter was influenced by two longitudinal, qualitative inquiries that, while not looking specifically at social support, found social influences on the literacy development of multicultural, multilingual students. In her three-year study of four university students for whom English was not the first language, Leki (2007) found that the academic success of these students was often based on the academic literacy support—such as shared lecture notes, informal study groups, and mentoring—they received via relationships they had established with their classmates and their instructors. A second study (Snow, Porsche, Tabors, & Harris, 2007) followed 41 low-income students from age 3

through 10th grade and concluded that "[t]he poorer academic outcomes of the students highlighted . . . compared with those in the group who fared better has much to do with the availability of supportive adults in general, and strong parental support in particular" (p. 66).

Social Relationships in the Writing of Multilingual Adolescents

As I have described elsewhere (Wilson, 2013), a variety of qualitative studies of multilingual adolescents' writing (and reading) demonstrate the many contexts in which these students are interacting through literate activities with important people in their lives. Such contexts and activities include emailing a parent living abroad, chatting with friends on the Internet, and composing creative pieces online (Yi, 2007); working with a partner to compose a group project for school (Villalva, 2006); chatting online with peers around the world (Lam, 2000); negotiating conflict with an English teacher (Ortmeier-Hooper, 2013); and relying on a teacher to compose a course paper (Kibler, 2013).

Most of these studies have been more concerned with the literate practices and events in which the participants were engaging than with the existence or substance of the relationships that influenced these practices and events; as a result, each study documents said relationships in limited contexts and not across all possible contexts or within a participant's complete network. Taken as a body of work, however, the contexts in which such relationships have been described by second language writing (SLW) researchers correlate with the categories of supportive individuals described by social support researchers (e.g., Malecki & Demaray, 2006): adolescents have substantial *socioliterate relationships* with parents, teachers, friends, and, to a lesser degree, classmates.

The concept of socioliterate relationships in my research evolved from Leki's (2007) use of the term "socioacademic relationships" to denote social interactions between multilingual undergraduates and their peers and faculty members "that proved to be critical to the students' sense of satisfaction with their educational work and sometimes even to the possibility of doing that work" (p. 14). I have adapted the term in this chapter to refer specifically to relationships with a writing component.

Study Context and Design

In the fall of 2008, my colleagues and I began tutoring high school students at Pathways to Education (P2E)[1]—a community-based after-school program created to address the high local drop-out rate[2]—in preparation for conducting a yearlong study of the literacy development of "at-risk" high school students (see Cumming, 2012).

Regent Park, the neighborhood where P2E originated, is just a dozen blocks east of downtown Toronto and is home to the oldest and largest public housing project in Canada; it has consistently been cited as one of the poorest neighborhoods in Canada (TCH, 2007). It is a linguistically and culturally diverse

neighborhood as well: In 2007, approximately 60% of Regent Park residents were immigrants, speaking over 70 languages; 50% of residents had arrived in Canada in the past 10 years (TCH, 2007).

Participants

The yearlong study mentioned above, Adolescent Literacy in Three Urban Regions (ALTUR), followed 21 P2E students, freshmen through juniors, whom P2E staff members had identified as "at-risk for literacy development." After that study ended, I continued to follow seven of those students for another 12–18 months.

Although my participants were all high school students between the ages of 14 and 16 at the start of the project in October 2009 (see Table 5.1), there was

TABLE 5.1 Participants' Demographic Information

Student	Gender	Grade[a]	Age[a]	Age when moved to Canada	Country of birth	Language(s) spoken at home[b]	Language(s) used for literacy events[b]
Acer	M	9	14	n/a	Canada	Cantonese, English	English, Cantonese, Mandarin
Angel	F	9	14	12	Angola	Portuguese, English, French, Lingala	English
Hines	F	9	14	2	Italy	English, Somali, Arabic	English, Arabic, French
K-9	M	9	14	n/a	Canada	English, Jamaican Patois	English
Lala	F	11	16	12	Syria	Arabic, English	English, Arabic, Turkish
Ning	F	10	15	14	China	Mandarin, English	English, Mandarin
Shona	F	10/11[c]	16	9	Bangladesh	Bengali, Tamil, English	English, Arabic

[a]At the start of the ALTUR project. [b]Listed in order of student-reported usage. [c]Shona was in the third year of high school, but until the spring term she did not have enough credits to be classified as a grade 11 student.

great variation in the length of their residence in Canada: two were born in Toronto (to immigrants from China and Jamaica), and the others immigrated to Canada at ages ranging from 2 to 13. Representing a cross section of the linguistic diversity in Regent Park, these seven students reported speaking a total of 11 different languages at home; even the two born in Canada were functionally bilingual.

On the other hand, most of these students were essentially monolingual readers and writers of English. For example, although Hines[3] reported engaging in literacy events in Arabic and French, she used Arabic only to read the Quran and never for writing, and she read and wrote in French only for schoolwork for her French class. Shona's literate use of Arabic also was confined to reading the Quran, and she admitted that she needed a fair amount of help from her mother with the Arabic vocabulary. Acer's literate use of Cantonese and Mandarin were restricted to his schoolwork for Chinese school, which he had attended since middle school. One factor in this marked preference for English among these multicultural, multilingual participants in this study may be related to findings by Jia and Aaronson (2003) that L1 attrition was occurring by the time students had been in the United States for 36 months, and that attrition was most severe in students' reading and writing: Angel told me that she could no longer read and write in Portuguese despite six years' education in that language in Angola and Brazil.

As mentioned above, these students had all been identified by P2E as "at-risk for literacy development." Their English/language arts grades in the first year of the project ranged from 50 (Hines) to 82 (Acer, in special education class), with most students in the 60–70 range. Participants' fairly low scores on the Sight Word Efficiency and Phonemic Decoding Efficiency subtests of the Comprehensive Test of Phonological Processing (Wagner, Torgesen, & Rashotte, 1999), completed as screening measures for the ALTUR project, confirm their struggles in reading and writing (Table 5.2).

TABLE 5.2 Participants' Reading Efficiency Skills

	Sight word percentile	Phonemic decoding percentile
Acer	39	82
Angel	14	12
Hines	39	58
K-9	27	36
Lala	9	14
Ning	6	−1
Shona	16	21

Data Collection and Analysis

The findings reported in this chapter are based primarily on data from two years of interviews and a member check interview at the end of a third year. The interviews used three sets of instruments: a social network protocol, retrospective reading and writing interviews, and checklists of participants' reading and writing activities. Other data for the project were collected from a year of tutorial reports and a variety of literacy assessments, including the phonological processing measures above, writing tasks, reading comprehension tasks, a vocabulary test, and a test of morphological awareness.

In the social network protocol, the students were asked to identify all individuals in five domains of their social network: home, other family, school, friends, outside of school. In addition, the students were asked to identify up to 10 of these individuals who were "most important" to them. The students were then asked specifically about their reading and writing interactions with these 10 individuals, as well as how often and in what ways they talked to these 10 individuals about their future plans.

Analysis consisted of writing individual case studies and comparing across cases (Miles & Huberman, 1994; Stake, 2006). The interview transcripts were coded by two raters (with satisfactory inter-rater reliability per Miles & Huberman) for literacy events and types of social support. I used these codes to create a database of all literacy events that participants reported and the social support types associated with those events (for more details, see Wilson, 2012). Finally, about 10 months after the main data collection had concluded, I conducted member check interviews with each participant, during which the participant and I read together the relevant case report, and the participant corrected inaccurate or missing information. Because several of the participants were either preparing to apply to college or were in their first year of college at this point, this interview was an important source of information for this chapter.

Findings

The Composition of Students' Social Networks

Because space in this chapter does not permit a full analysis of each participant's social network (see Wilson, 2012, for detailed information), I have aggregated the data across the participants in order to provide a picture of who featured in these students' networks (Figure 5.1). Network members are categorized by the domain in which they were placed by students on their network maps during the interviews.

Unsurprisingly, considering the premium placed on friendships in adolescence, participants' *friend* relationships were reported to be very important in their lives. Indeed, the percentage of *friend* contacts was the highest among all network domains, for both the general networks and the "most important" contacts.

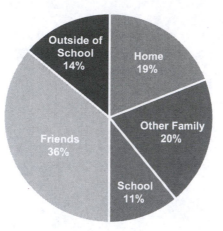

FIGURE 5.1 Percentages of Network Contacts by Domain

Because participants generally included only teachers in the *school* domain, that domain was regularly the smallest in their networks. Another less populated domain was *outside of school.* I had hypothesized that, due to participants' regular contact with tutors and an assigned support worker in the P2E program as well as the strong community aspect of the Regent Park neighborhood, students might have as many or more contacts outside of school as at school; however, that did not turn out to be the case for anyone except Lala, who had a part-time job and was very involved with her mosque.

Also salient was the relatively large number of network members located in the *other family* domain; this domain was essentially the same size as the *home* domain. A few contacts in this domain lived overseas (e.g., Lala's grandmother in Syria and Ning's cousins in China) or in other parts of Ontario, but for the most part these network members—aunts, uncles, cousins—also lived in Regent Park and participants had regular contact with them. So, while there were no noticeable neighborhood effects for the *outside of school* domain, neighborhood did seem to influence the density of the *other family* domain.

Writing within the Networks

Throughout the course of this study, participants described having social interactions with network members on 98 discrete writing activities; as indicated in Figure 5.2, 30% of these socioliterate interactions were with individuals named as friends. Notably, when parents (16%) and siblings (14%) are merged together into the *home* domain, we see that participants were interacting through writing with immediate family members as much as they were with their friends. Further analysis revealed that these teens were interacting with these network members through writing for four main purposes: (a) social communication (e.g., MSN,

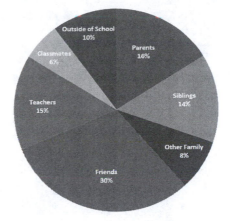

FIGURE 5.2 Percentages of Writing Activities (*n* = 98) on Which Participants Reported
Interacting with Specific Individuals

Facebook); (b) academic purposes (e.g., homework assignments); (c) entertainment
(e.g., writing stories for fun); and (d) linguistic purposes (e.g., learning to read and
write Mandarin).

In earlier analyses I looked at reading and writing events *together*, in which case
this group of teens was reading and writing more for *social purposes* than for any
other reason. However, when looking only at writing activities, these adolescents
tended to write more for *academic purposes*; in fact, a little over half of all the social
writing they reported in the 18 months of the study was conducted to accomplish
a school assignment. Most of the support they received was from parents and siblings, though some participants worked with friends, too.

All of these adolescents were doing a fair amount of writing for *social purposes*,
almost exclusively using social media. Only Acer and Ning did not report any daily
social media usage, although both had computer access at home. On the other end
of the spectrum, by the end of the study Angel and Shona were engaging in daily
use of every social media tool queried: email, instant messaging, texting, Facebook.

One of the more interesting findings regarding social media use was the marked
preference some participants had for certain platforms or tools. While some of
these teens used all forms of social media, others stated very strong preferences
for or against specific platforms. Echoing the findings of a contemporaneous Pew
Internet report that email is "losing its luster" as teens gravitate toward tools that
allow synchronous communication (Lenhart, Madden, Macgill, & Smith, 2007,
p. 20), MSN was Acer's preferred method of communication:

IV: Which do you prefer, email or MSN?
AC: Uh, MSN is more, more social interacting, and you can just get the message
to the other person more faster than emailing, so MSN I guess.

IV: So, when you say "more social," is it the *quickness* of it that makes it more social, or is it something else?

AC: Uh, you can, like, add a lot of friends to the conversation and talk.

Even when students used a social media tool regularly, they recognized issues with it. In grade 11, Shona had the following discussion about Facebook with her interviewer:

IV: And how often do you use Facebook?

S: Every single day.

IV: And you like it?

S: No, it's the biggest distraction of my education.

IV: Really. Why are you using it then?

S: Because it's *sooo* addictive.

Participants generally were using these digital tools to communicate with friends, although in a few cases with older siblings (Acer, K-9, Lala), parents (Angel, K-9, Lala), cousins (Angel, Ning), and even a grandmother (Lala). K-9 shared a humorous anecdote about how his stepmother learned from Facebook that he and his long-term girlfriend had broken up.

Prior to the data collection, I speculated that there would be a clear divide for socioliterate interactions between extracurricular and academic writing, with social interactions for the former revolving around social media and for the latter around homework help. To a large extent this pattern held, but there were instances where academic and extracurricular literacy events overlapped. For example, Acer's older sister (a business major at a local university) decided to teach him to write business letters—this was an extracurricular undertaking but an academic topic. Lala wrote fiction stories as a hobby and brought them to her P2E tutor for feedback, just as she would for a school assignment.

While all seven participants mentioned writing to *entertain* themselves at least once during the study, four specifically described writing for fun with network members. One of Acer's favorite pastimes was playing online multiplayer games; he and his friends used the in-game text feature to communicate remotely. Shona co-authored articles with a friend for a local youth magazine, and, as mentioned above, Lala wrote stories for fun and shared them with the people around her. Angel described writing stories together with her 12-year-old sister about places they had gone ("like in the bedroom and shopping") and even illustrating those stories together. Similarly, Angel's cousin (who is also her best friend) wrote stories and shared them with Angel afterward.

Two of the participants, Acer and Lala, engaged in writing with others specifically for the purposes of *language learning*. Acer attended a Saturday Chinese school throughout high school, where he studied Cantonese and Mandarin. Because his closest friends also attended this school, he worked extensively with

them on Chinese reading and writing assignments, even emailing them about this work during the week. In addition, his parents and older sister regularly helped him with his Chinese school homework. Lala was both a language learner and teacher. She was in the process of learning Pashto from a high school friend, and she talked about reading a Pashto book with him as well as practicing writing in Pashto. Lala described her reading in Pashto as "bad" but then described how she was able to help another friend whose family received letters in Pashto but could not read them. In addition to her own language learning, throughout this study Lala was teaching Arabic as a heritage language to a younger girl in her neighborhood.

Social Support for Writing

Overall, the seven participants reported receiving 354 instances of social support over the 18 months of this study. Of these, 155 were related to literacy activities ("socioliterate support"), but only 83 of these instances occurred specifically with writing activities. Sixty percent (60%) of the general support was provided by family members and friends, with school personnel providing only 29% of the overall support. These proportions reverse when we look at support that was related to literate undertakings specifically: For all reading and writing support, over half (51%) came from school personnel, while only 39% was provided by family and friends; 54% of support for writing came from the school domain and only 30% from family and friends (see Table 5.3).

Within the network domains, there tended to be specific individuals who provided writing-related support to these teens. Just over half of the reported writing support came from individuals in the *school* domain ($n = 45$ instances); further analysis identified that 36 instances were reported from English teachers, compared to 3 from classmates and 6 from teachers in classes other than English/language arts. Indeed, English teachers were the single most-cited source of support for

TABLE 5.3 Percentage of Received Social Support by Network Domain

Domain of network member	Percentage of social support instances[a]	Percentage of socioliterate support instances[b]	Percentage of writing support instances[c]
Home	31	25	23
Other family	6	2	0
Friends	23	12	7
School	29	51	54
Outside of school	11	10	16
Total	100	100	100

[a]$n = 354$ reported instances of general support. [b]$n = 155$ reported instances of socioliterate support.
[c]$n = 83$ reported instances of writing support.

writing, accounting for 43% of the total reported instances. In comparison, the group with the second-most reported instances was parents, who were described as providing 13% (11 instances) of the writing support. Despite occurrences in previous research indicating that school personnel other than teachers could provide socioliterate support to teens (e.g., a librarian in Hynds, 1997), there were no similar instances reported by these participants.

The ways in which English teachers provided writing support varied greatly, of course.[4] Support instances described by students ranged from short interactions such as a teacher pointing out specific ways a student could improve a paper (reported by all seven participants) to more involved one-on-one meetings, such as when Shona went to her grade 10 English teacher after school to get advice about the Ontario literacy test that students had to pass in order to graduate: "He gave me ideas of how and what's appropriate and how to write an essay and what are like the contents and *everything*."

Notably, two students (Acer and Ning) reported receiving very meaningful support from their English teachers, support that had an impact beyond a single assignment or class. For example, Acer described how he and his grade 9 GLE (special education) English teacher regularly talked about preparing him to move up to the next level of English ("applied") in grade 10; to help him prepare for the type of work he would do in that course, this teacher gave Acer a young adult novel to read outside of class and asked him to write an elective reading journal that she checked regularly. Acer successfully made the transition to the higher course level, and by grade 11 he had moved into the college-preparatory English track ("academic"). Likewise, Ning had an ESL teacher (in grades 9–11) who took an interest in her academic progress and with whom she talked about the possibility of skipping a year of ESL in order to be eligible to take the Ontario literacy test at the same time as the other 10th graders. This teacher regularly gave her opportunities to rewrite her essays; by the time I met Ning, she felt comfortable asking this teacher to read essays she had revised on her own initiative. This relationship established in grade 10 English turned into a mentoring relationship, and Ning even sought help from him in other classes, like grade 11 history.

Socioliterate Interactions and Social Support Relating to Higher Education

As foreshadowed in the previous section, students' social networks not only provided support on their actual writing, but sometimes in doing so *also* provided support for students' future plans, such as helping students pass graduation requirements (Shona, Ning) and transition to college-bound courses or tracks (Acer, Ning). Ning was particularly motivated to activate her network to help her with writing that was related to pursuing higher education—about eight months after our last interview for this project, Ning emailed me to ask if I could help her with her college essay, which I did.

Some of the writing-related support was not necessarily designed to help students prepare for college but clearly would be helpful in a postsecondary context. In grade 11, K-9 learned how to differentiate between class notes and homework from his Canadian Law teacher. He made a point to label this teacher as helpful, even though his grade in the course was a C (approximately a 65):

> I learned a lot of things in that class. Like what he told me, "You're a good kid, you've got the stuff [homework], [but you need to] know what to hand in and what not to hand in." Cuz I had a problem with *notes*, like I'd write the notes and I'd write the answers to certain things, but I didn't know which one to hand in, so I just left them to myself [laughs]. So, I'm like "I don't know." . . . So I started handing it [my work] to him, and he was like, "Yeah, you hand this, you hand this in." And I'd go after school, before I have to go to work, and he'd look through my stuff and be like "You have to hand this in, hand this in, don't hand this in."

In my personal experience as a P2E tutor, I found that many of the students did not understand a teacher's written instructions for an assignment prompt and they benefited greatly when their tutors modeled this skill. Such skill-building is, of course, crucial for success on college writing assignments. Hines astutely described a one-on-one interaction with a P2E tutor that helped her understand how to read assignment instructions for a grade 10 history essay on "20th Century Heroes":

> [The tutor] had a laptop with him, he showed me a bunch of websites. . . . Basically, cuz like the whole point [of the essay] was heroes, right? But I didn't really think of that part. I was thinking more of the 20th century part, and then like he helped me like really *think* about what a hero *is* and what they do, and then it helped me with my essay.

Most of the support that network members gave that helped students navigate the high school-to-college transition, however, was not related to writing at all. In most cases, the support consisted of network members (1) encouraging these teens to go to college or to pursue a specific career or (2) giving advice about college entrance requirements (course selection, grades, or admission paperwork). Finally, there were a few documented instances of network members offering negative support for college or a career.

Family members, by and large, were the network members with the most influence on the participants' future plans. At some point in this study every one of these participants mentioned discussing their future plans with parents, siblings, aunts, uncles, and even older cousins. In some cases, these talks were initiated by the student, in other cases, by the family member. There was an overwhelming sense among participants that these discussions made them feel "really, really, really good" (Angel). The information discussed ranged from Ning's mother advising

her on possible career choices, to Acer's sister telling him about local colleges and universities, to Hines' cousins telling her what grades were necessary to attend college.

It is on the topic of future plans that the participants mentioned interacting with P2E personnel most often, even when those personnel were not on their network maps. It seems that, even though students generally did not perceive the relationship with their P2E tutors or Student Parent Support Workers (SPSWs) to be strong enough or important enough to include on a network map, they still viewed these individuals as a valuable source of information on postsecondary preparation. Lala summed it up: "Since I don't know, [my tutor] would explain to me about colleges and university, like which ones are better on what I want to do." Angel and Ning were the only participants who never mentioned their tutors or SPSWs as individuals to whom they talked about their future plans; however, in the spring of grade 9, Angel admitted that she knew little about the two colleges she had just claimed to want to attend, and she asked her interviewer—who was also her P2E tutor—to find out for Angel if either school had any medical programs. As I mention above, Ning asked me (her former P2E tutor) to give her feedback on her college admission essay. Preparing Regent Park students to pursue postsecondary education was a stated goal of the P2E program, and it seems that the program's personnel were successful in creating relationships that facilitated that goal. This support was critical for students whose parents had not attended university in Canada—and possibly not at all—and who were not getting advice from other venues. (For example, when I specifically queried Ning during grade 12 about her contact with her school guidance counselor, she told me that her counselor was nice but young and very busy and was not able to answer Ning's questions.)

In comparison to their importance in other facets of these adolescents' lives, friends were notably absent from or uninfluential in the discussion of future plans. Angel repeatedly stated that she did not know if graduating from high school was important to her friends, nor did she know what they wanted to do after high school. Although Acer claimed that it was "pretty important" to his friends to graduate from high school, he denied ever talking to them about postsecondary plans. In fact, only half the participants (Shona, Lala, Hines, and Ning) reported talking to their friends about their future plans. For Hines, although she and her friends occasionally discussed their plans, her father and cousins were more important sources of information and support about her desire to go to college and be a nurse. Shona, however, talked more to her best friend Rima about her future plans than to anyone else, and she found these conversations provided her with incentive; as Shona explained in grade 11, "Talking [about going to college] helps; it motivates me even more." This social support turned out to be even more crucial for Shona during the following year—after Shona's family found out about her older, unapproved boyfriend during her senior year of high school, they forced her to withdraw her college applications and threatened to send her back to Bangladesh to get married. After they relented, she continued to be motivated

to attend university with Rima and applied to the same school to which Rima had just been admitted.

Negative social support is an acknowledged, though little studied, phenomenon in the field of social support. In my study, I found no instances of negative social support for writing, but a few for reading and a few for pursuing postsecondary education. One such situation, in which Shona's parents valued their goals for her love life and marriage over her own career goals and college education, is described in the previous paragraph. In another example, Ning's dearest dream was to be a singer, but she said on multiple occasions that her mother "didn't agree" and was encouraging her to pursue business instead, which was stressful to Ning because she was worried that it would require a lot of math. She was the only participant who reported that discussions about the future were "sometimes good, but sometimes not." Hirsch (1985), a leading scholar in social network and support, termed this phenomenon "social rejection" (p. 121) in order to contrast it with social support, and he linked its relevance to its impact on "our social identities in major spheres of life" (p. 119).

I was able to interview only two of these teens, Lala and Shona, after they had graduated and started attending community college (Lala) and university (Shona). Their writing experiences were different in several ways but similar in one important respect related to social support. Lala thrived in her English class, obtaining the highest grade in the course, while Shona failed her writing-intensive humanities course. Lala thought the English course would be harder than those she took in high school but was pleasantly surprised that it was enjoyable and not overly difficult. In contrast, Shona found that university-level writing was

> so hard, yeah, it's so hard . . . They expect so much from you; it's like, you write a paper and then you just like, you read it and you don't even like reading it because you're just like "Ok, no, that's not what they want."

In particular, Shona's experience was similar to that documented by Kibler (2013) of a multilingual student in California moving from high school to college—Shona's expectations of how much and what she was expected to write in university were shaped by her very different experiences in high school. It is possible that Lala's English course at the community college was closer to her high school English course than were Shona's content-based, writing-intensive courses at a university.

There was one striking similarity between Shona's and Lala's college writing experiences: Both of these young women desired and sought out socioliterate support in college, with varying degrees of success in finding it. On her first paper in her women's studies course, Shona received a C+; as a result of her desire to improve, she had several appointments with the course teaching assistant (TA) for the second paper, on which she earned a B+. She said that she began to "pay more attention" to her writing than she did in high school, especially to precision

of word choice. Despite the assistance she received from the TA, she stated, "This year I didn't actually get a lot of help, I had to do it myself, basically." She pointed out that the P2E tutors were not available to help her during her first year of university. Lala also regretted the loss of access to the P2E tutors, despite her strong performance in her college English course. She did try to go to her college's writing center, but she claimed she would have had to wait a month for an appointment. Instead, she went on two occasions to the P2E tutoring site; once the site manager allowed Lala to work with a tutor, but the second time he turned her away.

Closing Thoughts

A number of studies on second language students paint a sterile picture of students' socioliterate lives, often due to issues of social isolation (e.g., Fu, 1995; Leki, 1999; Valdés, 2001). It is refreshing, then, to find the culturally and linguistically diverse group of participants in this study involved in a wide variety of writing events with a number of close people in their lives.

These multilingual adolescents who had been labeled "at-risk for literacy development" were writing a variety of traditional and multimedia texts—and often they had social motivation to do so, whether this was to communicate with others, to entertain themselves and others, or to get assistance on school assignments. As Moje, Oversby, Tysvaer, and Morris (2008) asserted, "youth read and write when they have a well-articulated purpose, a purpose that is usually centered in a network of social activity" (p. 146). As well, all seven reported discussing their future plans with and receiving advice about those plans from a variety of network members, and by grade 11 all seven were actively planning to pursue postsecondary education, despite having struggled academically in at least the first year or two of high school and having no parents with degrees from Canadian institutions.

So, how can we apply the research from this chapter to educational settings? For example, if socioliterate support from parents and siblings is important, how can it be activated? One possibility is for school personnel to use a social network map in a manner similar to the way such a map was used by Tracy and Whittaker (1990) with mothers who were being counseled by a social work agency. The very act of completing a social network map often revealed supportive relationships that the clients had not initially recognized. The women were coached about how to ask for assistance from these resources, and social workers believed the network map activity was empowering for many of these mothers. Likewise, when teachers or administrators are talking to students who are struggling with literacy events or practices, they could help students think about who in their social networks might be able to help them with particular writing tasks, practices, or situations.

This study also found socioliterate support in established spaces like school and an after-school program. What do spaces that promote socioliterate interactions and support look like? They may resemble after-school programs like Digital

Underground Storytelling for Youth in Oakland and Voices, Inc., in Tucson, where young people are apprenticed into literacy events with real-world applications, often mentored by peers who look and speak like them (Rubinstein-Ávila, 2007). They may be classrooms with an established system of teacher-student writing conferences (e.g., Sperling, 1991), journal writing (cf. Fu, 1995), or collaborative writing (e.g., Rish & Caton, 2011), or other teacher practices that build a general sense of trust, such as reaching out when a student needs additional help or is struggling in class (Ivey & Broaddus, 2000) or simply getting to know students' lives outside the classroom (Langer, 2002). Such a safe space could be located in cyberspace as well, like the social site Welcome to Buckeye City (Yi, 2007), used by Korean teens in a midwestern U.S. city to write texts such as comics, poems, and reviews.

Supportive spaces are also ones that welcome teens as active and equal partici-pants who are voicing their own needs, concerns, and interests, instead of trying to guide or even force adolescents into an expected model of learning or writ-ing. For example, on the surface the SPSWs (Student Parent Support Workers) in the P2E program appear to serve an important role as advocates for students and their families within the individual schools, as well as being a very visible presence in both the schools and the P2E office—a study in 2005 found that "more than two-thirds of Pathways participants at all grade levels indicated being 'very satisfied' with their SPSW" (Rowen & Gosine, 2006, p. 297). On the other hand, in this in-depth, qualitative study, only three participants named an SPSW as a "most important" person, and SPSWs only appeared on network maps 6 out of 21 possible times. Moreover, no participants reported specific socioliter-ate interactions with an SPSW, even when asked directly about their SPSWs in member check interviews. Perhaps these positions are configured on a deficit model that these teens were subconsciously resisting—would teens respond bet-ter to adults whom they have identified as support figures, thereby exercising their own agency, rather than adults who have been thrust upon them in some manner? Thus, it is important for program administrators to recognize that it is not enough to make such support available to students but that individuals in these positions have to (1) continuously reach out to students and (2) find ways to engage students as "active participants" (Lesko, 2001). This advice holds true, as well, for individuals providing support for the transition from high school to college.

A final relevant point raised by this study is that after-school programs focused on helping students graduate from high school need to help successful graduates find similar services in postsecondary education. Providing "at-risk" high school students with tutors for several years, only to yank that support out from under their feet when they need it most—at college—sets them up for failure. Instead, these programs should provide their students with tangible descriptions and examples of the ways in which postsecondary writing assignments will differ from those in high school. They also need to make concrete, practical suggestions for

places—such as college writing centers, peer tutors, academic advising offices—and *ways*—like making regular appointments with TAs or instructors—to seek out socioliterate support.

That social relationships provide support, purpose, and context for writing is not necessarily a surprise, more a reminder: After all, "people use written language to participate in a meaningful social formation" (Oates, 2001, p. 234). This chapter illustrates how writing and "social formation" can interact in the lives and transitions of multilingual academically at-risk teens.

Notes

1. P2E has given permission to identify their site and participation in this project.
2. P2E was open to *every* high school student within the geographic boundaries of the neighborhood. Approximately 95% of eligible students choose to participate (Rowen & Gosine, 2006). Students whose guardians sign participation agreements have access to twice weekly after-school tutoring assistance; a weekly social mentoring group; full-time Student Parent Support Workers (SPSW) who are assigned to each family and track students' academic progress; and public transportation tickets, school supplies, and $1,000 per year of participation for postsecondary education (up to a total of $4,000).
3. All names given in this chapter are pseudonyms. The participants selected their own pseudonyms, and I assigned those of other individuals and aimed to represent the language and culture of the original name.
4. When coding for support, I excluded instances that occurred as part of a teacher's lesson plan or were provided to an entire class, such as when Shona described how her grade 12 English teacher's grading practices helped her learn grammar points or when Acer described how his grade 9 English teacher would answer students' questions while the class was reading aloud.

Bibliography

Cumming, A. (Ed.) (2012). *Adolescent literacies in a multicultural context.* New York: Routledge.

Fu, D. (1995). *"My trouble is my English": Asian students and the American dream.* Portsmouth, NH: Boynton/Cook.

Hayden, R., & Fagan, W. T. (1995). Literacy learning outside the classroom: Social relationships of literacy. *The Reading Teacher, 49*(3), 260–262.

Hirsch, B. J. (1985). Social networks and the ecology of human development: Theory, research and application. In I. G. Sarason & B. R. Sarason (Eds.), *Social support: Theory, research, and applications* (pp. 117–136). Dordrecht: Martinus Nijhoff.

Hynds, S. (1997). *On the brink: Negotiating literature and life with adolescents.* New York: Teachers College Press.

Ivey, G., & Broaddus, K. (2000). Tailoring the fit: Reading instruction and middle school readers. *The Reading Teacher, 54*(1), 68–78.

Jia, G., & Aaronson, D. (2003). A longitudinal study of Chinese children and adolescents learning English in the United States. *Applied Psycholinguistics, 24*, 131–161.

Kibler, A. (2013). "Doing like almost everything wrong": An adolescent multilingual writer's transition from high school to college. In L. C. de Oliveira & T. Silva (Eds.), *L2 writing in secondary classrooms* (pp. 44–63). New York: Routledge.

Lam, W. S. E. (2000). L2 literacy and the design of the self: A case study of a teenager writing on the Internet. *TESOL Quarterly, 34*(3), 457–482.

Langer, J. A. (2002). *Effective literacy instruction: Building successful reading and writing programs.* Urbana, IL: NCTE.

Leki, I. (1999). "Pretty much I screwed up": Ill-served needs of a permanent resident. In L. Harklau, K. M. Losey, & M. Siegal (Eds.), *Generation 1.5 meets college composition: Issues in the teaching of writing to U.S.-educated learners of ESL* (pp. 17–43). Mahwah, NJ: Erlbaum.

Leki, I. (2007). *Undergraduates in a second language: Challenges and complexities of academic literacy development.* New York: Erlbaum.

Lenhart, A., Madden, M., Macgill, A. R., & Smith, A. (2007). *Teens and social media.* Pew Internet & American Life Project. Retrieved from http://pewinternet.org/~/media//Files/Reports/2007/PIP_Teens_Social_Media_Final.pdf.pdf

Lesko, N. (2001). *Act your age! A cultural construction of adolescence.* New York: Routledge Falmer.

Malecki, C. K., & Demaray, M. K. (2006). Social support as a buffer in the relationship between socioeconomic status and academic performance. *School Psychology Quarterly, 21*(4), 375–395.

Marin, A., & Wellman, B. (2011). Social network analysis: An introduction. In J. Scott & P. J. Carrington (Eds.), *The SAGE handbook of social network analysis* (pp. 11–25). Los Angeles: SAGE.

Miles, M. B., & Huberman, A. M. (1994). *Qualitative data analysis* (2nd ed.). Thousand Oaks, CA: Sage Publications.

Milroy, L. (1987). *Language and social networks* (2nd ed.). Oxford: Blackwell.

Moje, E. B., Oversby, M., Tysvaer, N., & Morris, K. (2008). The complex world of adolescent literacy: Myths, motivations, and mysteries. *Harvard Educational Review, 78*(1), 107–154.

Morgan, D. L. (1990). Combining the strengths of social network, social support, and personal relationships. In S. Duck & R. C. Silver (Eds.), *Personal relationships and social support* (pp. 190–215). London: Sage.

Oates, S. F. (2001). Literacy as an everyday practice. In E. B. Moje & D. G. O'Brien (Eds.), *Constructions of literacy: Studies of teaching and learning in and out of secondary schools* (pp. 213–237). Mahwah, NJ: Erlbaum.

Ortmeier-Hooper, C. (2013). "She doesn't know who I am": The case of a refugee L2 writer in a high school English language arts classroom. In L. de Oliveira & T. Silva (Eds.), *L2 writing in secondary classrooms: Student experiences, academic issues, and teacher education* (pp. 9–26). New York: Routledge.

Richman, J. M., Rosenfeld, L. B., & Bowen, G. L. (1998). Social support for adolescents at risk of school failure. *Social Work, 43*(4), 309–323.

Rish, R. M., & Caton, J. (2011). Building fantasy worlds together with collaborative writing: Creative, social, and pedagogic challenges. *English Journal, 100*(5), 21–28.

Rowen, N., & Gosine, K. (2006). Support that matters: A case study in raising the achievement of economically vulnerable youth. In D. E. Armstrong & B. J. McMahon (Eds.), *Inclusion in urban education environments: Addressing issues of diversity, equity, and social justice* (pp. 277–299). Greenwich, CT: Information Age Publishing.

Rubinstein-Ávila, E. (2007). In their words, sounds, and images: After-school literacy programs for urban youth. In B. Guzzetti (Ed.), *Literacy for the new millennium: Vol. 3. adolescent literacy* (pp. 239–250). Westport, CT: Praeger.

Snow, C. E., Porsche, M. V., Tabors, P. O., & Harris, S. R. (2007). *Is literacy enough? Pathways to academic success for adolescents.* Baltimore, MD: Brookes.

Sperling, M. (1991). Dialogues of deliberation: Conversation in the teacher-student writing conference. *Written Communication, 8*(2), 131–162.

Stake, R. E. (2006). *Multiple case study analysis.* New York: Guilford Press.

Toronto Community Housing (TCH). (2007, September). *Regent park social development plan: Part I: Context.* Retrieved on July 24, 2011, from www.toronto.ca/revitalization/regent_park/pdf/regentpark_sdp-part1_sept_16.pdf

Tracy, E. M., & Whittaker, J. K. (1990). The social network map: Assessing social support in clinical practice. *Families in Society, 71*(8), 461–470.

Valdés, G. (2001). *Learning and not learning English: Latino students in American schools.* New York: Teachers College Press.

Villalva, K. E. (2006). Hidden literacies and inquiry approaches of bilingual high school writers. *Written Communication, 23*(1), 91–129.

Wagner, R., Torgesen, J., & Rashotte, C. (1999). *Comprehensive test of phonological processing.* Circle Pines, MN: American Guidance Service.

Wilson, J. S. (2012). *Social support networks for literacy engagement among culturally diverse urban adolescents.* Unpublished doctoral dissertation, University of Toronto. Retrieved from http://hdl.handle.net/1807/34964

Wilson, J. S. (2013). The role of social relationships in the writing of multilingual adolescents. In L. de Oliveira & T. Silva (Eds.), *L2 writing in secondary classrooms: Student experiences, academic issues, and teacher education* (pp. 87–103). New York: Routledge.

Yi, Y. (2007). Engaging literacy: A biliterate student's composing practices beyond school. *Journal of Second Language Writing, 16*, 23–39.

6

"I DON'T WANT TO BE SPECIAL"

English Language Learners in Rural and Small-Town High Schools

Todd Ruecker

"A Midwestern Meatpacking Town Welcomes Immigrants." "In A Small Missouri Town, Immigrants Turn To Schools For Help." Headlines like these have increasingly appeared in the news in recent years as demographic shifts have increasingly changed the face of rural areas in the United States. From 2000 to 2013, the percentage of minority students in rural schools rose from 16.4% to 26.7%. The percentage of students officially classified as English language learners (ELLs) doubled. Approximately 2.6 million minority (not necessarily language minority) students and over 300,000 students classified as ELL are now attending rural schools (Johnson et al., 2014). Some populations are changing more subtly, while other towns are undergoing dramatic shifts. For instance, Sulzberger (2011) explored how Latina/o immigrants, often drawn by jobs in meatpacking and other occupations undesirable to native-born U.S. workers, are changing the face of traditionally dying towns in the plains states.

Drawing from a series of reports released by the Rural Community and Educational Trust, a national organization that seeks to create a more favorable policy environment for rural schooling, as well as preliminary data from a study focused on rural high school literacy instruction in New Mexico, this chapter explores the increasing diversity of rural schools, identifies the challenges facing these schools in preparing increasingly diverse student populations for college, and calls for more research on language diversity in rural schools.

Linguistic Diversity in Rural Schools: What the *Why Rural Matters* Reports Tell Us

In 2000, the Rural School and Community Trust released the first in a series of biannual reports titled *Why Rural Matters* (WRM). In the opening to this report, they wrote: "[Rural] children, and the communities and schools they live and study

in, are largely unnoticed in the national debate over the direction of American education." They continued by calling for change:

> While policymakers, advisors, and scholars debate—and they should—the wisdom of alternative policies for urban schools, and for special education students or second language learners, or for poor and minority students, we rarely read serious analysis of the particular policy issues faced by students who live in rural places.
>
> *(Beeson & Strange, 2000, p. 63)*

Although emphasizing diversity in rural schools, neither of the first two reports (2000 and 2003) mentioned ELLs. The rural ELL population, while growing, has been doubly marginalized by both the lack of research on rural schools and the invisibility of this particular population in the limited research on rural contexts. This is in part because the shift is relatively recent. While it has been happening for a few decades, the magnitude of demographic shifts in rural communities was not fully seen until the 2010 census (Sulzberger, 2011).

The *WRM* writers began to more fully recognize this shift with the 2005 report. Here, while noting that poverty is the largest challenge facing education anywhere, they wrote, "Rural schools face challenges associated with factors other than poverty, including students with disabilities, students who cannot speak English well, and minority students disadvantaged by generations of racial and ethnic discrimination" (Johnson & Strange, 2005, p. v). They described this trend as recent and dramatic, explaining that it has presented schools with challenges: "Rapid growth in English Language Learner student populations and lack of access to ELL training programs for teachers has left many rural schools and districts without qualified staff" (p. vii). In this report, they introduced a measure for "Percentage of the population age 5 or older who speak English 'less than very well,'" noting that this was 2.4% of rural students nationwide, with this number highest in New Mexico at 14%, followed by Arizona at 12% (p. 8). They explained that methods exist for serving this population but that "they require dedicated school staff and the support of policymakers" (p. 8).

Recognizing the increasing presence of ELL students in rural schools, the authors of the 2007 *WRM* report included a much stronger focus by devoting a section titled "Meeting the Needs of Rural ELL Populations." They began by giving the readers a sense of this change, noting that ELL enrollment in rural schools more than doubled between 1989–90 and 2004–05, a rate "more than seven times higher than the rate of increase for total student enrollment" (p. 25). The authors point to a number of states that have seen rapid growth, with rural ELL numbers increasing by 254.5% in South Carolina and 249.1% in Kentucky (p. 25). They described specific challenges that rural schools face in serving ELL students, including the fact that rural schools are often spread out and remote, meaning they cannot share support resources like urban/suburban schools.

What We Know about Rural Schools and the Challenges They Face

In general, research on rural schools is limited compared to research on schools in more urban or suburban areas (Arnold et al., 2005; Coladarci, 2007). In a meta-analysis, Arnold et al. (2005) found that a third of rural education studies were only incidentally conducted in rural contexts, meaning they did not engage with rural-based issues in analyzing and presenting their data. This dearth is exacerbated when looking at research on ELL students in rural areas, with Arnold et al. (2005) failing to uncover any studies focused on ELL populations in rural areas. However, we do know something about rural schools from existing research; in this section, I would like to explore a bit of what we know about rural schools in general and what this might mean for ELL students entering these schools.

Teachers

A number of researchers have noted the difficulty attracting teachers to and keeping them at rural schools, in part because of the gravitation toward urban areas as well as salary disparities (Johnson & Strange, 2007). Given the shortage of TESOL- and/ or bilingual-certified teachers in most states (ED, 2015), it is especially hard for rural schools to recruit the teachers necessary to support their students' language needs, whether in learning English or building biliteracy through a dual language program. A lack of teachers qualified to work effectively with ELLs means these students may be more likely to face a sink-or-swim environment in rural schools.

Administrative and Staff Turnover

As they do with teachers, rural schools also have a difficult time recruiting and retaining administrators. In rural areas, this is often connected to politics surrounding local administration and school boards (e.g., Howley & Harmon, 2000), but it is often something that connects to broader accountability moves that make careers in education less desirable, whether as a teacher or administrator. Strong administrators can make a huge difference in the lives of ELL students because they tend to be the ones applying for grants to fund necessary services or unique programs that can support their students. They also make resource decisions like the need for a district-level bilingual education coordinator.

Supplementary Educational Services

With the arrival of No Child Left Behind, schools were required to provide supplementary educational services (SESs) to particular groups of students, such as ELLs and special education students.[1] While positive in its intent, this mandate has been largely unfunded (like many state/national education mandates are) and places a special burden on rural schools, where students needing these services are

not as concentrated as in urban schools (Barley & Wegner, 2010). Rural schools are often home to a number of transient student populations, including children of migrant farmworkers (Bustamante, Brown, & Irby, 2010). Consequently, schools may be hesitant to provide services for students who may leave after a few months (and take the funding associated with their ELL label with them).

Funding Shifts

Providing the necessary resources and services to support ELL students costs money, money often limited in rural schools with a limited tax base due to a lower population density and a higher prevalence of untaxed federal and state land. Moreover, educational costs per student in rural districts are higher, in part because they have smaller classes and spend more money on services like transportation. They are further disadvantaged by existing funding formulas and their dependence on state funding (e.g., Strange, 2011).

Assessments and Standards Movements

As I have argued elsewhere, assessments have the tendency to ignore local cultures and push a remedial curriculum on schools that serve large percentages of ELL students (Ruecker, 2013; Ruecker, Chamcharatsri, & Saengngoen, 2015). As in the broader education literature, rural schools tend to be ignored when it comes to designing standardized assessments and the textbooks aimed at teaching to them (Woodrum, 2009). Donehower, Hogg, and Schell (2007) expressed concerns over standardization movements representing a white, suburban middle-class norm with limited representation of the experiences of rural communities. This means that ELL students in rural schools may be even further removed culturally from these assessments.

Preliminary Findings from the Field

The narrative in my current institution is that students coming from small-town schools throughout the state struggle to adjust to college, even if they were in the top of their class at their former school. With this in mind, I obtained institutional review board (IRB) approval to analyze enrollment data from our institutional data office for our first semester first-year writing (FYW) class for the last five fall semesters. They track a variety of data points on our students, so I was able to obtain information on FYW grade, high school of origin, admission status, whether or not they had dual credit in high school, high school GPA, ACT or SAT score, and financial aid status, among others. From preliminary descriptive analyses of these data, I found that rural students are struggling to adapt to college at our institution. For instance, students coming from rural schools are less likely to get an A or B in a first-year writing class than their urban counterparts. Instead, they

are more likely to withdraw, representing 36% of the overall FYW population but 47% of the population that ends up with Ws in their FYW class. My ongoing analyses of these data reveal some other things at play as well: rural students in our state are disproportionally Native American, and many tend to attend branch campuses closer to home, where dropout rates in FYW classes commonly exceed 50%. I realized I had to dig more deeply than the numbers to get a sense of how rural high school students were being prepared for college and what factors impacted their ability to transition to and succeed at college.

With this in mind, I set about designing a project that would enable me to build portraits of rural high schools around the state of New Mexico in order to better identify the diversity of rural ELL student populations and how they are being served. This chapter is based on a subset of data from a larger study, data from one out of six schools I am visiting over a period of three years. These three- to four-week site visits are focused on exploring English teachers' working conditions and the varying impacts of these conditions on ELL students' literacy learning experiences, especially in regard to college preparation. During my time on-site, I observe English and ESL classes all day, taking notes as a passive observer or jotting down notes between classes when more active. I interview students about their lives in a small town, their writing experiences in school, and their post–high school goals. I interview teachers about their classrooms including the types of writing they assign as well as the constraints and supports for their teaching. I also interview administrators to get a higher-level perspective on serving ELL student populations. In addition to interviews, I collect writing samples from interviewed students and take samples and pictures of teachers' lesson materials and materials posted on their walls or written on their chalkboards.

As is common with qualitative studies, I have been analyzing data recursively throughout the ongoing data collection process. I spend time each evening while visiting a research site writing up analytical field notes, reflecting on the observations made or the interviews conducted that particular day. For this chapter, I triangulated these notes with recursive readings of the transcribed interviews to help recreate the students' life worlds. For this chapter, I will focus on one school, Leon High School, and two students in it.

This study is very much focused on context. From the discussion earlier, it is evident that rural schools have a unique policy and instructional context in comparison to urban or suburban counterparts, a context that shapes the way ELLs are served within these schools and prepared for college-level literacy. Theories of cultural ecologies, first developed in writing studies by Cooper (1986), are particularly useful in helping me understand each student story within a larger ecological context. Cooper (1986) explained that this ecological model is based on the notion that "writing is an activity through which a person is continually engaged with a variety of socially constituted systems" (p. 367). As argued elsewhere (e.g., Ortmeier-Hooper & Enright, 2011; Ruecker; 2015), literacy and literacy instruction takes place in a larger network of interconnected systems, with broader issues

such as policies pushing high-stakes assessment and ongoing systemic inequalities in society impacting individual students and teachers at the classroom level. In collecting and analyzing data for this study, I was conscious of issues beyond instruction, such as students' working lives outside the classroom.

The School

Leon High School (LHS)[2] is located in a community with approximately 10,000 people and surrounded by a number of rural communities, including Native American pueblos. Approximately 30% of the community lives in poverty, well above the state average of 20%, and there are high rates of alcohol and drug use. The average household income is around $20,000.

The district spans around 50 miles, with elementary schools scattered over a wide range, many located in small communities. Over the years, the district has consolidated various schools, and one result of these changes is that students come from a wide swath of semi-urban to very isolated communities in order to study at the only high school in the district. Because it draws students from such a broad area, it is quite large for a rural school. Like many rural schools, administrative turnover was a challenge in the years surrounding my visit. Both the district and high school regularly saw new administrators every couple years. The consequence of this turnover meant that teachers had limited allegiance to administrative personnel and there did not seem to be a consistent vision shaping the district and school.

About a quarter of approximately 900 students were classified as ELL. However, the services provided to these students were limited. Despite being a relatively large district, there was no bilingual education director at the district level. LHS offered only one ESL class, which was taught by a TESOL-certified Spanish teacher, Ms. Gonzalez. Ms. Gonzalez (and de facto ESL director) shared information with me about the school's Title III program models and the students within them.[3] By far the most popular form of support (covering about 85% of students designated as ELL) was the "Enrichment" program, which meant that students were taking language classes in their home language, whether it be Spanish or the most prevalent local Native language. However, this did not mean they were receiving any special support in English, support that teachers felt was still necessary. An additional 10 students were in the "Heritage" program, which meant they took classes in a home language in addition to being in another classroom (English or another subject) at some point during the day with a TESOL-certified teacher. The low number of students in the "Heritage" program may be attributed to the fact that LHS, like many rural schools, had ongoing difficulties finding TESOL-certified teachers.

Now I turn to profiling two students to illustrate the role of college ambitions in immigrant student dreams and the challenges they may face in getting appropriate language support in rural schools.

Miguel

Miguel had been at LHS for two and a half years when I met him, spending one year in a local middle school before starting at LHS. Like most immigrant students at the school, he was from Mexico. His father had stolen some money from important people in a government job and would have gone to jail or faced worse consequences if they had stayed in Mexico. The father suggested that the family move to Leon, where they had family. Miguel generally liked his experiences in the U.S. school system but did not particularly like Leon, as he was used to living in bigger cities. After high school, he had plans to move to one of the larger cities in New Mexico with his girlfriend and attend college.

His initial transition was difficult:

> It was like rude, it was hard because it was everything um, like in one week I was here so I got here and everything was different I got directed to school, I didn't know anybody, the teachers didn't know me the teachers didn't speak Spanish, so I feel sca, I got scared.

This experience is similar to one other immigrant students face on transitioning to the United States: a period of shock and disorientation while struggling to figure out a new context. It appeared that Miguel's middle school did not have an ESL program, as he noted that he was not placed into such a program until arriving at the high school.

Even though the majority of students at the school were Latina/o there was still a bit of a hierarchy between Latina/o students and newly arrived students from Mexico, with the former tracing their lineage back to Spanish colonizers and some viewing Mexicans and Mexican culture negatively. Nonetheless, Miguel did not personally experience much prejudice and found the fact that a number of students spoke Spanish as useful for integrating into the school context, enabling him to make friends easier as he gained fluency in English.

Overall, Miguel seemed to be doing well at the school and progressing in English, able to function well in his classes but still consistently having trouble with grammar and syntax in his writing. This in part seemed to be supported by what seemed to be a relatively strong language learning experience in Mexico as his teacher had regularly drawn on communicative language teaching methods. He seemed satisfied with ESL classes at LHS, saying that they spoke a lot in English (something I did not observe) and played a lot of games (something I observed). In general, Miguel valued the sink-or-swim model in place at the school, noting, "The more rude that the teachers are with you the more faster that you will learn English."

As he progressed toward graduation, Miguel seemed well positioned to succeed and meet the graduation requirements, which were most notably dominated by the New Mexico state test, the Standards Based Assessment (SBA). The SBA

was the annual high-stakes assessment in place at the time of this study and tested students on core subjects. Students had to pass the test in order to graduate, and teachers were increasingly evaluated based on these scores as well. Because of the state's large Spanish-speaking population, the SBA was offered in Spanish as well as English, which enabled Miguel to do well the first time he took it.

Miguel had also developed coping strategies in his English classes, reading difficult works like Shakespeare's *Julius Caesar* in Spanish in order to write about them in English. The school had recently started developing an intensive reading program tied to the STAR test (a standardized assessment designed to measure literacy levels) and the Accelerated Reading program for which students would have dedicated reading in English classes every day on a book of their choice (and connected to their Lexile level) and be tested on it at the end. Because he was concerned about doing well on the associated test, Miguel ended up choosing a book in Spanish. He still was building his vocabulary and found his anatomy class particularly difficult because of all the new words. In transitioning to college, he anticipated his biggest challenge would continue to be English writing and speaking:

> My biggest challenge will be the, um, everything will be in English, so um, if I have to write big essays or if I have to do something like speech to public in English it will be a little bit hard for me.

Liang

Unlike most of the immigrant students at LHS, Liang came from China and he, his family, and a few others were the only Chinese people in town. He came to the United States for opportunity, especially in regards to education, as his family did not like the Chinese government and the general culture of corruption there. For instance, Liang reported stories of teachers hitting students and demanding money from parents for after-school tutoring to bring student grades up, and felt that postsecondary education was only accessible if one had money. Like Miguel, Liang came to Leon because he had extended family living there, managing one of the two Chinese restaurants in town. His parents did not come with him, so he lived with his aunt and occasionally helped out at the restaurant. Like Miguel, he was used to living in a larger city at home.

Liang had strong college ambitions but had just come to the United States a few months previously and was already in 12th grade (and, at 19, old compared to his fellow students). Although he had years of English instruction in China, it seemed to be generally confined to vocabulary memorization and some writing, which was likely due in part to large classes. Nonetheless, he was supported by a strong motivation to learn outside of school, spending his weekends at home studying. In general, his family seemed supportive of his education and did not ask him to help out in the restaurant unless he had finished his schoolwork.

Because he was the only Chinese student at the school, Liang seemed to have more difficulties than Miguel in assimilating into the school culture. We talked about this:

T: How does it feel to be the one Chinese student here?

L: I don't want to be special but I need a special here. Just me. Special. I don't want be.

T: You don't want to.

L: I want to be a normal classmate. Maybe we can hang out. Maybe we can talk anything. But I can't because the language is the problem. And the courage. Maybe sometimes I'm impolite anyone but I don't know. Like this.

He did seem to have a few friends and I saw him hanging out with the other students in the ELL class. Nonetheless, his desire to make friends sometimes created unwelcome stereotyping, as he came into class one day upset that students were insinuating that he was gay.

While I was on-site, Liang's mainstream English class was reading *Beowulf*; he always appeared lost during classes I observed, understanding very little of the reading or discussion. He would mess around a lot, perhaps because he had no idea what was going on but perhaps in part to gain the affection of other students. His senior English teacher, Ms. Johnson, was unsure where to start in supporting him except in encouraging him to use his cell phone to write down Chinese translations of words in *Beowulf*. While every English class started with 15 minutes of silent reading, Liang did not have a book, even though this time would be perfect for him to read something appropriate for his level. His ESL classes unfortunately did not seem much better. I visited the class first during the week of Halloween, and the students had just been given a packet of Halloween word searches and the teacher said they planned to watch a Halloween-themed movie later in the week. A look into his ESL notebook found pages of vocabulary lists and no sustained writing.

While I had intended to continue playing a relatively passive observer role in the class, I was a bit disturbed that Liang was spending a whole week focused on activities that would not do much to build his academic literacy, especially since he was so interested in pursuing college right after high school. Encouraged by the teacher, who was interested in learning new ways to teach her students, I taught most classes for the rest of my time on-site, focusing on reading texts matched to the students' levels along with reading from their history class and discussing them while focusing on pertinent vocabulary. It was my hope that the teacher would get more ideas about instruction through these different activities, and she was very open to it.

As Liang had strong ambitions to graduate from high school and go to college, he was particularly worried about the state test, the SBA, which he had to take a month after he arrived. He recognized the stakes were high: "The teacher tells

me if I can pass the SBA, I can graduate. I can go to the college." Unsurprisingly, he was pretty certain that he failed. While the SBA was provided in Spanish for Miguel, the school had no idea if the test was available for Liang to take in Chinese (it was not) or otherwise how to support him in taking it (such as providing a translator, for instance). Consequently, he seemed to be held to a different standard than an immigrant student from Mexico who comes from a demographic more traditionally represented at the school. At the end of the interview, I asked him about his future possibility for success, and he felt that "maybe" he will be successful in pursuing college. Liang's future in a school and town that offered little support for ELL students was a bit uncertain. I thought about recommending him intensive ESL classes at a local college but learned that the college administration had recently cut the ESL program amid budget challenges and a transformation from a community college to a regional university.

Discussion and Concluding Thoughts: A Call to Action

As rural ELL student populations continue to grow, it is important that researchers in a variety of fields begin exploring how these populations are being served by their schools. As discussed earlier, some rural schools have a longer history of linguistic diversity, while others are seeing rapid growth of their ELL student populations. The case studies presented in this chapter revealed a largely sink-or-swim model in place at LHS with no coordinated bilingual or language education at the district model, even in a district with a history of diverse student populations. Looking at the experiences of the students profiled in this chapter from an ecological perspective reveals the way their pathways were shaped by themselves, their teachers, and a variety of external forces.

The sink-or-swim model described by Miguel and Liang appeared to be in part due to the broader issue of funding challenges, along with staffing issues. Similarly, with a constant turnover in administration, it is hard for someone to guide the school with a vision for ELL students, a vision that can greatly help facilitate their language learning experiences and their ultimate readiness for college reading and writing. While Miguel expressed support for the sink-or-swim model, saying that it would help him learn English "faster," Liang was clearly struggling to keep up in his classes. While Liang's motivation would likely carry him through the year, students less motivated may be more likely to struggle and fall through the cracks in such a model.

Another broader force impacting literacy instruction for ELLs at Leon High School is the use of standardized assessments, which were used in a variety of ways, including a reading program as well as the state graduation requirement. Because New Mexico had a history of Spanish-speaking students, Miguel was fortunate: He was able to take the state test in Spanish for at least three years, which would enable him to pass for graduation. On the other hand, Liang was required to take it in English a month after being at school in the United States and was constantly

worried that he was going to fail. The school, and certainly Liang, was not aware of any particular language supports for him on the exam. With the arrival of the new Common Core-aligned exam, the Partnership for Assessment of Readiness for College and Careers (PARCC), this disparity does not seem to be going away. While the math portion of the exam is going to be offered in Spanish, there has not been mention of a version in Chinese or other languages, with the exception of translation of test instructions (PARCC, 2015).

Of the two students discussed in this chapter, I am most concerned about Liang's trajectory. Coming to the United States with limited English fluency in such a high grade and at such a late age means that his college-going trajectory is likely going to be interrupted substantially. Whether he continues to struggle in passing the state-mandated test or simply cannot handle the literacy demands of an English-only college classroom, Liang likely has a challenging journey ahead of him to fulfill his college dream. Liang's trajectory could have certainly been supported through better sponsorship at the school as well as the availability of an accessible and affordable ESL program at the local community college. He could consider entering an Intensive English Program in college, but the cost of a program might be beyond the financial means of his family. The transitions of students like Liang are not always neatly planned. Whatever the causes that brought him here, they are part of an unpredictable, constantly shifting life journey that is intimately intertwined with one's literacy transitions.

Something we can take away from these findings is the importance of learning more about the experiences of students like Miguel and Liang in rural high schools and what it means for preparing them for college-level literacy. This chapter is only a picture of one school in one state. Moving forward, it is vital that researchers in a variety of disciplinary and geographic contexts collaborate across disciplines and also with K–12 teachers to conduct studies designed to document the experiences of linguistically diverse students in rural contexts. These studies can focus on some of the following questions:

- What kind of language learning opportunities are offered in rural schools for ELL students? How are these opportunities affected by challenges particular to rural schools?
- What curricular strategies can be utilized in rural schools to effectively prepare their ELL students for college-level literacy work?
- What happens to rural ELL students when they transition to college? Do they face different difficulties or have unique sources of support compared to other rural students or urban ELL students?
- What can colleges and universities, including their writing programs, do to better support the success of rural students, especially ELLs, transitioning into college literacy work?

These are just a few questions to help guide researchers and teacher educators as they begin focusing on how to support rural teachers and administrators in working with increasingly diverse student populations.

While completing this work, it is essential that researchers continue to develop ways to affect change in the world around them. Our society is rife with inequality, and the "cycle of inopportunity" that Ortmeier-Hooper and Enright (2011) reference does not only refer to disparities in curricular opportunities but broader inequities as well. Broader issues with teacher shortages (caused by practices such as low pay for teachers, the bureaucracy of increased testing, and punitive evaluation systems) impact rural schools especially hard; when even urban and suburban districts have trouble finding bilingual and/or TESOL-certified teachers, rural schools have a greater struggle attracting teachers qualified to support their ELL student populations. Consequently, a student like Liang or Miguel, by immigrating to a smaller community because of family connections, may not be afforded the opportunities an immigrant to a larger school district might. It is vital that we not only document these inequities, but also that we fight to change the broader systems that perpetuate them.

Acknowledgement

I would like to acknowledge the University of New Mexico's Research Allocations Committee and NAED/Spencer Postdoctoral Fellowship Program for providing the funding to support the research presented in this chapter.

Notes

1. For those unfamiliar with supplementary educational services, the Department of Education explains them in more detail: "Low-income families can enroll their child in supplemental educational services if their child attends a Title I school that has been designated by the State to be in need of improvement for more than one year. The term 'supplemental educational services' refers to free extra academic help, such as tutoring or remedial help, that is provided to students in subjects such as reading, language arts, and math" (ED, 2012).
2. All names, including the high school, are pseudonyms. This project received IRB approval from relevant bodies.
3. Title III refers to federally funded support for ELLs. Schools receive supplementary funding to support ELLs as long as they can show they are providing some support for these students.

Bibliography

Arnold, M. L., Newman, J. H., Gaddy, B. B., & Dean, C. B. (2005, April 27). A look at the condition of rural education research: Setting a difference for future research. *Journal of Research in Rural Education, 20*(6), http://jrre.psu.edu/articles/20–6.pdf

Barley, Z. A., & Wegner, S. (2010). An examination of the provision of supplemental educational services in nine rural schools. *Journal of Research in Rural Education, 25*(4), www.jrre.psu.edu/articles/25.5.pdf

Beeson, E., & Strange, M. (2000). Why rural matters: The need for every state to take action on rural education. *Journal of Research in Rural Education, 16*(2), 63–140.

Beeson, E., & Strange, M. (2003). *Why rural matters 2003*. Washington, DC: Rural School and Community Trust.

Bustamante, R. M., Brown, G., & Irby, B. J. (2010). Advocating for English language learners: U.S. teacher leadership in rural Texas schools. In K. A. Schafft & A. Y. Jackson (Eds.), *Rural education for the twenty-first century* (pp. 232–252). University Park, PA: Penn State Press.

Coladarci, T. (2007, May 24). Improving the yield of rural education research: An editor's swan song. *Journal of Research in Rural Education, 22*(3), http://jrre.psu.edu/articles/22–3.pdf

Cooper, Marilyn M. (1986). The ecology of writing. *College English, 48*(4), 364–375.

Department of Education. (2012). www2.ed.gov/nclb/choice/help/ses/description.html

Department of Education. (2015). www2.ed.gov/about/offices/list/ope/pol/tsa.pdf

Donehower, K., Hogg, C., & Schell, E. E. (2007). *Rural literacies*. Urbana, IL: NCTE Press.

Howley, C. B., & Harmon, H. L. (Eds.) (2000). *Small high schools that flourish: Rural context, case studies, and resources*. Charleston, WV: AEL.

Johnson, J., Showalter, D., Klein, R., & Lester, C. (2014). *Why rural matters 2013–2014*. Washington, DC: Rural School and Community Trust.

Johnson, J., & Strange, M. (2005). *Why rural matters 2005: The facts about rural education in the 50 states*. Arlington: Rural School and Community Trust.

Johnson, J., & Strange, M. (2007). *Why rural matters 2007: The realities of rural education growth*. Arlington: Rural School and Community Trust.

Ortmeier-Hooper, C., & Enright, K. A. (2011). Mapping new territory: Toward an understanding of adolescent L2 writers and writing in US contexts. *Journal of Second Language Writing, 20*(3), 167–181.

Partnership for Assessment of Readiness for College and Careers. (2015). *PARCC accessibility features and accommodations manual*. Retrieved from www.parcconline.org/parcc-accessibility-features-and-accommodations-manual

Ruecker, T. (2013). High-stakes testing and Latina/o students: Creating a hierarchy of college readiness. *Journal of Hispanic Higher Education, 12*(3), 303–320.

Ruecker, T. (2015). *Transiciones: Pathways of Latinas and Latinos writing in high school and college*. Logan, UT: Utah State University Press.

Ruecker, T., Chamcharatsri, B., & Saengngoen, J. (2015). Teacher perceptions of the impact of the common core assessments on linguistically diverse high school students. *Journal of Writing Assessment, 8*(1), http://journalofwritingassessment.org/article.php?article=87

Strange, M. (2011, March). Finding fairness for rural students. *Education Week*. Retrieved from www.edweek.org/ew/articles/2011/03/01/kappan_strange.html

Sulzberger, A. G. (2011, November 13). Hispanics reviving faded towns on the plains. *The New York Times*. www.nytimes.com/2011/11/14/us/as-small-towns-wither-on-plains-hispanics-come-to-the-rescue.html?_r=0

Woodrum, A. (2009). Cultural identity and schooling in rural New Mexico. *Journal of Research in Rural Education, 24*(8), 1–5.

PART II

Transition and Disruption

Sponsors, Programs, Politics, and Policies

Bilingual and immigrant youth often "fall through the cracks" in pursuit of post-secondary education due to inadequate access to college-preparatory curricula, insufficient guidance in the college application process, immigration status, lack of financial resources, and ineligibility for financial aid. This section considers the powerful roles of sponsors, politics, and policies in the educational trajectories and achievements of resident multilingual writers. Authors share studies that examine how support networks—from individual teachers to federally funded programs—can aid student writers as they try to navigate these waters. Later chapters consider how immigration politics and federal policies shape students' opportunities and illustrate how some students write themselves into stronger positions of agency and advocacy.

In Chapter 7, Amanda Kibler draws upon the theoretical work of L1 literacy scholar Deborah Brandt to examine how sponsors and support systems impact the writing skills and aspirations of multilingual high school seniors. Kibler's series of case studies depict the multiplicity of sponsors that students depend upon—networks, monolingual sponsors, multilingual sponsors—from various communities and points of contact, noting that successful linguistic minority students often intertwine these various sponsors and leverage the support to meet varying needs and objectives. She finds that resident ML writers don't just need one sponsor—they may need many. Her study stresses the importance of finding "a strong match" between the individual student writer and the sponsor, and Kibler demonstrates that there is no fixed sponsorship situation that works for all students. Indeed, that need for variability is part and parcel of adolescence and identity.

In Chapter 8, Shauna Wight continues the exploration of sponsorship and support systems. Her study investigates the role that Upward Bound, a U.S. federally funded program, plays in supporting LM writers' transitions into higher education.

The Upward Bound (UB) program referenced in Wight's chapter is part of the federally funded TRIO programs designed to "identify and provide services for individuals from disadvantaged backgrounds" (U.S. Department of Education). In recent years, such programs have seen significant budgetary cuts—over $65 million from 2007 to 2014. In this yearlong study of UB students at one institution, Wight draws upon Wegner's Community of Practice theory to analyze the peer networks fostered by such programs and records how these networks help students negotiate the new demands of college writing. Like Gilliland (this volume) in Part I, Wight found that academic tracking in U.S. high schools created challenges for ML writers when they returned from the UB program. Wight illustrates the nuanced ways in which the UB program worked to mitigate those realities, but those efforts were often met with varying levels of acceptance by student participants, including some who resented the ways the program grouped marginalized students together and others who found the program gave them more agency in their schools and educational opportunities.

In Chapter 9, Genevieve García de Müeller expands on this thread of student agency and provides insights into how federal policies can impede the postsecondary paths of "undocumented" immigrant students. Within the United States, it is estimated that there are over 1.4 million undocumented high school and college-age youth, even though many have lived and gone to school in the U.S. since kindergarten (Passel & Lopez, 2012). In L1 and L2 writing studies, what is often overlooked is how closely intertwined discussions on immigration policy are with the roles and opportunities and identities inhabited by resident ML students in the United States. Here, policy debates play real and concrete roles in the ways in which resident ML youth are able to pursue higher education or not (Kanno & Harklau, 2012). García de Müeller examines the U.S. DREAM Act, a legislative proposal that would allow undocumented students to gain provisional status, attend college, and be eligible for loans and financial assistance. She then explores how these Dreamer students, as writers, use digital media and tools to construct and speak back to one another and policy that guides their fates.

In Chapter 10, Ruhma Choudhury and Leigh Garrison continue this section by taking readers into another transitional space: the community college. Their chapter discusses a pre-test/post-test literacy study in a New York City community college, where the authors worked with Bengali immigrant students. The authors articulate the challenges students typically face in transitioning into college-level writing and describe the preliminary results of an intervention designed to improve the students' success. The chapter argues that writing courses can be redesigned to build L1 and L2 literacies, thereby supporting immigrant student success in multiple languages. Ultimately, Choudhury and Garrison suggest that programs consider providing support to students in their multiple literacies in order to create more successful transitions into college composition.

In Chapter 11, Julia Kiernan returns readers to issues of national education policies. Kiernan explores the Canadian context as she provides readers with an

understanding of how even progressive legislation on multilingualism can be at odds with the realities of classroom opportunities. Kiernan provides a window into the Canadian Multicultural Act by exploring the multilingual policy, a backdrop that differs greatly from monolingual policy trends in the U.S. educational systems. Kiernan compares language use and public policies on language in the United States and Canada, specifically the establishment of the Canadian Consultative Council on Multiculturalism in the 1970s and 1980s. Here, Kiernan considers the enactment of these policies within the framework of ongoing discussion of transnationalism, English-only debates, and translingualism within writing studies. The legacy of these initiatives have led to dynamic, language-rich, polylinguistic educational policy decisions that support the education of allophone students in kindergarten through secondary schools, but Kiernan critiques the postsecondary opportunities for Canadian multilingual residents—particularly immigrants and refugees—noting that at the postsecondary level, these rich policy decisions and resulting multilingual curricular options become less prevalent.

Bibliography

Kanno, Y., & Harklau, L. (Eds.) (2012). *Linguistic minority students go to college: Preparation, access, and persistence.* New York, NY: Routledge.

Passel, J. S., & Lopez, M. H. (2012). *Up to 1.7 million immigrant youth may benefit from new deportation rules.* Pew Research Center. Retrieved from www.pewhispanic.org/files/2012/12/unauthroized_immigrant_youth_update.pdf

7

PROMISES AND LIMITATIONS OF LITERACY SPONSORS IN RESIDENT MULTILINGUAL YOUTHS' TRANSITIONS TO POSTSECONDARY SCHOOLING

Amanda Kibler

Fabiola was born in the United States but grew up with her family in Mexico, only returning to the United States at age 15 for her first year of high school. She spoke little English upon her arrival, and her school, while full of committed teachers, was under-resourced and not known for academic excellence. In four years' time, however, Fabiola graduated from high school with a full scholarship to a prestigious state university, and just four years after that she graduated with a bachelor's degree in Gender and Women's Studies, a writing-intensive major.

What are some of the factors that helped Fabiola succeed? In high school, she was enrolled in a bilingual humanities course her first year, and in many classes she quickly earned a reputation as a serious student, often asking multiple adults for feedback on her writing. Teachers recommended her for a college scholarship, which was available to her thanks to her U.S. citizenship. Once in college, her scholarship provided an individual mentor as well as workshops, and she continued to seek out support for her writing from instructors, other adults, and peers. University policy also limited the remedial coursework Fabiola had to take before she could enroll in courses related to her major. She actively used technology throughout high school and college to find sources for her writing, compose, and edit. Although she could read Spanish easily, Fabiola drew upon English-language texts as sources for her writing almost exclusively in high school and college; but midway through her college career she began to use her own bilingualism as a support, drafting her essays at least partly in Spanish to help her think through complex ideas.

Deborah Brandt (1998, 2001) is a well-known literacy scholar in composition studies who examines how various "literacy sponsors" shape writers' practices in schools, communities, and workplaces. Fabiola's experiences suggest some of the ways in which sponsors—including various people, institutions, texts, and other

objects—can influence resident multilingual youths' transitions to (and success in) postsecondary settings. In her case, these sponsorships were overwhelmingly supportive, but as I demonstrate through other students' experiences, there can be a mismatch between sponsors and students' goals that can hinder academic success.

This chapter explores the role of literacy sponsors in transitions to postsecondary education for five Spanish- and English-speaking resident multilingual students who enrolled in a range of institutions, including university, community college, cosmetology school, and a Catholic religious institute. These cases demonstrate that literacy sponsors play key roles in helping students meet demands of postsecondary transitions, but their relative impact largely depends on the *match* of writers and their sponsors' goals.

Understanding the Sponsorship of Literacy

Brandt (1998) defines "literacy sponsors" as:

> Any agents, local or distant, concrete or abstract, who enable, support, teach, model, as well as recruit, regulate, suppress, or withhold literacy—and gain advantage by it in some way. Just as the ages of radio and television accustom us to having programs *brought* to us by various commercial sponsors, it is useful to think about who or what underwrites occasions of literacy learning and use. Although the interests of the sponsor and the sponsored do not have to converge (and, in fact, may conflict) sponsors nevertheless set the terms for access to literacy and wield powerful incentives for compliance and loyalty.
>
> *(p. 167)*

The concept of sponsorship therefore encourages researchers to look from multiple perspectives to better understand individuals' unique opportunities for literacy learning and the material circumstances in which that learning occurs. In this sense, it is appropriate to examine literacy learning through micro-level interactions and individual relationships, but not at the expense of the larger forces influencing (or being influenced by) them.

Literacy sponsors can include a range of institutions, individuals, and objects; the following list, drawing from Brandt (1998, 2001) unless otherwise noted, underscores this diversity.

- Institutions (including their policies and practices): churches; schools and universities; governments; media outlets; out-of-school programs; non-profit organizations; corporations and industries
- Individuals: relatives; teachers; friends; religious, cultural, or governmental leaders; work supervisors; librarians; researchers (Laursen & Fabrin, 2013); pop culture figures (Hall, 2003)

- Objects: storybooks; secular and religious texts; libraries; self-authored texts (Young, 2014); online discussion boards (Pavia, 2013); the Internet; technology more generally

In some cases, sponsors may simultaneously serve multiple purposes: Laursen and Fabrin (2013), for example, found that teachers and other adults can both support students' writing and act as gatekeepers or "counter-sponsors" who prevent access to or otherwise impede literacy learning. At the same time, students who are "sponsored" are also able to exert agency, in that individuals can engage in "corralling of sponsorship forces" (Brandt, 2001, p. 69) to serve their own ends, and decide, when offered a sponsoring relationship, whether to affiliate or not, and then whether to assimilate, appropriate, or reject the relationship (Donehower, 2013).

Access to sponsorship is often stratified by individuals' and communities' political, social, and economic privilege, which can either facilitate or limit access to meaningful and plentiful contacts with powerful literacy sponsors (Brandt, 1998). In relation to multilingual writers specifically, literacy resources acquired through sponsorship may be inconsistently valued across contexts. For example, in comparing the case of Dora Lopez (a Spanish-English bilingual) with that of a monolingual English speaker from the same community in *Literacy in American Lives* (2001), Brandt argues that Dora's Spanish language and literacy resources—which were carefully sponsored and developed by her family—lost value when shifting from the home sphere to school, play, and work contexts that required English. Technology can serve to reinforce these devaluations, rather than alleviate them, as Pederson (2010) found in Jordanian academics' limited use of Arabic even as part of their email and Internet work routines.

Sponsorship is a uniquely appropriate means of investigating writing specifically. Brandt (2001) found that writing sponsors were far scarcer than reading sponsors, especially in home but also in school contexts. And for multilinguals, institutional sponsorship of home or minority language writing, even in officially bilingual educational institutions, appears to be even more elusive (Gentil, 2005; Kibler, 2014).

Resident Multilingual Writers' Transitions from a Sponsorship Perspective

Because this entire volume explores resident multilingual writers' transitions more generally, such territory will not be covered thoroughly here. The following selective review of relevant literature presents a few key studies whose findings might help elucidate the role of sponsors in these contexts.

Schooling institutions' tracking and placement policies seem to offer important sponsorship (or more often counter-sponsorship) of multilingual writers labeled as "English language learners" or "ESL" that appears to significantly impact transitions. In high school, such students may be placed in tracks that preclude them from taking college-preparatory courses (Callahan & Shifrer, 2012; Kanno & Cromley, 2013), which are necessary to access university and gain the literacy expertise that helps students avoid remedial or ESL placements in college or university (Bunch &

Endris, 2012). Such placements, aside from carrying the stigma of "re-becoming ESL" (Ortmeier-Hooper, 2008), can also be problematic because of trends that show students' limited progress through remedial or ESL courses at community colleges (e.g., Patthey-Chavez, Thomas-Spiegel, & Dillon, 2009).

Yet, successful literacy sponsorships have also been documented. These include the skillful pedagogical practices of a writing teacher to support multilingual and multiliterate practices and identities (Skerrett, 2013); multiple, dynamic, and multilingual adult and peer sponsorships in support of an adolescent's school-based writing in English over time (Kibler, 2014); and adolescents' self- and peer-sponsored use of technology to navigate and develop multiple languages and genres (Lam, 2004; Lee, 2006; Yi, 2007) and to develop positive identities (de la Piedra, 2010; Yi, 2013). Even successful sponsors, however, may not always facilitate postsecondary transitions: Harklau and McClanahan (2012) suggest that well-resourced schools, extracurricular programs, churches and religious activities, and families can simultaneously sponsor and counter-sponsor linguistic minority students' access to and success in college.

The Study, Data Collection, and Data Analysis

This multiple-case study draws upon eight years of data collection, starting when students began 9th grade at South Sierra, a small majority-Latino high school in California, and extending four years after high school graduation. All spoke Spanish as a primary language and were at beginning or intermediate English language proficiency in writing when they began high school, according to standardized assessment data (see Kibler, 2009). In four years' time, all students graduated on time: four from South Sierra, and one from West Hills, where the fifth student transferred in 10th grade. After graduation, students scattered geographically and academically, attending a four-year university, community college, cosmetology program, and Catholic novitiate program (see Table 7.1 for demographics).

TABLE 7.1 Participant Settings

	Grade entered U.S. schools	U.S.-born?	High school	Postsecondary
Ana	5th	No	South Sierra	1.5-year cosmetology program: local community college
Diego	Kindergarten (1 year only); 7th	Yes	South Sierra	4-year degree program: in-state private university
Fabiola	9th	Yes	South Sierra	4-year degree program: in-state public university
Jaime	3rd	No	South Sierra/ West Hills	No degree plan: local community college
Maria	6th	Yes	South Sierra	4-year training at Catholic novitiate, the "Institute" on the East Coast

I was (and am) involved in students' lives in many realms: as an instructional coach at their school, an observer, a tutor, and sometimes a cheerleader and confidant. Although it is not possible to achieve true insider status (Heath & Street, 2008), my lack of a teacher role, my use of Spanish, and my ongoing communication with students across settings helped me earn trust and gain access to a range of writing practices and artifacts.

Primary data for analysis include interview transcripts and writing samples, focusing on the last high school year and first two postsecondary years (study years 4–6). Secondary data include observational field notes as well as interviews and writing samples from other years. Interview transcripts were analyzed inductively (Marshall & Rossman, 2011), and writing samples from years 4–6 were revisited to support or refute students' claims wherever possible. I coded each instance of sponsorship for either reading or writing (although the emphasis of the overall study was more on writing), creating a matrix of sponsors within and across students, also noting the different "layers" to which the sponsors corresponded (see Figure 7.1). Field notes and writing samples from other study years further triangulated and contextualized findings.

In regard to Figure 7.1, it should be noted that individual students experienced different sponsors and also experienced similar sponsors differently. These

FIGURE 7.1 Resident Multilingual Writers' Literacy Sponsors in Postsecondary Transitions

relationships are explored below for each student in relation to the four layers of the figure (government, institutions, individuals, and objects).

Findings

In addition to several sponsorships most students shared, three distinct patterns in postsecondary transitions were found: that of students who experienced "matches" (sponsorship), "mis-matches" (counter-sponsorship), and alternative sponsorship. It is to these histories and trajectories that we now turn.

Similar Sponsors across Cases

When looking across cases, certain governmental and school-based institutional sponsors operated similarly for multiple students, alongside sponsorship through technology use. Each is addressed in turn.

All five students were able to attend postsecondary schooling because of financial literacy sponsors, through scholarships (Fabiola, Diego), private donations from community members or former teachers (Jaime, Ana), or church donations (Maria). The extent to which financial sponsorship came from public sources, however, depended on the government's policy toward undocumented immigrant students: state and federal policy at the time kept Ana and Jaime from competing for most scholarships or applying for governmental financial aid. The private donations they received allowed them to attend classes but in one case had to be paid back (Ana). Both students also received supplemental in-kind support from parents, and Jaime earned money from a part-time job. More importantly, however, both Ana and Jaime explained in interviews that the immigration policy then in place appeared to influence their perspectives on future education and employment while still in high school. Ana explained to me in 10th grade that, "I do want to go to college, but I want to study for nurse and probably police, but you have to have papers to do those. [To] do it would just be a waste. They're not going to accept me because I don't have papers. So why I am going to study if I'm not going to do it?" (2/17/08).

As is the case with most students in the United States, governmental sponsorship was also visible through state assessments of curricular learning, most notably through the state's high school graduation exam. While testing pressures did not wholly drive the entire school curricula or all classroom activities for students in this study, the skills and content on those assessments clearly guided instruction, as they do in most public schools, and were also visible in tutoring sessions and even students' placement in test-prep classes. In Jaime's case, in-class test preparation occurred in the context of tracked classes, which did not provide him with credits necessary for university entrance, but for students at South Sierra, curricula were taught in untracked class. All five passed the high school exit exam,

but perhaps most importantly for these multilingual writers, the emphasis on English-only testing (alongside more ideological anti-bilingual pressures in the state) precluded any from developing advanced Spanish-language writing skills through U.S. schooling.

Despite these larger pressures, all students in the study cited at least one teacher who was helpful in their writing development. Even Ana, whose high school advisor thought she should be recommended for special education because of her writing, spoke fondly of a teacher who motivated her to complete several 12th grade writing tasks. Once students had transitioned into and become aware of the writing demands in postsecondary institutions, however, all were critical to varying degrees of the writing instruction they received, ranging from Diego's contention that the high school and students were "doing like almost everything wrong" (6/29/11; see also Kibler, 2013) to Jaime's explanation that a remedial college English course was difficult because "I didn't really know how to write a good paragraph" (2/2/12).

Another omnipresent sponsor in all participants' lives was technology: from nonstop text messaging to MySpace and Facebook socializing to Google Docs drafting, students relied upon phones and computers to create and share almost all of their out-of-school writing (in English and Spanish) and much of their in-school (English) writing as well, a pattern that continued throughout the post-secondary transition for all but one student. (Maria had no cell phone and only very limited computer/Internet access in her religious Institute). Once out of high school, laptops were provided through Fabiola and Diego's scholarships, and even with more limited resources, Ana and Jaime used home computers or laptops in their transition. The omnipresence of technology meant that it became a multi-faceted sponsor: one that supported writing in both languages for both social and academic purposes.

Cases of "Match": Facilitating Sponsorships

Two case study students—Maria and Fabiola—appeared to consistently benefit from matches between their literacy goals and those of sponsors during the transition to postsecondary schooling.

A range of sponsors supported their aspirations, either to pursue a religious life (Maria) or to complete a four-year university degree (Fabiola), and provided requisite supports. For example, when Maria decided to enter the Institute, an order founded in Argentina and with many Spanish-speaking leaders, she began to read several Spanish-language religious books published by the Institute. When she began her studies, the Institute supplied Maria's housing, schooling, and living expenses free of charge. As mentioned in the introduction, Fabiola earned a reputation as a serious student in high school (with her own self-designated "study corner" in her advisor's classroom) and was recommended by teachers for a

competitive four-year scholarship to a top-tier state university. Once at the university, her scholarship foundation paid for Fabiola's tuition, fees, and living expenses and provided her with a college-educated Latina mentor and regular workshops on college and career success.

Specific institutional policies also sponsored these students. Although Maria attended a Catholic religious institute and Fabiola a four-year university, sponsors' goals still aligned with students'; moreover, diverse institutional structures—such as a shared religious mission and progressive writing-placement practices—supported transitions in which students struggled with postsecondary writing demands. Maria explained how she coped with writing challenges in her first year in terms of her choice to enter a religious order: "Sometimes I'm having a hard time with writing, yeah sometimes I'm tired, but it doesn't matter cause I feel like, I'm more free in a way, like I'm more free even though . . . the world thinks you're crazy" (2/8/11). Fabiola entered a university writing program that facilitated her progress toward a degree through requiring relatively few courses for students found to be in need of remediation. She had to take only one "remedial" writing course, which was also credit bearing, before entering the typical writing sequence. This allowed her to begin coursework early in her transition in the Gender and Women's Studies Department, her eventual major, and to eventually complete all graduation requirements in four years.

Both Maria and Fabiola actively solicited support for their English writing in high school and postsecondary institutions from academically oriented peers, teachers, and other adults, drawing upon bilingual and monolingual literacy sponsors serving as "encouragers," "idea shapers," "clarifiers," "writing experts," and "idea sources" (see Kibler, 2014, for an in-depth analysis of Maria). In high school, these sponsorships occurred in class or after school through conversations with peers and teachers, and out of class by asking teachers, mentors, and even me for feedback on what they had written. Once in postsecondary institutions, both remained proactive in seeking individual sponsors but also adapted their strategies to produce writing that was valued by their institutions. Maria's teachers graded more stringently for conceptual knowledge than writing conventions, and she reported becoming particularly adept in seeking others who could help her understand the ideas she wrote about on exams. She explained,

> Whenever I didn't understood, I will ask one of the sisters to help me. . . . I'll ask them what it means and if I was right or if it's the same idea, and pretty much I will ask the one that has good grades . . . pretty much she's like the person I go when I need help, and then when I don't understand I go to the prefector of studies.
>
> *(1/8/11)*

Fabiola often began major in-class writing tasks with frustration, but she drew upon multiple sponsors to complete them, undertaking in-class activities supporting the

writing task, engaging in multiple drafts, visiting professors during office hours, and soliciting feedback from peers or other adults. For an interpretive essay on the film *Far from Heaven*, for example, she said the assignment at first seemed overwhelming:

> So we were supposed to write about how the house was a symbol of claus-trophobia and suffocation. And so when he first gave us the prompt, I was like, how am I going to do this? You know what I mean? Like, you're asking me how the house is a symbol of this? Like, no, I'm not going to write this.
>
> *(12/16/10)*

After watching the movie several times and participating in lessons focused on how to write about film techniques and how to create transitions between ideas, however, Fabiola said she felt more confident about writing this new type of essay. She explained that this assignment "introduced me to a new way of writing . . . because I was used to just writing essays where I could introduce quotes." By the end of the first semester, Fabiola identified this text as the one she was most proud of, saying that "I really put effort into interpret things, and I think that in the end I was clear" (12/16/10). For this essay, drafts indicate that she received help from her teacher, whom Fabiola said was more approachable than she expected, along with her scholarship mentor, a tutor she identified as unhelpful, her suitemate, and me.

   Just as institutions, policies, and individuals supported Maria and Fabiola's transitions, the objects they used to engage in and learn from writing differed but matched the goals of sponsors in their respective contexts. In high school, both used a range of print and electronic sources to obtain ideas for their writing, a process that occurred primarily in English. For Maria, this pattern changed at the postsecondary level. First, Internet access was very limited. Second, although classes at the Institute were held in English, many institutional documents were originally written in Spanish, and Maria was able to access class texts in both English and Spanish in the library. She described using both to help her understand new ideas she would write about:

> So, like, the constitution is translated in English, but it's more difficult for me to read it in English, so I'm reading it in Spanish. So right now it came in handy that I know how to read both of them cause if I find a book that's difficult in one of the languages, I just translate to the other one. So, I'm jumping more than I did in school I guess where I did English. I'm jumping more from one language to the other one.
>
> *(4/23/11)*

In contrast to Maria's use of bilingual texts as writing sponsors, Fabiola drew on print and electronic texts that were almost entirely in English, the language in which she also was required to write her essays. One notable trend in Fabiola's use

of texts is how she reported that she began to see her *own* writing as a sponsor. When asked what she thought helped her one semester in terms of improving her writing, she replied:

> Writing a lot. Because for one class, I had to write six small papers, and then for two of my other classes I had to write three small papers too. . . . It was easier to write and be more confident expressing my ideas or my feelings.
> *(12/19/11)*

Along with the amount of writing, Fabiola also reported beginning to use her own Spanish abilities to sponsor her drafting process in English. She described how this process began during her second year of college:

> I feel at the beginning of college and in high school, I was scared of just thinking in Spanish. And I feel this [second] year that I really just try to think sentences in Spanish and put them in English. I think this is one of my first years I'm kinda more open in trying to use Spanish. And sometimes when I just had a lot of ideas, I'll just write. And if I can't get a word or a sentence, I'll just write it in Spanish and think about it later—just to keep writing.
> *(6/21/12)*

Fabiola frequently sent me drafts that included words and phrases in Spanish. Somewhat ironically, Fabiola only began to engage in this multilingual self-sponsorship many years after first beginning to write in English (even though her 9th grade humanities teacher encouraged her to do so in her class). For both Fabiola and Maria, their multilingualism appeared to serve as an important means for self-sponsorship in concert with other objects, individuals, and institutions.

Cases of "Mismatch": Counter-Sponsorship

For Diego and Jaime, however, mismatches in writers' goals—to complete four-year degrees in business and computer science, respectively—and those of their sponsors led to more problematic transitions to postsecondary education. Like Maria and Fabiola, they were sponsored in gaining access to the institutions they attended: Diego through a four-year scholarship, which included all tuition and living expenses, a mentorship program, and summer school, and Jaime through a community member who paid his tuition and took him to the community college to register for courses.

Mismatches were apparent, however, in relation to institutional policies at these postsecondary institutions. Although both students spoke with confidence about their writing abilities as seniors in high school, placement tests assigned Diego and Jaime to remedial English courses multiple levels below required, credit-bearing

college composition classes. The students reacted to this placement differently, however. Diego explained that he blamed his high school for not preparing him better: "I went there, now [they're] telling me that I actually didn't learn the basics things on high school about how to write a paragraph or an essay" (6/29/11). Jaime, on the other hand, had a more pragmatic approach. He did not question his placement or high school writing preparation, only saying that he would prefer to be in the upper-level ESL class offered by the college because it offered transferable English credits while his current classes, designed for the general community college population, did not. Diego and Jaime took almost no courses in their planned areas of study during the first two years, which were dominated by English, mathematics, and other elective courses.

Individuals present a mixed picture of sponsorship for Diego and Jaime. They relied on sponsors similar to Maria and Fabiola's, utilizing support from peers, teachers, other adults, and mentors, both in composing and in receiving writing feedback. In high school, I often observed Diego soliciting and receiving help from others, either in class or in after-school office hours with teachers, and his drafts frequently included feedback from multiple individuals. Jaime did so less frequently of his own volition in high school, but he participated in classroom writing activities and often spoke excitedly about the topics of his writing, like an essay on Pancho Villa or an alternative ending of *Lord of the Flies* he and his classmates wrote.

Diego had even more extensive individual supports in college than in high school, which included not only teachers and peers but also a scholarship-provided mentor during the school year and a tutor in the summer, though he did not specifically mention their roles in his writing. And while he described occasionally getting help in college with "grammar" from friends at his dorm and the campus learning center, teachers were his primary writing sponsors. What made Diego unique from the other students in the study, however, was the way in which he solicited assistance from his teachers: both he and a high school teacher, for example, admit that the teacher was "writing the essay *for* him" (Kibler, 2011), and this trend appeared to continue in college (Kibler, 2013).

In college, Jaime's individual sponsorships were generally multifaceted and productive. He solicited feedback from a smaller range of individuals than Diego, but he frequently participated in peer-review and writing activities in classes and consistently relied on his English-dominant girlfriend, who was majoring in pre-med at another local university. He explained:

> She was like, "Oh, you should use this word, it sounds better," because I guess she has a better understanding of words. . . . Then she would sort of like fix my sentences, like, to sound more interesting—more catchy I guess. I mean, she's a good writer.
>
> *(2/2/12)*

And while Jaime often described falling behind with smaller assignments, final papers were usually success stories. In one of his classes, for example, he described how his writing was even shown as a model:

> [The teacher] used it as an example of how you should write TEA [thesis-example-analysis] paragraphs and stuff. So, yeah, then after that, everybody thought I was like, ah, smart, but you know, I wasn't (laughs) . . . I guess it was good. She said it was good. She liked it. She used it as an example. So it felt good for a while.
>
> *(6/20/12)*

Such stories were typical for Jaime, and the writing he shared with me demonstrated both revision and paragraph structures that paralleled what he reported being taught.

In terms of the objects sponsoring writing, Jaime and Diego drew upon a range of similar printed and online school texts that aligned to varying degrees with those of sponsors in their respective contexts. Textbooks often provided somewhat rote "exercises," but assigned or independent-research readings in the postsecondary classes in which significant writing occurred were often relevant and engaging to students, ranging from the memoir *Burro Genius* to nonfiction texts on the DREAM Act. All materials were provided in English, however, and students never mentioned using Spanish in their school-based reading or writing. While no evidence points to objects hindering Jaime's writing development, there are several moments in which the amount of assigned reading appears to have overwhelmed Diego, leading to his falling behind in classes and relying upon others to help him when writing about the texts (Kibler, 2013).

Despite generally supportive individual and object sponsorships, Diego and Jaime experienced less-than-successful transitions. By the end of their second postsecondary year, neither had yet completed the remedial English sequence in which they were placed. For Diego, this occurred because of the sequence length and his needing to retake two English classes for passing grades. His overall academic success in other classes was problematic too, which he attributed to both being overwhelmed by multiple assignments due at the end of each term and his own time management skills. After his second year, in fact, he transferred back to a local community college at his scholarship foundation's urging. Jaime stopped taking classes midway through his second year; although he was earning credits successfully, by the end of his first semester, he had decided, "I just want to get it over with, community college" (12/20/10). By the middle of his second year he was working almost 40 hours per week and had stopped taking classes entirely. He explained that, because of his work schedule, "I haven't really been thinking about writing lately. It's too much stuff going on" (2/12/12). He said he hoped to return to community college, but for a vocational "short course" rather than coursework that would transfer to a four-year university.

It is clearly impossible to identify singular or definite reasons for Diego and Jaime's problematic transitions, either within a sponsorship framework or otherwise, but a common trend through their stories is that of institutional counter-sponsors that required them to develop "remedial" writing skills instead of pursuing literacy tasks related to their longer-term goals and areas of study (business and technology). Other issues were clearly in play, ranging from the language and literacy demands of classes (for Diego) to financial support that only included tuition but left living expenses unpaid (for Jaime). Based upon the data, students' abilities in Spanish were not recognized by sponsors or even students themselves as strengths or resources in the transition; while such an omission cannot be linked to any certain outcomes for Diego and Jaime, the difference from Maria and Fabiola's cases is nonetheless striking.

A Case of Alternative Sponsorship

Finally, Ana, seen as a weak writer by teachers in high school, enrolled in and completed a postsecondary cosmetology program despite limited institutional and governmental support. Rather, she was enabled by a partial match between institutional policies, individual and object sponsors, and by her own self-identification as a "hands-on" person (6/19/12).

Institutional and governmental sponsorship for Ana was extremely limited. As mentioned above, Ana was not eligible for financial aid or scholarships because of her immigration status; only through the intervention of a former high school teacher, who offered Ana a loan, was she able to afford the cosmetology program. She relied on family for additional financial support and housing while in school.

The cosmetology program's institutional policies matched Ana's own goals for writing and for her postsecondary career. Ironically, one of her goals was *not* to write: she often professed a dislike for any academic writing and for traditional coursework, saying she "wouldn't have made it" in a regular college degree program, which she thought would have "too much writing, too much work" (6/19/12). Her one-and-a-half year program was comprised of cosmetology courses only, with a heavy emphasis on hands-on application of what they learned. She explained, "It was like, a lot of work, a lot of like quizzes and then, a lot of doing things, running around, getting ready for this and that thing . . . up-dos, dyeing hair, cutting hair, make-up, nail" (1/5/11). In this sense, although the program offered little in the way of traditional or extensive collegiate opportunities for writing, it allowed Ana access to and a means of progressing through her chosen course of study.

Individual sponsors played a unique role in Ana's writing during the postsecondary transition, in which she undertook several multiple-choice tests without a writing component but also completed a written project, an account of a makeover she did on her own. Although she utilized teachers (and other adults and peers, though to a lesser extent) as literacy sponsors in the same roles as the other

study participants while in high school, once in cosmetology/vocational school, she relied on teachers only tangentially for her main written project, via lecture notes. Instead, she primarily relied upon a new kind of individual sponsor, a peer with whom she talked about how to *do* the makeover that she was planning, rather than about how to write the text.

Object sponsors also played an important role in this process. She reported relying on the textbook, as well as her own in-class lecture notes in order to use the appropriate technical language for her written project, saying, "I had to use the specific vocabulary, not just like, 'cut it this way then cut it the left way and then this.' You have to [write] like, 'high graduation to low graduation' " (1/5/11). Photographs of her makeover were also included in her project and described through her writing, further underscoring the close relationship between Ana's "hands-on" identity and her writing tasks.

Ana was successful in her assigned writing—tailored to her stated kinesthetic proclivities—as well as the other elements of her coursework, and she completed her cosmetology program midway through her second year after high school graduation. The question of exactly what her various sponsorships allowed her to achieve, however, is a more complicated issue. Due to immigration policy, Ana wasn't able to take the examination that would enable her to earn an official cosmetology license, so her future employment options were dramatically restricted. In fact, when I met with her after completion of her course, she was working part-time from home and part-time at a low-paying, cash-only beauty salon in her neighborhood. At that time, Ana vehemently stated that she did NOT write or read in any way in her daily life (although she texted frequently during our conversations). She wanted to eventually own her own beauty salon, however, and a state-level DREAM Act that had passed after she finished her program would allow her to work toward that goal. (See García de Müeller, this volume, for further discussion on the DREAM Act.)

Discussion

These case studies suggest a range of insights into postsecondary transitions that have larger resonances for many resident multilingual writers. First, it is notable that all students had multiple literacy sponsors outside of their own families, and while many were institutionally provided, students also found unique means of "corralling" sponsors (Brandt, 2001) by drawing upon their own strengths, such as their multilingualism, their hands-on approaches to learning, and their relationships with others (and those individuals' sense of investment in them) to help them engage in writing tasks, either in preparation for or as part of postsecondary schooling. Regarding the impact of matches or mismatches between writers and their literacy sponsors, these cases suggest no singular or clear-cut relationships but several trends that appear to influence transitions.

The counter-sponsorship of immigration policies for undocumented students was influential on Ana and Jaime. Although they both attended postsecondary

institutions and Ana completed hers, their overall literacy sponsorship networks were somewhat weaker than those of the other students due to more limited financial and employment sponsorships, as well as approaches to schooling colored by prospects of limited future opportunities. For example, one cannot help but wonder whether Ana's "hands-on" (and anti-writing) identity developed on its own or in response to her restricted postsecondary options.

Institutional policies and practices appeared to more effectively sponsor transitions when they allowed students quick access to content related to their interests or long-term goals (e.g., religion, cosmetology, gender and women's studies). This is not to say that Jaime and Diego did not benefit from the writing instruction they received in their English courses or that remediation itself was not beneficial; rather, as part of the larger picture of transitions, the extent to which these courses prevented students from progressing more quickly to their postsecondary goals seems to have been problematic, as others have documented (Patthey-Chavez, Thomas-Spiegel, & Dillon, 2009). At the same time, Ana's experiences in the cosmetology program highlight the under-studied but common vocational pathways many resident multilingual youth take, which have their own unique opportunities and challenges that merit further study.

Individual-level sponsorships, whether provided institutionally or solicited by writers themselves, appeared to facilitate students' transitions as long as the role(s) they played matched the larger institutional demands for writing. For example, Maria's writing at the Institute was judged primarily on the accuracy of its content, and so her use of a "good student" or the prefector of studies to discuss that content facilitated her eventual passing of written examinations. For Diego, however, his reliance on teachers to provide both the content and at times the language for writing assignments resulted in initial placement in the lowest-level remedial English course and did not appear to facilitate his progress through the sequence of courses once in college.

A final observation particularly relevant to this volume is the mismatch between sponsoring institutions and the home language and literacy skills of the multilingual writers in this study, consistent with previous research (Brandt, 2001; Gentil, 2005; Kibler, 2011). From what the data suggest, neither Ana nor Diego nor Fabiola nor Jaime were presented with any postsecondary opportunities to read or write in their home languages or explicit opportunities to draw upon their home language expertise in support of their writing. (Secondary opportunities to do so were present but also very limited; see Kibler, 2009.) Fabiola began to self-sponsor her own writing in college through use of Spanish, but this approach was not institutionally initiated or supported. Maria benefited from institutionally supported sponsorships of her reading in Spanish, but even she did not have *writing* sponsors to legitimate or support her use of written Spanish.

The above analysis also raises provocative questions about how we (as researchers and educators) understand postsecondary education, the role of writing in school and life, and writers themselves. For example, what makes a transition

"successful," and whose criteria and time frames are we using? What does "failure" mean in terms of postsecondary transitions, and how does this vary by stakeholder? Such issues are at the heart of educators' work as well as the implicit understandings upon which individual actions and institutional policies and practices are built, but they remain contested nonetheless.

Just as this chapter raises provocative questions, it also leaves some issues unexplored. For example, the role of families in these transitions is somewhat opaque. The students' parents were all born and raised in Mexico, and none had undertaken postsecondary education there or in the United States. Both Ana and Jaime had older sisters who began or completed community college programs, but the others were the first in their families to attend postsecondary schooling. Students rarely mentioned family sponsorship in general, although both Ana and Jaime lived at home during the transition period, and never mentioned family support in relation to writing specifically. To what extent families' support may have extended into these realms, perhaps in modeling the "mundane" writing that Brandt (2001) explains often goes unnoticed, is unclear. Technology is also addressed in this chapter, but only briefly, and the broader ways in which it supports non-institutional multilingual writing merits further analysis that cannot be included here. For reasons of space, I also do not provide a full analysis of some larger trends influencing various sponsorships, such as global flows of immigration or workforce demands that make postsecondary education so important in the first place. They are visible to greater or lesser degrees, but further treatment of these issues is clearly important, particularly when examining writing sponsorship over a lifetime. Also intriguing is the possible role of gender in sponsorship and the ways in which women may seek or accept sponsorships for school-based writing differently than men. And finally, Diego's course performance—in which he was unable to succeed even in remedial courses—suggests a further potential mismatch between those institutional structures and the English proficiency and literacy skills required by the institution.

Conclusions and Implications

Resident multilingual writers and their diverse literacy sponsors function within institutional ecologies that can facilitate or mediate against successful postsecondary transitions, and while a full array of literacy sponsors may not be necessary for students to succeed, institutional and governmental constraints appear to overpower even strong individual sponsorship. Brandt (1998) suggests that although teachers are "neither rich nor powerful enough to sponsor literacy on our own terms, we serve instead as conflicted brokers between literacy's buyers and sellers" (p. 182). This study suggests that teachers can benefit from building upon students' diverse, multilingual literacy sponsors, and that school administrators should recognize individual teacher "support" cannot overcome institutional barriers, particularly postsecondary. Finally, researchers can better understand transitions by conceptualizing literacy sponsors as part of an overall writing ecology.

At the same time, it is important that all potential writing sponsors (including researchers) working in multilingual communities think carefully about how they understand and support individual writers. As Donehower (2013) notes in her study of governmental, religious, and school-based sponsors in Appalachia: "The presence of any literacy worker or researcher in Appalachia is likely to be interpreted as a re-inscription of the Appalachian illiteracy stigma, even if the workers or researchers themselves have no wish to promote such stereotypes" (p. 359). While such tensions cannot be avoided entirely, it is incumbent upon individual and institutional literacy sponsors to proceed thoughtfully, cautiously, and with input from the communities and writers they serve.

Bibliography

Brandt, D. (1998). Sponsors of literacy. *College Composition and Communication, 49*, 165–185. doi: http://dx.doi.org/10.2307/358929

Brandt, D. (2001). *Literacy in American lives.* Cambridge: Cambridge University Press.

Bunch, G. C., & Endris, A. K. (2012). Navigating "open access" community colleges: Matriculation policies and practices for U.S.-educated language minority students. In Y. Kanno & L. Harklau (Eds.), *Linguistic minority students go to college: Preparation, access, and persistence* (pp. 165–183). New York: Routledge.

Callahan, R. M., & Shifrer, D. R. (2012). High school ESL placement: Practice, policy, and effects on achievement. In Y. Kanno & L. Harklau (Eds.), *Linguistic minority students go to college: Preparation, access, and persistence* (pp. 19–37). New York: Routledge.

de la Piedra, M. T. (2010). Adolescent worlds and literacy practices on the United States–Mexico border. *Journal of Adolescent and Adult Literacy, 53*, 575–584.

Donehower, K. (2013). Literacy choices in an Appalachian community. *Journal of Appalachian Studies, 9*(2), 341–362.

Gentil, G. (2005). Commitments to academic biliteracy: Case studies of Francophone university writers. *Written Communication, 22*, 421–471. doi: http://dx.doi.org/10.1177/0741088305280350

Hall, R. M. (2003). The "Oprahfication" of literacy: Reading "Oprah's book club". *College English, 65*(6), 646–667. doi: http://dx.doi.org/10.2307/3594275

Harklau, L., & McClanahan, S. (2012). How Paola made it to college: A linguistic minority student's unlikely success story. In Y. Kanno & L. Harklau (Eds.), *Linguistic minority students go to college: Preparation, access, and persistence* (pp. 74–90). New York: Routledge.

Heath, S. B., & Street, B. V. (2008). *On ethnography: Approaches to language and literacy research.* New York: Teachers College Press.

Kanno, Y., & Cromley, J. G. (2013). English language learners' access to and attainment in postsecondary education. *TESOL Quarterly, 47*(1), 89–121. doi: http://dx.doi.org/10.1002/tesq.49

Kibler, A. (2009). *Talking writing: Adolescent English learners in the content areas.* Unpublished doctoral dissertation, Stanford University, Palo Alto, CA.

Kibler, A. (2011). "*Casi nomás me dicen qué escribir*/They almost just tell me what to write": A longitudinal analysis of teacher-student interactions in a linguistically diverse mainstream secondary classroom. *Journal of Education, 191*(1), 45–58.

Kibler, A. (2013). "Doing like almost everything wrong": An adolescent multilingual writer's transition from high school to college. In T. Silva & L. de Oliveira (Eds.), *L2 writing in the secondary classroom* (pp. 44–64). New York: Routledge.

Kibler, A. (2014). From high school to the *noviciado* (the novitiate): An adolescent linguistic minority student's multilingual journey in writing. *Modern Language Journal, 98*(2), 629–651. doi: http://dx.doi.org/10.1111/j.1540–4781.2014.12090.x

Lam, W. S. E. (2004). Second language socialization in a bilingual chat room: Global and local considerations. *Language, Learning, and Teaching, 8*, 44–65.

Laursen, H. P., & Fabrin, L. (2013). Children investing in literacy. *Linguistics and Education, 24*, 441–453. doi: http://dx.doi.org/10.1016/j.linged.2013.04.003

Lee, J. S. (2006). Exploring the relationship between electronic literacy and heritage language maintenance. *Language, Learning, and Technology, 10*, 93–113.

Marshall, C., & Rossman, G. B. (2011). *Designing qualitative research*. Thousand Oaks, CA: Sage Publications.

Ortmeier-Hooper, C. (2008). English may be my second language, but I'm not "ESL". *College Composition and Communication, 59*, 389–419.

Patthey-Chavez, G., Thomas-Spiegel, J., & Dillon, P. (2009). Accessing academic literacy in college pathways of U.S.-educated English language learners. In M. Roberge, M. Siegal, & L. Harklau (Eds.), *Generation 1.5 in college composition: Teaching academic writing to U.S.-educated learners of ESL* (pp. 135–150). New York: Routledge.

Pavia, C. W. (2013). Literacy sponsorship of the "my online friends" discussion board: Competing and complementary relationships. *Computers and Composition, 30*, 132–145. doi: http://dx.doi.org/10.1016/j.compcom.2013.04.002

Pederson, A. (2010). Negotiating cultural identities through language: Academic English in Jordan. *College Composition and Communication, 62*(2), 283–310.

Skerrett, A. (2013). Building multiliterate and multilingual writing practices and identities. *English Education, 45*(4), 322–360.

Yi, Y. (2007). Engaging literacy: A biliterate student's composing practices beyond school. *Journal of Second Language Writing, 16*, 23–39. doi: http://dx.doi.org/10.1016/j.jslw.2007.03.001

Yi, Y. (2013). Adolescent multilingual writer's negotiation of multiple identities and access to academic writing: A case study of a Jogi Yuhak student in a US high school. *The Canadian Modern Language Review/La revue canadienne des langues vivantes, 69*(2), 207–231.

Young, M. (2014). Writing the life of Henry Obookiah: The sponsorship of literacy and identity. In J. Duffy, J. Nelson Christoph, E. Goldblatt, N. Graff, R.S. Nowacek, and B. Trabold (Eds.), *Literacy, economy, and power: Writing and research after literacy in American lives* (pp. 61–76). Carbondale, IL: Southern Illinois University Press.

8

LITERACY SPONSORSHIP IN UPWARD BOUND

The Impact of (De)segregation and Peer Dynamics

Shauna Wight

> My English classes at UB [Upward Bound] are much better than high school. I guess it's the students, the attitude in the class. The people in UB are pretty much ready to work and help people work, and my school's like, they can't wait until they get out, until the bell rings and they go somewhere else.
>
> Jared, a bilingual UB participant

> UB influenced me my first year a lot, because like these kids are pretty smart, like I want to be up there, so my first year I went off and I did everything; I got like As.
>
> Ariel, a bilingual UB participant

Inaugurated in 1964 as a result of the Civil Rights Movement, the federally funded Upward Bound (UB) program helps underrepresented students succeed in their pre-college performance and postsecondary pursuits. Spawning a number of similar programs, UB remains the largest, serving approximately 60,000 students each year (Calahan & Curtain, 2004). While not represented in UB's demographic profiles, many linguistic minorities (LMs) come from families with low levels of income and parental education, the two main eligibility requirements for the program (Kanno & Harklau, 2012). Currently unexplored in second language writing research, UB's approach to writing instruction could provide insights into supporting LMs' transitions. The study presented here addresses this gap by examining how Upward Bound (UB) impacted LMs' access to academic writing during their senior year of high school and the college admissions process.

As the epigraphs opening this chapter contend, UB's academically driven peer cohort profoundly impacted students' writing. Specifically, I argue here that participants' high school and UB peers acted as sponsors of literacy: "any agents, local

or distant, concrete or abstract, who enable support, teach, and model as well as regulate, suppress, or withhold literacy" (Brandt, 2001, p. 15). However, the nature of peer sponsorship was often determined by tracking, a form of ability grouping in which students are placed within different classrooms and courses of study. To support this claim, I first provide an overview of the scholarship on tracking and pre-college outreach programs to highlight structural inequities and possible interventions. Next, I introduce Wegner's (1998) Communities of Practice framework, situating literacy as social act that encompasses multiple communities. Using this perspective, I analyze peer interactions in both Upward Bound and the participants' high schools, illustrating how these communities shaped possibilities for sponsorship.

Tracking and LMs' Access to Academic Writing

Numerous studies on linguistically diverse students have documented the deleterious effects of tracking. Harklau (1994) found that schools conflated academic ability and language proficiency, disproportionately placing LMs within lower levels. Despite increasing English proficiency, institutional inertia and students' own acceptance of labels often prevented advancement. Davidson (1996) and Oakes (2005) have also revealed the many ways in which tracking led to social division among peers, creating distrust and stereotyping among diverse students.

Tracking has also restricted multilingual students' access to academic writing, which is inextricably linked to their academic trajectories (Enright & Gilliland, 2011; Fu, 1995). This limited access to writing is compounded by peer relationships within these courses. Ortmeier-Hooper (2010), for instance, discovered that LMs emulated peers in remedial courses by avoiding rigorous writing assignments. Noting tracking's threat to educational advancement, Ortmeier-Hooper and Enright (2011) have coined the term "cycle of inopportunity" to refer to these reciprocal influences between tracking, identity, peer interactions, and access to academic writing (p. 175). In order to improve college access for LMs, interventions must break this cycle.

Breaking the Cycle: The Potentials and Limitations of Pre-College Outreach Programs

Among the variety of pre-college outreach programs available, most are funded by government agencies and typically include college preparatory coursework, mentoring, tutoring, cultural enrichment activities, and workshops on the college admissions and financial aid process. The limited data on these programs' outcomes have generally been positive, showing that their participants enroll in college at higher rates than control groups (Calahan & Curtain, 2004; Engle, 2007; Gándara, 2002).

The minimal literacy-based research that has been conducted on pre-college outreach programs typically focuses on Puente, which provides underserved

students in California with the writing instruction, mentoring, and counseling they need in order to get into college and complete a degree. Cazden (2002), for instance, found that the project's literacy curriculum gave participants opportunities to develop hybrid identities and bicultural competencies by blending instrumental culture, the skills necessary for social advancement, with expressive culture, their own values and interpersonal connections. Pradl (2002) has also tied the program's success to its model of professional development, which emphasizes teacher research, ongoing collaboration, and writing alongside students.

Despite the potential of these programs, broader structural inequities can attenuate their effectiveness. Research has often revealed negligible improvement in participants' GPAs and test scores, since most programs target high school students with less time for academic preparation (Calahan & Curtain, 2004; Gándara, 2002). Additionally, these programs cannot reach all the underserved students who need their services. TRIO, which encompasses UB, only serves 10% of the eligible student population, a number dwindling from ongoing budget cuts (Engle, 2007; Swail, 2000). Exploring pre-college outreach programs can inform wide-scale reforms that promote educational equity. This chapter begins to address this need. Specifically, the study presented here provides rich portraits of two participants in order to examine how UB sponsored their writing within and beyond the program.

Applying a Communities of Practice Framework to the High Schools and UB

This project uses Communities of Practice (CoP) as a framework to examine how these LMs' participation in UB and high school classes impacted peer interactions, writerly identities, and participation in academic writing. In this section, I highlight key terms and concepts from this theory in order to explain how it informed my analysis. While originally focusing on professional apprenticeships, CoP's relevance to other learning environments has made it useful for examining second language writing in classrooms (Haneda, 2006; Morita, 2004; Toohey, 1996) and online spaces (Yi, 2010). Lave and Wegner (1991) first articulated this concept as part of their situated-learning theory to balance social and cognitive perspectives on learning. In CoPs, learning emerges through legitimate peripheral participation (LPP), a process through which novices acquire the requisite skills needed to display mastery and become full members. Extending this work, Wegner (1998) has defined CoPs as groups of people who negotiate meaning through mutual engagement, a joint enterprise, and a shared repertoire. This negotiation of meaning emerges from participation, ongoing social interpretations of the world, and reification, fossilized understandings.

In this framework, learning is tied to identity. Specifically, Wegner (1998) has argued that learning transforms community members. Identity formation within CoPs is an ongoing process of identification—association and differentiation—and

negotiation, ability to control or contribute meanings within the community. In addition to these ongoing formations, however, certain identities can become fossilized into social labels. Individuals' sense of selfhood emerges from associating and differentiating themselves from communities. Sometimes, however, participation is marginalized among some members of the community whose contributions are rejected or ignored. For this reason, one's place within the community is as important as membership itself.

Beyond any particular community, individuals have to reconcile their identity across a "nexus of multi-memberships" that may carry conflicting forms of participation (p. 149). For this reason, individuals follow unique trajectories of participation within and between communities. As a data analysis tool, this framework provided me with the terminology and concepts necessary to explain how (de)tracking policies impacted trajectories of participation and writerly identities in the high schools and UB.

The Study

Much of the data presented here comes from a series of five case studies that I conducted as part of a yearlong project on how participation in UB impacted potential first-generation college students' academic writing and educational trajectories. For this chapter, I draw on transcribed interview data, field observations, and writing samples from two LM case study participants: Jared and Ariel. Chosen for their clarity and robustness, these exemplar cases illustrate themes that emerged across the data as students' writerly identities were shaped by institutional policies and the social interactions they entailed. As their demographic profiles (see Table 8.1) show, these participants received most of their education in the United States.

The first participant, Jared, returned with his mother to her native country of Peru shortly after his birth in the northeastern United States. Wanting Jared to start school in the United States, his mother moved them back at the start of 1st grade. Jared was placed in an ESL program from that time until the end of his 7th grade year. The second participant, Ariel, was born and raised within the United States. Ariel's parents were Vietnamese refugees, and Vietnamese was the primary language used within her home. Unlike Jared, Ariel never received

TABLE 8.1 Demographic Profiles of LM Participants

Name	Race	Birthplace	L1	# of years in UB	ESL services
Jared	Asian/Latino	United States	Spanish	3	1st–7th grade
Ariel	Asian	United States	Vietnamese	2	None

ESL services. Both participants indicated greater proficiency in English, but still reported difficulty writing in academic English.

The research took place in two locations: (1) UB's six-week summer residential program on the campus of a public northeastern university and (2) two different urban high schools in the Riverview school district. As a participant observer, I recruited students from the UB summer program with the help of its administrators. The program served 114 students from six different high schools, three of which were in Riverview. After the summer program, I followed the case study participants through their senior year of high school. To better contextualize the participants' school experiences, it is important to understand the district's demographics, educational outcomes, and funding. The Riverview school district had the second lowest per pupil spending and highest dropout rates in the state. Of its 15,536 students, 56% didn't meet the state-mandated writing proficiency levels, 47% qualified for the Free or Reduced Lunch program, 10% were identified as having limited English proficiency, and 34% were racial minorities.

Primary data sources for the study included (1) nine semi-structured student interviews with each participant, which lasted 30 to 60 minutes, (2) students' academic writing from UB, high school, and the college admissions process, and (3) a semi-structured 90-minute student focus group. These data sources were triangulated with hour-long semi-structured interviews of UB teachers and administrators, high school and UB policy statements and handbooks, and 50 hours of observations from UB classes and events. I was also able to interview Ariel's junior-/senior-year English teachers and conduct hour-long observations in her English classes on four occasions. I used summary vignettes of emerging themes to conduct member checking during interviews and consulted colleagues during data analysis to enhance the validity of my interpretations.

In what follows, I use three main concepts from the CoP framework to discuss findings from this study: trajectories of participation, identification, and multimembership. In particular, I show how trajectories of participation within these communities and the nexus of multi-memberships between them impacted students' identifications with peers and their writerly identities.

Contrasting Trajectories of Participation in UB and the High Schools

> *If students are fearful of being humiliated, either by a teacher or fellow students, they will not offer opinions or take risks, will not engage in discussion, and will do their best to be invisible. However, if students are not fearful, they will begin to find their voices.*
>
> No Discount Policy, UB Staff Manual

According to the CoP perspective, identity formation is an ongoing process that takes place within and between communities. UB and the high schools offered contrasting forms of participation that had significant outcomes for participants'

writerly identities. UB used mixed ability grouping within classes to give all participants access to the same college preparatory curriculum. Jared and Ariel's Senior Seminar English course included a college admissions essay and compare/contrast research paper in which the students researched different colleges and evaluated their options. Multiple opportunities for peer feedback, small class sizes, and one-on-one attention from the teacher and a tutor provided opportunities for legitimate peripheral participation (LPP) as students revised their essays to gain and demonstrate increasing competence. The curriculum and instructional methods, then, used authentic writing assignments and support from more established writers to facilitate participation in academic writing and higher education.

UB policies emphasized integration both inside and outside of the classroom. In order to give students a place within the community, UB established smaller groups that engaged in team-building activities. Group construction was centered on diversity:

> We design the groups so that they are diverse as possible. All the high schools we serve are represented, and students from the same school are often in different grades and programs. Racial, ethnic, and gender diversity are all part of the mix.
>
> *(UB Staff Manual)*

Classes were comprised of multiple groups, and staff assigned tables during meals to help students across the program get to know one another.

To address "unhealthy disagreements" that might emerge from these diverse groupings, UB had initiated a No Discount Policy and Ceremony (UB Staff Manual). In an initiation rite at the start of the program, administrators, staff, and then each of the five student groups stood in concentric circles and lit each others' candles as symbols of support before affirming their "full respect for the inherent worth of each person and for that person's feelings, opinions, ideas and well being." They then pledged to "not put one another down, put ourselves down, or disregard our own needs." Within this ceremony, the symbolic gestures of lighting one another's flames and configuring themselves into circles were intended to create an embodied response to the words of the pledge and provided concrete tokens to symbolize the group's communal values. Afterward, participants shared what the policy meant to them. In often tearful testimonials, returning students expressed how the policy helped them be themselves and explore new possibilities. After hearing these prototypical experiences, newcomers joined in by sharing what they hoped to achieve in the program. At the end of the ceremony, students were asked to state, "No D," any time they heard community members discounting themselves or anyone else.

In contrast to UB, high schools in the Riverview school district were tracked into four courses of study, which had become reified into institutional labels. Ariel's English teacher described the students in Level 1 as remedial; Level 2 as average;

Level 3 as college bound, but still pretty average; and Level 4 as advanced. Pointing to differing forms of participation within coursework, she noted that Level 3s and 4s provided more opportunities for writing, inquiry, and collaboration. While students could choose their levels in each subject, this policy still marginalized certain members' trajectories of participation. In April 2014, the U.S. Department of Education found that information barriers, standardized testing, and the policy of failing students who dropped to a lower level midterm excluded LMs in the district from college preparatory courses. Ariel and Jared were an exception to this trend as both were primarily enrolled within Level 3 courses at the time of the study.

Tracking created divisions among students within and beyond the classroom. Both participants indicated that white, native English speakers predominantly filled their college preparatory classes. As a result, there was a clear ranking system and minimal opportunities for diverse groups to interact. For instance, when I asked Ariel how she felt about being in predominantly white classes, she offered this response:

> I feel normal. I consider myself as white because I act more like a white person than I do an Asian person. If you see other kids at my school, the Asian kids usually hangout with the Asian kids, the Spanish kids with the Spanish kids, the white kids with the white kids, and whatnot. I find myself hanging out more with the white kids than the Asian kids.

She went on to explain that previous affiliations with Vietnamese peers shifted once they left for college, and white classmates, the "popular kids," replaced them. In many ways, then, Ariel's identifications reflected her desire to associate herself with members of the high school community who held academically and socially prestigious positions.

Like Ariel, Jared noted that students in his school were divided into different cliques. However, he based these divisions on interests rather than race or nationality. Still, he seemed to have accepted institutional labels, attributing LMs' remedial status to laziness: "I know a lot of minorities [at my school] really don't want to learn. Some people just use the ESL thing as a way to pass a test." For both participants, the school's rigid categories cast LMs as marginalized members. Despite these shared community practices and interpretations, each student negotiated membership differently. Because learning in CoPs is both individual and social, the next sections analyze each participant's trajectories of participation and writerly identities to show how they reconciled these contrasting memberships.

Jared: Inbound Trajectories in UB and High School

Participants' ability to reconcile identities impacted their willingness to participate in community writing practices. For Jared, participation and peer identifications at UB shifted his writerly identity in high school. Following teachers' and counselors'

recommendations, Jared enrolled in Level 2 courses upon entering high school and experienced marginalized participation in academic writing. For instance, he noted that, within his Level 2 courses, disruptive behaviors often caused teachers to give up on writing assignments. Despite limited experience with peer feedback or collaboration, he doubted that classmates would value writing workshops. Jared conformed to this environment and admitted investing minimal effort.

According to Jared, mixed ability grouping in UB interrupted this cycle, increasing his motivation and confidence with academic writing:

> In UB, highest levels, lowest levels, it's like a mix. I guess they choose people with good attitudes 'cause they know that in the future they're going to change to become a better student, a better writer, like me. My freshman year, I was a really bad writer; I didn't care. I was just like the kids in my school. Then I went to UB.

These mixed ability levels highlighted possibilities for transformation, and Jared sought competency with writing to affiliate with academically driven peers. Equally important, this peer cohort contributed to a classroom environment that was conducive to writing. In contrast to his Level 2 English class, Jared noted, "Everyone did well in Senior Seminar because students are in a good mood to work, so the teacher's in a good mood to teach." In a process he compared to "cranking the gears," he indicated that participating in a community with high expectations and levels of engagement gradually changed the way he saw himself as a writer.

The level of trust he experienced at UB also influenced his writerly identity. Jared believed he could negotiate meanings within the UB community and found social interactions there authentic. For instance, he felt the No Discount Policy challenged cliques, enabling him to be himself and share his writing:

> Upward Bound unleashed the best side of me that I didn't see before. I was shy then not shy; I was a really bad writer that had potential, and now I'm a decent writer. I guess when I used to write papers I was scared. I always wanted to fit in with my friends, but now I just want to be myself. I guess it's like the "No D" policy and stuff like that.

Specifically, Jared worried that in high school, other students might laugh at what he wrote or the amount of time it took him to complete a paper. At UB, he reported that he just focused on expressing his ideas, confident that classmates would help him improve. He found peer feedback incredibly useful for his college admissions essay, a piece about his father's open-heart surgery. For instance, questions over the outcome of the surgery helped him add detail and gain audience awareness. By creating a safe space to write and get feedback, UB policies provided opportunities for LPP that increased Jared's competence.

In many ways, he was able to reconcile this writerly identity and redirect his trajectory of participation in his school. According to Jared, participation in UB caused him to enroll in Level 3 English and science courses, which offered more opportunities to write and collaborate. For instance, in College Composition, his high school's college preparatory writing course, he turned to classmates for help in developing topics for a research paper on the novel *Cold Mountain*. Similarly, in Mythology, he delivered a collaborative presentation on Greek heroes, noting that the UB experience instilled the necessary confidence to address the whole class.

However, in other situations, reconciliation became more complicated. Due to cliques within science, Jared was uncomfortable asking questions in class and, though struggling with reports, refused to seek his lab partner's assistance. While expressing a greater willingness to seek feedback from Level 3 peers, he still did not trust them as much as UB friends. For instance, he continued turning to UB peers while revising his college admissions essay, explaining, "Mostly I asked people from UB because I trust them more than regular persons from high school. They are in the same playing field as me, go into a program, changing yourself, and then going to college." In some ways, then, Jared disassociated himself from peers in both his Level 2 and Level 3 classes. While participation in UB had positive impacts on Jared's academic writing, his identifications with high school classmates sometimes interfered with these practices.

Ariel: Conflicting Memberships and Trajectories

With Ariel, the process of negotiation and reconciliation created more conflicts than Jared experienced. During her first year in UB, Ariel tried to associate herself with academically driven peers in the program by working hard to maintain good grades in all her classes. However, Ariel's identifications shifted as a desire to associate with popular students in high school caused her to disassociate from UB peers. As a result, the emphasis on social integration within UB made her uncomfortable. For instance, when asked if her friends at high school would like the students at UB, she indicated:

> At UB they have kids from different categories, different races, and at school, it's just one category that stays together. There's the popular kids, the not popular kids, the weird kids, the geek kids, the game kids. At UB they're all mixed together. I feel like when I'm at UB, I have to talk to everyone, even if I don't want to.

For Ariel, this emphasis on integration conflicted with high school practices, and she found it difficult to reconcile identities across communities. She did not perceive opportunities to negotiate meanings within the UB community, indicating that its policies and staff "forced" these peer interactions on her. Feeling little control over her participation, she characterized its social interactions as inauthentic,

complaining, "People in UB are too nice, and when people are too nice, they want something from you."

This general sense of distrust shaped Ariel's interactions with UB peers during writing workshops for the college admissions essay, a piece in which she wrote about her father's suicide. After the first workshop, Ariel told me that the peer feedback she received "pissed me off." Specifically, she became angry when a classmate highlighted unnecessary details and suggested a stylistic edit: "I woke up one night to find my Mom sitting on the front porch steps crying harder than ~~me crying~~ [I did] during a stupid romance movie." Ariel questioned both this peer's feedback and credibility: "She's not like a great student, and I'm not 'D'ing her or anything." Such superficial references to the No Discount Policy illustrated Ariel's reluctance to accept UB practices and abandon negative institutional labels. In offering her own feedback, Ariel complained that the No Discount Policy prevented her from being honest.

While this was the most emotionally charged incident, Ariel also rejected help or feedback from other UB peers. Out of the five case study participants, she was the only one who did not revise in response to peer feedback. However, when teachers and tutors offered similar suggestions, she revised her essay accordingly. For instance, several peers noted that the end of her original essay did not explain how her father's death impacted her. Successive drafts revealed that she did not change her ending until her teacher made the same comment. When I pointed this out to Ariel during a member check, she attributed her response to a lack of trust and a sense of laziness. In many ways, then, peer schisms hindered her writing process. During the second workshop, Ariel exclusively worked with the tutor to edit her partner's paper. In contrast, the rest of the students discussed editing decisions with their partners. While interactions with staff still provided LPP, her negative identifications with peers undermined additional sources of support.

Yet, her interactions with high school peers did not reflect this distrust. When she decided to move up to a Level 4 economics class with less scaffolding on writing assignments, she actively sought out peer feedback to meet these new literacy demands. She also complained that her Creative Writing class never included peer workshops. When I pointed out that she typically ignored peer feedback in UB, she responded, "I trust the kids in my class more than I did at UB because I'm closer to them, and they don't act like they are know-it-alls." Although Ariel initially wanted to associate herself with UB peers, changing identifications undermined their legitimacy and created resentment. Difficulties reconciling the popular identity she was forming in high school and limited opportunities for negotiation compounded these problems, leading to nonparticipation within the UB community. By the end of her second summer, Ariel indicated, "I was like, 'F-it, I just want to go home.'" Ariel's experiences highlight how a student's sense of belonging within an academic community can impact her membership. Importantly, this sense of belonging often hinges upon identifications with peers and the ability to influence group practices.

Discussion

Within this chapter, I have shown how CoP theory reveals insights into the ways institutional policies impact multilingual students' writing practices, identifications with peers, and trajectories of participation. Specifically, I have argued that (de)segregation policies shape peer identifications in ways that affect possibilities for LPP and identities of mastery. In the high schools, tracking policies created hierarchies among students that could also influence UB practices. As Wegner (1998) has observed, learning transforms identities, but difficulties reconciling multiple memberships limited Jared and Ariel's transformative potential.

While shared practices in these Communities of Practice had become reified labels and interpretations, both participants still followed their own trajectories due to the tensions between institutional power and individual agency. As Haneda (2006) has argued, CoP theory has under-conceptualized these dimensions, which poses a significant limitation for classroom research since LMs often grapple with hegemony and cultural conflict. In many ways, L2 studies using this framework have paid more attention issues of power and agency. For instance, Toohey (1996) has shown how physical configurations within elementary classrooms limited LMs' agency and access to LPP. Similarly, both Morita (2004) and Norton (2001) have illustrated how adult multilingual students engaged in acts of subversion, such as nonparticipation, to maintain their agency in the face of hegemonic academic communities. Extending these findings, the current study has shown how institutional power mitigated the agency provided within pre-college outreach programs. Mixed ability grouping in UB showed Jared that minority students could excel with academic writing, but he was not always able to transfer these practices. While Ariel initially experienced a similar transformation in UB, white privilege in her high school later caused her to adopt an identity of nonparticipation in the program.

Furthermore, while existing L2 research has largely focused on classroom Communities of Practice, the current study shows how practices in these individual communities are inextricably bound to broader networks, or what Wegner (1998) has termed "constellations." Haneda (2006) has argued that researchers should distinguish participation from learning, since social interactions in an academic community are not the same thing as disciplinary knowledge. However, the broader perspective employed in this study questions whether such factors can be separated among adolescent learners, whose peer relationships and identities remain integral to disciplinary learning.

The saliency of peer relationships and multiple memberships within this study highlight important areas for future research. Although the current study does not focus on students' postsecondary experience, like UB, the transition from high school to college provides an opportunity to reshape identities by joining new academic communities. For this reason, future research should consider this study's implications for first-year writing. Unfortunately, writing programs

may perpetuate the negative labels students encounter in secondary schools by using placement practices that segregate LMs into developmental or ESL courses (Costino & Hyon, 2007; Harklau, Losey, & Siegal, 1999; Ortmeier-Hooper, 2008; Ruecker, 2011). Based on growing awareness of how these policies can affect LMs' identities and trajectories, the *CCCC Statement on Second Language Writers and Writing* (2009) has called for multiple placement options, including mainstreaming, ESL sections, and cross-cultural composition (which mixes student populations and makes linguistic diversity a topic of inquiry). Future research might compare the peer dynamics within these very different options in order to build stronger writing communities.

Secondly, these findings call for inquiry into practices, such as the No Discount Policy, that help culturally and linguistically diverse classrooms address conflict and challenge negative labels. For Jared, the No Discount Policy and ceremony gave him the confidence he needed to change his writerly identity. However, he still stereotyped minority students in his high school, suggesting a need for greater critical awareness. Additionally, Ariel's dismissal of the No Discount Policy highlights the importance of helping students maintain agency while addressing ongoing conflicts. Taking these limitations into account, action research projects, such as those described in Gutiérrez's (2005) four-week summer program for migrants, can identify ways to blend community-building rituals, like the No Discount Policy, with reading, writing, and discussion activities to raise critical awareness. By using practices from nontraditional academic communities to challenge negative labels and transform social interactions, such research can help first-year writing teachers and administrators design inclusive communities that support LMs' transitions to college.

Bibliography

Brandt, D. (2001). *Literacy in American lives*. Cambridge, UK: Cambridge University Press.

Calahan, M. W., & Curtain, T. R. (2004). *A profile of the upward bound program: 2000–2001*. Washington, DC: U.S. Department of Education Office of Postsecondary Education Federal Trio Programs. Retrieved from www2.ed.gov/programs/trioupbound/ubprofile-00–01.pdf

Cazden, C. B. (2002). A descriptive study of six high school Puente classrooms. *Educational Policy, 16*(4), 496–521.

Conference on College Composition and Communication (CCCC). (2009). *Statement on second-language writing and writers*. Retrieved from www.ncte.org/cccc/resources/positions/secondlanguagewriting

Costino, K., & Hyon, S. (2007). "A class for students like me": Reconsidering relationships among identity labels, residency status, and students' preferences for mainstream or multilingual composition. *Journal of Second Language Writing, 16*(2), 63–81.

Davidson, A. L. (1996). *The making and molding of identity in schools: Student narratives on race, gender, and academic engagement*. Albany, NY: SUNY Press.

Engle, J. (2007). Post-secondary access and success for first-generation students. *American Academic, 3*, 25–48.

Enright, K. A., & Gilliland, B. (2011). Multilingual writing in an age of accountability: From policy to practice in U.S. high school classrooms. *Journal of Second Language Writing, 20*, 182–195.

Fu, D. (1995). *My trouble is my English: Asian students and the American dream*. Portsmouth, NH: Heinemann.

Gándara, P. (2002). A study of high school Puente: What we have learned about preparing Latino youth for postsecondary education. *Educational Policy, 16*(2), 474–495.

Gutiérrez, K. (2005, April). Intersubjectivity and grammar in the third space. *Scribner Award Talk presented at the Annual Meeting of the American Educational Research Association*. Montreal, Canada.

Haneda, M. (2006). Classrooms as communities of practice: A reevaluation. *TESOL Quarterly, 40*, 807–817.

Harklau, L. (1994). Tracking and linguistic minority students: Consequences of ability grouping for second language learners. *Linguistics and Education, 6*, 221–248.

Harklau, L., Losey, K. M., & Siegal, M. (Eds.) (1999). *Generation 1.5 meets college composition*. Mahwah, NJ: Lawrence Erlbaum Associates.

Kanno, Y., & Harklau, L. (Eds.) (2012). *Linguistic minority students go to college: Preparation, access, and persistence*. New York: Routledge.

Lave, J., & Wegner, E. (1991). *Situated learning: Legitimate peripheral participation*. Cambridge, England: Cambridge University Press.

Morita, N. (2004). Negotiating participation and identity in second language academic communities. *TESOL Quarterly, 38*, 573–603.

Norton, B. (2001). Non-participation, imagined communities and the language classroom. *Learner contributions to language learning: New directions in research, 6*(2), 159–171.

Oakes, J. (2005). *Keeping track: How schools structure inequality* (2nd ed.). New Haven, CT: Yale University Press.

Ortmeier-Hooper, C. (2008). English may be my second language, but I'm not ESL. *College Composition and Communication, 59*(3), 389–418.

Ortmeier-Hooper, C. (2010). The shifting nature of identity: Social identity, L2 writers, and high school. In M. Cox, J. Jordan, C. Ortmeier-Hooper, & G. G. Schwartz (Eds.), *Reinventing identities in second language writing* (pp. 5–25). Urbana, IL: NCTE.

Ortmeier-Hooper, C., & Enright, K. A. (2011). Mapping new territory: Toward an understanding of adolescent L2 writers and writing in US contexts. *Journal of Second Language Writing, 20*, 167–181.

Pradl, G. M. (2002). Linking instructional intervention and professional development: Using the ideas behind the Puente high school English to inform educational policy. *Educational Policy, 16*(4), 522–546.

Ruecker, T. (2011). Improving the placement of L2 writers. *Writing Program Administration, 31*(1), 91–118.

Swail, W. S. (2000). Preparing America's disadvantaged for college: Programs that increase college opportunity. *New Directions for Institutional Research, 2000*, 85–101.

Toohey, K. (1996). Learning English as a second language in kindergarten: A community of practice perspective. *Canadian Modern Language Review, 52*, 549–576.

Wegner, E. (1998). *Communities of practice: Learning, meaning, and identity*. Cambridge, England: Cambridge University Press.

Yi, Y. (2010). Identity matters: Theories that help explore adolescent multilingual writers and their identities. In M. Cox, J. Jordan, C. Ortmeier-Hooper, & G. G. Schwartz (Eds.), *Reinventing identities in second language writing* (pp. 303–323). Urbana, IL: NCTE.

9

DIGITAL DREAMS

The Rhetorical Power of Online Resources for DREAM Act Activists

Genevieve García de Müeller

Undocumented migrant students, called Dreamers based on the DREAM Act, often have institutional roadblocks in their transition from high school to college due to their immigration status. In August 2012, the Migration Policy Institute (MPI) reported that, "according to MPI's analysis of Current Population Survey (CPS) data from the U.S. Census Bureau and U.S. Bureau of Labor Statistics, as many as 1.76 million unauthorized immigrants under age 31 who were brought to the United States as children are, or could become, potential beneficiaries of the deferred action initiative." Deferred Action for Childhood Arrivals (DACA) is an executive order proposed and signed by President Barack Obama in 2012 that allowed for "prosecutorial discretion." With increased migration, "the logic of Obama's policy of 'prosecutorial discretion' is to allow immigration enforcement officials to focus their resources on those who have committed crimes, rather than deporting young people who actively participate in society and were brought as children to the USA by their parents" (Schmid, 2013, p. 697). DACA offers temporary protection from deportation and allows the individual to work and or attend college. If passed federally, the Development Relief and Education of Alien Minors Act (DREAM Act), another important piece of legislation, would offer undocumented persons a pathway to citizenship via either a college degree or military service.

Dreamers have created writing strategies and developed activist genres to traverse tenuous legislation and aid undocumented students in navigating the transition from high school into college. Specifically through their online presence, Dreamers have formed alternative digital literacy initiatives by using their genres to support a sustainable activist network. Dreamers disseminate knowledge and teach pragmatic discursive and rhetorical strategies to negotiate texts. Dreamer discourse and genres foster initiatives for acting as responsible agents of change, and through these genres undocumented students may transfer their

already flourishing rhetorical and discursive skills to college writing. This migrant rhetorical and writing agency has become the new norm and is generating novel linguistic ecologies in academia and particularly in the writing classroom. When using "an ecological approach to language in society [it] requires an exploration of the relationship of languages to each other and to the society in which these languages exist" (Creese & Martin, 2003, p. 1). An ecological approach addresses the sociopolitical environment in which the language is generated. Through genres and writing strategies appropriated from dominant discourses in a transnational, transcultural, and translinguistic space, Dreamers respond to how the DREAM Act text and public discourse in immigration in the United States situates immigrants rhetorically, changing the public immigration debate and the university.

According to the Lumina Foundation report, *Camino a La Universidad*, in the United States, out of 100 Latino students, 48 drop out of high school and 52 graduate high school, but out of that only 31 go to college, and only 10 of those students graduate college. Furthermore, citizenship status "increases the number of reported institutional obstacles to gaining a higher education. For example, students born in Mexico reported more institutional obstacles than those born in the United States. Students who wrote in English reported more institutional resources than those writing in Spanish" (ASHE, 2013, p. 3). Latino students, both U.S. citizens and undocumented, confirmed that "framing educational pursuits as ways students can fight discrimination, enhance ethnic pride and assist their communities when they return with college degrees can make college more attractive" (*Camino*, 2007, p. 3).

As part of this framing of educational pursuits, this chapter argues that students already have the rhetorical and discursive strategies to combat discrimination and that they are already using these strategies in their communities. Through writing teachers in secondary and college contexts giving students the means to transfer these skills to the university setting and refine these skills in the writing classroom, writing instruction may aid undocumented students in navigating U.S. immigration policy and ultimately transitioning into higher education.

Historical Background on the DREAM Act and Undocumented Immigrants in U.S. Contexts

The need for immigration reform in the United States is quickly becoming necessary. It is estimated that "approximately 65,000 undocumented students graduate from high school each year" (Schmid, 2013, p. 697). Migrant students often cross over as infants or very young children and "because of barriers to their continued education past high school, including poverty (almost 40% of undocumented families live in poverty) they are excluded from legal employment and often discouraged from attending college (Immigration Policy Center, 2011)" (Schmid, 2013, p. 697). The DREAM Act was initially proposed to help undocumented students bear the burden of college tuition while also providing a pathway to citizenship for persons who were raised in the United States and by all cultural and social respects are U.S. citizens.

Two weeks before September 11, on August 21, 2001, the Student Adjustment Act, now called the Development Relief and Education of Alien Minors (DREAM) Act, was presented in the U.S. House of Representatives by Rep. Howard Berman (D-CA) and Rep. Chris Cannon (R-UT). From 2001–2010 the DREAM Act went through several revisions and redrafts. In September of 2010, the DREAM Act, along with the repeal of Don't Ask Don't Tell (DADT), was included in the National Defense Authorization Act for Fiscal Year 2011. Senate Republicans effectively filibustered the passage of the bill. In December 2010, the House passed the bill, but again it did not advance to the Senate. In May 2011, Sen. Harry Reid reintroduced the DREAM Act in its current incarnation. The DREAM Act has faced several legislative barriers to its passage. In response to these problems, President Obama issued DACA in 2012.

According to Schmid (2013), to qualify for DACA, an undocumented person must meet the following requirements:

- came to the USA under the age of 16;
- has continuously resided in the USA for at least five years prior to June 15, 2012;
- has graduated from high school, has obtained a general education development (GED) certificate, or is an honorably discharged veteran of the Coast Guard or Armed Forces of the USA;
- has not been convicted of a felony offense, a significant misdemeanor offense, or multiple misdemeanor offenses, or does not otherwise pose a threat to national security or public safety; and
- is not above the age of thirty.

Since "attempts to expand rights, even for individuals who were brought young to the USA and have attended American schools have been blocked at the federal level," DACA provides a pragmatic way for persons who are by all respects acting as citizens in the United States to participate in society. However, the problem remains that even though "DACA offers short-term amnesty and temporary relief from deportation . . . undocumented individuals have no clear path to resident alien status (possession of a green card) or citizenship" (Schmid, 2013, p. 701).

Besides legal issues, for many undocumented students difficulties arise rhetorically, discursively, and educationally. Because "there is no universal right to pay in-state tuition at institutions of public colleges and universities or even attend higher education for undocumented students," they are situated as not worthy of education and are always in contentious scenarios when trying to enter academia (Schmid, 2013, p. 697). To combat this concern, some states have policies that allow undocumented students to pay in-state tuition. In two of these states,

> Texas and New Mexico, undocumented students are also eligible for state financial assistance. Studies show that offering in-state tuition makes a

considerable difference: in states with such provisions, one and a half times more non-citizen Latinos enroll in college than do similar students in states without such provisions.

(Glenn, 2010, p. 11)

Despite these pragmatic shifts in policy, undocumented students living as civically engaged community members and participating productively in society are not granted the same rights and access as U.S. citizens. This occurs on the federal, state, and institutional level.

Study and Methods

Dreamers use writing strategies to combat an immigration system intent on marginalizing undocumented students. They respond to problematic textual and systemic effects of the features of the DREAM Act by producing counter texts and controlling the metadiscourse surrounding those texts. Dreamers:

- Assemble on the Internet
- Combat a criminalized identity with personal narratives of "good moral character"
- Lobby for legislation, make new conditions, create new provisions, and make compromises that still adhere to a central goal

Through these strategies they create ways to help undocumented students transfer into the university in three ways:

- Assemble support → Discursive Transfer
- Combat criminal narratives → Rhetorical Transfer
- Create pragmatic ways to navigate the university → Educational Transfer

With Dreamers' websites and online resources as my primary texts, I conduct a critical discourse analysis, informed by social language theory, focusing on how Dreamers respond to the rhetoric surrounding the immigration debate. Specifically, I use a framework employed by Eleanor Lamb (2013) in her analysis of UK immigration policy from 1968–2009. She asks "how far [UK] immigrant organisations were able to challenge marginalising representations of migrants and refugees" (p. 339). First, Lamb lays out a three-tier system of analysis:

- Investigate the sociopolitical context of each time period
- Map the different kinds of organizations and the genres that one case-study organization was able to access in each time period
- Text-level analysis

Although Lamb sees the importance of the social and historical context of immigration legislation, attitudes on race and ethnicity in particular, her analysis focuses on tiers "(2) and (3) as containing novel ways to approach analysis: the maps of different genres and the categories of analysis developed from the research questions" (p. 339). What is lacking in this analysis is how immigrant activists and organizations combatted the ways the UK legislation constructed racial and ethnic identities. Using Lamb's second and third tiers of critical discourse analysis, I reveal the active agents in the Dreamer movement and analyze the discursive practices of the Dreamers, indexing how they navigate through a system bent on marginalizing them. An analysis of immigration activists must include the social forces they are navigating, since

> viewing language use as social practice implies, first, that it is a mode of action and, second, that it is always a socially and historically situated mode of action, in a dialectical relationship with other facets of "the social" (its "social context")—it is socially shaped, but it is also socially shaping, or constitutive.
>
> *(Fairclough, 1993, p. 134)*

As such, I map out the genres Dreamers use and illustrate how Dreamer discourse shapes and is shaped by the rhetoric surrounding the debate on U.S. immigration policy and specifically the Dream Act and DACA while focusing on how this activism facilitates transfer for migrant students.

All resources were created by Dreamers and center on migrant students. The resources focus on helping students find financial support, activism, and undocumented student academic success. Selection of resources was based on if the methods used on the website aligned with the goals of migrants as outlined above, if they responded to the Dream Act and DACA, and if they were used frequently by Dreamers. I chose three websites created to support Dreamers—the National Council of La Raza (NCLR) Blog, Immigration Equality, and the Immigrant Youth Justice League. The National Council of La Raza Blog was created as a way to highlight the ongoing narratives of immigrants navigating U.S. immigration policy. It mainly focuses on students trying to apply for DACA or already in the DACA program. Immigration Equality is an activist website centered on strategizing ways to effect legislation. Its focus is providing resources for an activist network of youth-led organizing and protesting anti-immigration lobbyists. Finally, the Immigrant Youth Justice League provides a list of scholarships for undocumented students categorized by national, state, and city funding initiatives. This website is focused on providing financial resources to students and helping migrant students to navigate the university financial realm.

The second and third tiers of Lamb's framework function as ways to map these organizations and parse out the various genres used in support of their

goal. Using a rhetorical studies lens that sees "as a common intuitive concept—a sense that features of language aggregate in recognizable patterns, and that these aggregations indicate something important in the uses of language in context," I have outlined three genres commonly used by DREAM Act activist websites: narratives, calls, and guides (Stein & Giltrow, 2009, p. 1) and aligned them with Halliday's (2006) three functions of language—the ideational, the interpersonal, and the textual (pp. 57–59). In the ideational, "the speaker or writer embodies in language his experience of the phenomena of the real world; and this includes his experience of the internal world of his consciousness: his reactions, cognitions, and perceptions, and also his linguistic acts of speaking and understanding" (Halliday, 2006, p. 58). In the interpersonal, the speaker or writer is "using language as the means into his own intrusion into the speech event" (Halliday, 2006, p. 58). And finally, in the textual, "language makes links with itself and with the situation and discourse becomes possible because the speaker or writer can produce a text and the listener or reader can recognize one" (Halliday, 2006, p. 59). The explicit goals of the discursive strategies of the Dreamers are twofold: first, to reveal the experiences of undocumented students (ideational), and second, to insert those experiences into a speech act, namely the discourse surrounding U.S. immigration (interpersonal). Through textual strategies grounded in specific digital genres, Dreamers shift into the public realm by synthesizing and interpreting legislative documents and combatting racist ideologies, and disseminating knowledge to a community of linguistically and socially diverse undocumented students.

Analysis of Dreamers' Digital Resources and Genres

Migrant activists use the genres of narratives, calls, and guides to respond to the problem areas of the DREAM Act text. I define *narratives* as personal stories that reveal the experiences of Dreamers. *Calls* are genres that ask or command an audience to take an action. *Guides* are documents that explain a procedure and help with a process the undocumented students must take. Below I discuss how the Dreamers use a genre, the purpose or strategy behind the genre, the grammatical function of the genre, and finally the type of transfer this fosters in undocumented students, namely the way the student can use the genre to transfer from the private into the public.

Migrant Narratives

Narratives are used as a way to express the personal (internal logic and external action) aspects of the Dreamer's life. They are used to counter criminalizing narratives in U.S. immigration policy, to assemble support from the community, and to aid in the rhetorical transfer of undocumented students.

The series "Hanging in the Balance" on the NCLR Blog details narratives of undocumented persons dealing with DACA. In the post titled "The Tale of Two Latinas," the stories of Carla Mena and Karla Salgado are reported.

> Despite their tenuous status in their adopted country, the young women's commitment to their community remains strong. In recent months, Karla was appointed by Raleigh's mayor as the youngest member of the Downtown Plan Advisory Committee. Carla is also giving back to her community and was recently selected to serve on the Board of Trustees of the Wake Health Services. Both girls also volunteer on the Youth Council at El Pueblo, Inc., an NCLR Affiliate . . . the two women have made a positive impact in their communities.
>
> *(NCLR Blog)*

The narrative shows a sense of civic responsibility, an important aspect of citizenship. As Schmid outlined, the third aspect of citizenship includes the social "identity or behavior aspects of individuals and conceiving as members of collectivity, classically the nation." The DREAM Act text functions as a way to exclude the undocumented migrant and conceptualizing the migrant as "alien" and "criminal" and without "good moral character." The Dreamer narrative works against that rhetoric and composes the migrant as a social citizen, along Schmid's definition, and a person who adds to the collective nation.

The narrative is both ideational and interpersonal, invoking the personal, private experiences of the Dreamers (tenuous status, adopted country, positive impact, commitment to community) while entering the very problematic and ongoing discussion in the public realm (U.S. Congress has failed, urge President Obama to provide relief). These narratives aid in the discursive and rhetorical transfer of students into the university. They give a way to use private rhetoric and discursive strategies to shift the public rhetoric on immigration issues. By focusing and shifting the discussion to include "our community" and a failed U.S. immigration structure, it makes the private public and the transfer to the academy evident and a natural progression.

Migrant Calls

The genre of calls is used to solicit support from the community and to aid in undocumented student activism. Calls can be a way to ask for donations or resource support from the community or can be a command for undocumented students to actively participate in helping the DREAM Act to pass. The call to the community to ask for congressional support is a way to give discursive and rhetorical power to undocumented students. By focusing on "targets" as areas of support and giving strategies for activism, undocumented students gain the discursive strategies needed to enter the public discourse. The three types of calls are to

Congress/community, for funding, and for scholarships. These calls focus on the three areas of the DREAM Act that work to exclude undocumented students from entering the university. First, the call to the U.S. Congress aims to gather legislative support and have influence in how the U.S. immigration legislation is written. The calls to community help to find allies and influence how Dreamers are perceived in the public. The calls for donations work against the difficulty in the lack of federal funding for undocumented students. The calls for scholarships give agency to the undocumented student, which is taken away through the DREAM Act.

On the Immigration Equality website, they have a call to get the vote out and determine which U.S. Congress members are pro-immigration rights. This process is separated into three steps:

• Research a U.S. congressional voting record
• Determine who best to vote for
• Share the info with other voters

Immigration Equality first presents an interactive system to determine the voting record of your congressperson. Next, they have a call to voters to share the information and create a critical mass of voters. The Immigrant Youth Justice League provides a list of scholarships for undocumented students categorized by national, state, and city funding initiatives. Included in this list is a call to students to help create funding options. IYJL states,

> Remember that there are just not enough scholarships for all undocumented youth who want to go to school, which is why we are fighting for the opening of more opportunities, and for a change in the laws. Don't be afraid to challenge your school or scholarship institutions if they are not supporting undocumented students.
>
> *(IYJL)*

They then show ways to get involved in IYJL and provide resources to start activist campaigns. Immigration Equality's call to the community to seek congressional support and urge U.S. citizens to vote is a way to give discursive and rhetorical power to undocumented students. On a similar note, IYJL's call for scholarships and call to action to seek financial options while providing ways for undocumented students to engage the community empowers students with the rhetorical and discursive activist power. Through the genre of calls, these sites support agency in undocumented students. This tactic combines the interpersonal and ideational functions of language—the interpersonal calls to action using personal experiences as a source of ethos to urge voters to seek congressional help and as an ideational call by which the Dreamers are entering a speech event.

The various types of calls aim to facilitate transfer and help students to enter the public conversation on immigration. Calls function as a way to directly combat

the silencing nature of the DREAM Act. The DREAM Act erases the affected subjects, the undocumented migrants, and through the appropriation of the genre of calls, migrant activists take back their agency and directly oppose their erasure. Migrant activists use the dominant discourse to infiltrate the legislative process by directly contacting U.S. Congress members and garnering their support. Calls also work as ways to gather economic support for educational pursuits. There are both calls for donations and calls for scholarships to encourage students to find pragmatic ways to fund college.

Migrant Guides

Guides are used to aid in student transfer into the university system, to help fund undocumented student education, and to give ways of understanding processes. Migrant guides are focused on the kinds of issues undocumented students have and what sorts of issues undocumented students may face when trying to first enter college and then attain a college degree. Guides are especially problematic in that they may in a sense be tools for assimilation. At once they show explicitly the resources and tools of a white dominant structure in the university and also in many ways ask the undocumented to adhere to these structures.

The IYJL part of the guide to DACA has three sections: a history of DACA, an outline of who qualifies for DACA, and a link to the application page. Part one summarizes complicated legislative language into easily understood guidelines. Part two of the guide includes resources for Dreamers that help them to understand the application process and to successfully complete the application. This section is specifically helpful as it outlines how to navigate the application process.

The DACA guide provides undocumented students the skills to transfer into an educational setting and the rhetorical skills to gain agency in the immigration process. Another important guide created by IYJL is their Undocumented Student Guide to College that outlines how to both apply for the recently passed Illinois DREAM Act and/or DACA and then how to prepare for college. There are several steps outlined. Most of these steps give pragmatic solutions for undocumented students.

This guide to getting into college and succeeding once there provides explicit help in accessing the educational tools needed for undocumented students to successfully complete a higher education degree. The subtle shift from interpersonal functions of language like seeking help and to ideational functions of language like getting involved and researching schools supports student transfer. What these guides ignore is the institutional racism undocumented students will experience on campus as they try to work toward graduation. In some ways, the guides give students agency and the explicit steps to work toward entrance into the university and attainment of the baccalaureate. In other ways, the guides ask the students to assimilate to a primarily white dominant structure.

Conclusion

Migrant students have to combat financial issues, educational disparities, and immigration policies that act as roadblocks. As migrant undocumented students enter the university at increasing rates, instructors should begin to discuss how best to serve an ethnolinguistically diverse population, and

> as writing practitioners and scholars increasingly acknowledge the rapidly accelerating dissemination of linguistic heterogeneity across the nation and worldwide, more questions arise about the most responsible and adequate way to respond to language difference in teaching and assessment practices.
>
> *(Ayash, 2014, p. 116)*

A part of this inquiry should include acknowledging the linguistic practices students bring with them into the classroom and finding ways to embed those practices in instruction. The Dreamer websites discussed serve students by positioning them as authorities on immigration and rhetorical transfer from one discourse community to another. Studying how the discursive practices of Dreamers provide undocumented students the resources and skills necessary for transition, writing teachers in secondary and college contexts can learn to apply these practices in the writing classroom and in the programmatic structure.

What is most interesting about migrant activist genres and rhetorical moves are the ways in which Dreamers combat the often-racist ideology embedded in U.S. immigration policy and the public discourse surrounding migrant identities. The writing classroom works as a way to practice and reaffirm the writing skills Dreamers already have and provide the critical environment for Dreamers to position their writing in academic situations.

Migrants are adept at appropriating genres while avoiding assimilation. While avoiding the assimilationist tendencies of this appropriation, by using these genres and rhetorical moves as the basis for programmatic shifts, programs might make policies to best serve migrant undocumented students and to focus the writing classroom on the ideals of translingual pedagogical approaches and transnational identities. Transcultural repositioning is "a notion grounded in the idea that members of historically excluded groups are in a position to cultivate adaptive strategies that help them move across cultural boundaries by negotiating new and different contexts and communicative conventions" (Guerra, 2008, p. 299). In this view of transition, the dominant structure is not privileged but rather it's placed as a position the student may move across for specific rhetorical purposes. Since the Dreamer goal is to gain access to the university, writing programs may provide the means by which Dreamers transfer their rhetorical skills in public into an academic setting.

A critical undocumented migrant pedagogy would include a central focus on transculturalism and translingualism, a multifaceted approach to migrant student discourses focused on transference by use of migrant genres, and an acceptance

of the re-localization of linguistic skills in migrant student writing when they "mobiliz[e] linguistic resources" (Sohan, 2014, p. 203). Sohan (2014) suggests this mobilization of language skills is a way for students to choose their strongest linguistic skills and utilize them as a means of meaning making. This often manifests in what writing instructors see as error. To respond to this re-localized writing, instructors should consider employing what Sohan terms as re-localized listening, which "asks teachers to think of reading, writing, and revision differently—as a linear dynamic, interconnected processes that attend to the movement of meanings within and beyond texts and contexts" (Sohan, 2014, p. 193). Using this method would align with a critical pedagogy approach that is mindful of the experiences of migrant student writers. As Sohan (2014) has noted, working with student writers in these ways can help them:

> to understand the ways individual readers and writers re-localize their reading and writing practices emphasizes the agency of readers/writers as the producers/transformers of the language conventions they repeat in the process of listening: re-localized listening treats language not as preformed but as actively shaped and reshaped in both form and meaning every time a writer re-localizes it (employs it in contexts for which it has not been traditionally used).
>
> *(Sohan, 2014, p. 193)*

This strategy responds to migrant student texts and "enables students to become agents over their own language practices throughout (and after) their academic careers as they write across a variety of contexts and disciplines" (Sohan, 2014, p. 194). As students are re-localizing their linguistic skills and repositioning their rhetorical moves, writing instructors must re-localize their listening and reading, because this task "asks that we as teachers revise our pedagogy so that it more actively and dialogically responds to and engages with the multiple, competing, conflicting cultural influences on our students' re-localization of conventions (including form and meaning) in their writing" (Sohan, 2014, p. 194). The use of migrant activist genres, like narratives and guides, can facilitate this re-localizing of linguistic skills and support transfer into an academic context engaging with the ethnolinguistically diverse migrant population and work toward transference of skills but fully accept the fact that migrant activists are adept at appropriating the dominant discourse, using it as a way to combat racism, and manipulating it and shaping it to their needs.

The migrant activist student uses language for powerful political ends, enters the academy, and changes it. The migrant activist student sees the "self as situated within a discipline and within the world, confronting racism head on as well as other situations that distance women, the poor, and others from the dominant discourse and its racialized and gendered assumptions" (Villanueva, 1999, p. 172).

Work on migrant activist genres intersects activist work, writing practices, and Dreamer transfer into the university, while acknowledging and valuing the ways in which translingualism and transcultural citizenship generate novel ways for migrant students to reposition their linguistic skills into an academic setting shifting the linguistic landscape of the university.

Bibliography

ASHE. (2013). Latinos in higher education: Creating conditions for student success. *J-B ASHE Higher Education Report Series* (AEHE), Volume 181: ASHE 39:1. Somerset, NJ: John Wiley & Sons.

Ayash, Nancy Bou. (2014). U.S. translingualism through a cross-national and cross-linguistic lens. In B. Horner & K. Kopelson (Eds.), *Reworking English in rhetoric and composition: Global interrogations, local interventions* (pp. 116–128). Carbondale: Southern Illinois University Press.

Baillif, Michelle. (1997). Seducing composition: A challenge to identity-disclosing pedagogies. *Rhetoric Review, 16*(1), 76–91.

Black, Jane M. (1974). Cultural identity: An individual search. *College Composition and Communication, 25*(5), 422–425.

Brennan, John, & Naidoo, Rajani. (2008). Higher education and the achievement (and/or prevention) of equity and social justice. *Higher Education, 56*(3), The Future of Higher Education and the Future of Higher Education Research. 287–302.

Burgess, A., & Ivanic, R. (2010). Writing and being written: Issues of identity across time-scales. *Written Communication, 27*, 228–255.

Chavez, Karma R. (2012). Border interventions: The need to shift from a rhetoric of security to a rhetoric of militarization. In R. DeChaine (Ed.), *Border rhetorics: Citizenship and identity on the US-Mexico frontier* (pp. 48–62). Tuscaloosa: University of Alabama Press.

Creese, A., & Martin, Peter W. (2003). *Multilingual classroom ecologies: Inter-relationships, interactions, and ideologies.* Clevedon, England: Multilingual Matters.

Fairclough, Norman. (1993). Critical discourse analysis and the marketization of public discourse: The universities. *Discourse and Society, 24*(4), 133–168.

Glenn, E. N. (2010). Constructing citizenship: Exclusion, subordination, and resistance. *American Sociological Review, 76*, 1–24.

Guerra, J. C. (2008). Cultivating transcultural citizenship: A writing across communities model. *Language Arts, 85*(4), 296–305. Print.

Guerra, J. C. (2014). Enacting institutional change: The work of literacy insurgents in the academy and beyond. *JAC-AMES, 34*(1/2), 71–95. Print.

Halliday, M. A. K. (2006). Linguistic function and literary style: An inquiry into the language of William Golding's *The Inheritors*. In Jean Jacques Weber (Ed.), *Stylistics reader* (pp. 56–86). London: Arnold.

Lamb, Eleanor C. (2013). Power and resistance: New methods for analysis across genres in critical discourse analysis. *Discourse Society, 24*, 334–360.

Lumina Foundation for Education. (2007). El Camina de la Universidad. Indianapolis, IN: Ray Padilla.

Schmid, Carol L. (2013). Undocumented childhood immigrants, the dream act and deferred action for childhood arrivals in the USA. *International Journal of Sociology and Social Policy, 33*(11/12), 693–707.

Sohan, Vanessa Kraemer. (2014). Relocalized listening: Responding to all student texts from a translingual starting point. In B. Horner & K. Kopelson (Eds.), *Reworking English in rhetoric and composition: Global interrogations, local interventions* (pp. 191–206). Carbondale: Southern Illinois University Press.

Stein, Dieter, & Giltrow, J. (2009). *Genres in the Internet: Issues in the theory of genre.* Amsterdam: John Benjamins Pub. Co.

Villanueva, Victor. (1999). On the rhetoric and precedents of racism. *College Composition and Communication, 50*(4), A Usable Past: CCC at 50: Part 2. 645–661.

10

BENGALI-SPEAKING MULTILINGUAL WRITERS IN TRANSITION INTO COMMUNITY COLLEGE

Ruhma Choudhury and Leigh Garrison-Fletcher

Community colleges are a gateway to higher education for almost half of the undergraduate students in the United States (American Association of Community Colleges, 2014). They are particularly important in the education of immigrant students, who are 20% more likely to start postsecondary education at a community college than native-born students (Conway, 2009). In a recent paper, Teranishi, Suárez-Orozco, and Suárez-Orozco (2011) argue that because of the increasing number of immigrants in the United States, the weak economy, and the demand for a more educated workforce, "increasing the educational attainment, economic productivity, and civic engagement (of immigrants and their children) should be a national priority" (Teranishi, Suárez-Orozco, & Suárez-Orozco, 2011, p. 153). However, a large number of immigrant students entering community colleges are academically underprepared (Bragg, 2011). Community colleges need to determine policies and programs to aid transition to and through colleges for diverse student groups who often struggle with completing their degrees. Many students with low English proficiency are placed into basic skills courses, and research has shown that students who require basic skills courses are often unsuccessful in completing college (Bragg, 2011).

College students placed into ESL programs face especially difficult challenges, as they must rapidly gain the academic English skills needed in U.S. colleges. We are faculty in the English as a Second Language (ESL) program at LaGuardia Community College (LGCC), which is part of the City University of New York (CUNY). We have seen firsthand the struggles of our ESL students, who often have a difficult time making the transition to college-level literacy and overcoming hurdles in order to succeed in college.

In this chapter, we report on a study designed to help one group of our ESL students—Bengali speakers—in their transition to college-level academic English

by providing home language (Bengali) academic literacy instruction. We focused on the Bengali population because in the United States, New York City, and at LGCC, Bangladeshi Americans are one of the fastest-growing immigrant groups. According to data from the Census Bureau's 2006–2008 and 2009–2011 American Community Survey (ACS), as mentioned in Asian American Federation's Profile of New York City's Bangladeshi Americans (2013), there are over 270,000 Bangladeshi Americans living in the United States. In 2013, there were 440 students from Bangladesh attending LGCC, making up 2.7% of the total student body. In 2011, 11.5% of the college's ESL students were Bengali speakers.[1] However, we have very little information on the educational backgrounds of these students. This is not a monolithic group with a homogeneous educational experience. Thus, knowing our students' academic backgrounds would enable us to aid them in their transitions as multilingual writers at the community college and beyond.

Therefore, in order to aid in these students' transition, we collected background data and provided Bengali instruction alongside ESL. This idea of building on students' home language academic literacy is in line with research on second language (L2) learning that suggests that literacy knowledge in the home language (L1) can facilitate acquisition of L2 literacy (Cummins, 2005). We are in a unique position to conduct such a study because Ruhma, who implemented the intervention, is a multilingual writer herself, with expertise in both ESL and Bengali.

Importance of Home Language Literacy Skills in the Development of Second Language Literacy

Extensive research has revealed that home language literacy knowledge transfers to the target language. The research on transfer has shown that for both children and adults, among speakers of diverse languages, academic skills in the L1 transfer to the L2 (Bernhardt & Kamil, 1995; Burt & Peyton, 2003; Collins, 2014; Condelli, Wrigley, Yoon, Cronen, & Seburn, 2003; Cummins, 2009a; Lukes, 2009; Ramani & Joseph, 2010; Shiotsu & Weir, 2007; Thomas & Collier, 2003; Van Gelderen, Schoonen, Stoel, de Glopper, & Hulstijn, 2007; Yamashita, 1999). Among native Spanish-speaking college students in the United States, Carrell (1991) found that the level of L1 reading was the stronger predictor of L2 reading than L2 proficiency. In another study focusing on college-age students, Ramani and Joseph (2010) describe a bilingual BA program in English and Sesotho sa Leboa at the University of Limpopo, where "there is no doubt that the L1 is being used as a resource to understand concepts, process English academic texts, understand handouts in English, plan research . . ." (p. 53).

To quote Cummins (2005), who is a leading scholar on the transfer of skills from L1 to L2:

> Although the surface aspects (e.g., pronunciation, fluency) of different languages are clearly separate, there is an underlying cognitive/academic

proficiency that is common across languages. This common underlying proficiency makes possible the transfer of cognitive/academic or literacy-related proficiency from one language to another.

(p. 3)

In other words, academic proficiency in one language will transfer to other languages, and students do not have to relearn literacy skills and strategies. Furthermore, it is important to consider a view of learning as building upon prior knowledge. When students are able to bring their home languages to the task of learning, they are better able to link their academic concepts to the second language. However, "this linking cannot be done effectively if students' L1 is banished from the classroom" (Cummins, 2009b, p. 319). Based on the theory of L1 literacy transfer, and the idea that educators should treat students' home languages as resources, we provided students with instruction in academic literacy in both Bengali and English. We hypothesized that providing students with stronger literacy skills in their L1 and encouraging students to draw upon their home language would aid the students academically, thus providing a better bridge between ESL courses and credit-bearing courses in the college. Our primary research question was whether or not strengthening the students' L1 academic literacy skills would lead to better learning outcomes in the L2. In order to address this question, we gathered data on the demographics and the home language academic skills of the Bengali ESL students at LGCC.

Methodology

Context: Research Site (ESL Program at LGCC)

LGCC is a large, urban, culturally and linguistically diverse commuter campus. According to LGCC's 2014 Institutional Profile (Dickmeyer, 2014), the 19,770 students in academic programs come from 157 different countries, with 45% of the student population foreign born. LGCC is nicknamed "the world's college" due to the diversity of the student population. The current study was done with students in the academic ESL program at LGCC, which focuses on developing English academic reading and writing skills among non-native English speakers.

Participants

The students who participated in the study were all enrolled in the same level of ESL and were divided into three groups: (1) the experimental group, (2) the Bengali control group, and (3) the non-Bengali control group. The experimental group was comprised of eight Bengali speakers who enrolled in Ruhma's ESL class and thus received instruction in Bengali alongside English. Nine Bengali-speaking ESL students who did not receive any Bengali instruction comprised the Bengali control

group. The students in the Bengali control group were instructed by five different individuals, and the experimental group was in a class with non–Bengali speakers. We have many instructors in our program, but we all follow the same syllabus and assessments. We had one additional control group (the non-Bengali control group). This group contained 11 students enrolled in Ruhma's ESL section with the experimental group, but they did not receive any home language literacy instruction.

Data Sources

Questionnaire

We administered a background questionnaire in Bengali to the Bengali control group and the experimental group to elicit data on the students' educational history and literacy practices. Students were asked about their linguistic identities, educational backgrounds, and literacy practices. Students also self-assessed their reading and writing skills and commented on their future plans and goals. The students in the experimental group also wrote an educational background statement as part of their class.

Bengali Literacy Assessment (LENS)

To measure the Bengali literacy of the students in the Bengali control group and the experimental group, we used the Literacy Evaluation for Newcomer Students (LENS) (Klein & Martohardjono, 2014). The LENS was developed by language-acquisition and assessment experts from the Research Institute for the Study of Language in Urban Society (RISLUS) in order to measure the L1 literacy of students entering middle and high school. It covers a number of grade levels and a number of reading-related skills. It was the only Bengali literacy assessment available for our use. Because we could only meet students for one hour, we administered only the 8th and 9th grade passages of the test. The LENS covers 6th grade through 9th grade levels, and we thus chose the top two levels as our students are college-age and have graduated from high school, either in Bangladesh or the United States. The experimental group was tested on another version of the LENS (also 8th and 9th grade level) as a post-test to measure L1 literacy gains.

English Literacy Measures

We collected scores from two English literacy exams, which all students entering LGCC must take, to serve as the baseline English literacy level. One exam, the ACT Reading test, is a computerized multiple-choice reading test. The other is the CATW, which requires students to read a short passage (often an opinion-based piece), then to write an essay in which they summarize and respond to the passage. It thus measures the ability of students to read critically, to connect what

they read to something else, and to express themselves in a coherent written essay. At LGCC, these test scores are used to determine if entering students are prepared to take first-year composition. For those students who do not pass the CATW and are non-native English speakers, the ESL program reviews the tests and places students into the different levels of ESL. For the English post-tests, we looked at all participants' scores on the ESL Exit Exam. This exam involves writing an expository essay in class and is a programmatic assessment used to determine if students are ready to move to the next level of ESL or to exit the program.

Curriculum

We analyzed the Bengali LENS pre-test results to identify the gaps in the students' knowledge of academic Bengali. Students, for instance, struggled more with questions on inference, main idea, and supporting details than questions on basic comprehension. Using this information, we then developed a curriculum for the Bengali intervention with an emphasis on academic thinking skills (e.g., analysis, evaluation, critical thinking) and learning strategies. These skills are essential for students' success in ESL, as the ESL curriculum focuses on critical reading and expository writing. These skills were first introduced in the Bengali class, usually a week before they were covered in the English class. This is in line with the idea that "encouraging students to write in their L1 . . . enables them to use higher order and critical thinking skills much sooner" (Cummins, 2009b, p. 319).

Ruhma instructed the experimental group in Bengali for two hours each week, during the course's lab hours. The non-Bengali and Bengali control groups also had two lab hours a week; however, tutors instructed these students in English. During lab classes, Ruhma's non-Bengali control group worked with the tutors to revise their essays. The course's lab hours ran through a 10-week session.

The Bengali curriculum was created from scratch because Bengali instructional materials are not readily available for U.S. college students. Some of the articles that were used came from online Bengali newspapers; others we wrote ourselves. Each week, the focus was on a particular skill, such as analyzing a text to locate the main idea and supporting details, or inferring, paraphrasing, and/or summarizing key information.

During the first two weeks of lab hours, Ruhma focused on developing reading skills such as skimming, scanning, and locating the main idea and supporting evidence. The students also used context clues to interpret meanings of unfamiliar words. The first article they read described how toxic waste from garment factories contributed to water pollution in the neighboring areas of Dhaka, Bangladesh. Once they analyzed the article, the class wrote a letter to the editor, expressing their outrage and a call to action. At the time the task was assigned, the students reported that they were familiar with the format of formal letter

writing because they had written such letters in their high schools in Bangladesh. In contrast, summary writing, which was introduced next, was new to all. By week three, the students were summarizing articles and writing reader responses in Bengali; the reader response included the summary of the assigned article and the students' reaction to the piece. They read, for example, an article on gender inequality in education and wrote a response expressing their views on the issue. In their ESL class, the students wrote an essay on the same topic. The intervention group cited the article about gender gap from the Bengali newspaper in their essays to support their position.

Sometimes the class discussion in the intervention veered to topics not originally planned in the curriculum. Ruhma noticed the influence of Bengali on the students' L2 writing. One notable difference between Bengali and English is that Bengali has zero copula (where the copula or connective *be* is often missing) in the present tense, and the students' writings exhibited this omission, as the sample sentence from Salma's[2] writing[3] demonstrates: "He doesn't share his feeling with another people. Because of that he frustrated all the time and he always cries." The word order between the two languages also varies. As a head-final language, Bengali generally follows a subject-object-verb word order. The sentence, "She the cancer got" from Asif's essay is yet another example of Bengali influencing L2 where the object precedes the verb in the sentence. The lab created opportunities for Ruhma to address these differences. Commenting on these discussions, Salma revealed that she found them helpful as they made her more aware of how Bengali influenced her English.

Findings

Background Findings

Non-Bengali Control Group (N = 11)

We did not administer the background questionnaire to this group because the questionnaire was designed to elicit the literacy practices and educational backgrounds of the Bengali-speaking students. However, we have the language backgrounds of these students. They spoke five different home languages. Six students spoke Spanish, one Japanese, two Chinese, one Nepali, and one Korean.

Bengali Control Group (N = 7)[4]

At the time of the study, the average age of the students from the control group was 27. One student went to high school in the United States, and the remaining students attended high school in Bangladesh. The students came from a range of districts in Bangladesh. All students reported learning only Bengali at home as a child. All students went to school consistently from age 7. Furthermore,

the students had never lived outside of Bangladesh until they immigrated to the United States, and only one student moved within Bangladesh before arriving in the United States.

These students have multilingual literacy practices, reading and writing in Bengali and English. Only one of the seven students reported that they did not like to read in their spare time; the others enjoyed reading books and newspapers. One reported reading only in English; three reported reading in English and Bengali, and two reported reading only in Bengali. Five of the seven students reported that they liked to write in their spare time; two said that they wrote only in English, and three said they wrote in both English and Bengali.

The students all had professional goals. Two of the students were nursing majors, one student wanted to become a radiologic technologist, and one student was majoring in civil engineering. There was an accounting and a business major. Finally, one student was majoring in liberal arts.

Experimental Group (N = 8)

At the time of the study, students from the experimental group ranged in age from 19 to 26, with an average age of 22. They had been in the United States an average of three years (with a range of one and a half to five and a half years). All but two students attended high school in Bangladesh; the other two went to high school in NYC. Again, the students came from a range of districts in Bangladesh. All but one student learned only Bengali at home as a child; one reported learning Hindi alongside Bengali. All students went to school consistently from age 7. Furthermore, the students had never lived outside of Bangladesh until they immigrated to the United States, and only one student moved within Bangladesh before arriving in the United States.

Similar to the students in the Bengali control group, those in the experimental group have multilingual literacy practices. Three of the eight students reported that they did not like to read in their spare time; the others enjoyed reading books and newspapers. Two reported reading only in English, two reported reading in English and Bengali, and one reported reading only in Bengali. Half of the students reported that they liked to write in their spare time; two students said that they wrote only in English, one student claimed to write only in Bengali, and one student did not specify the language in which she wrote.

The experimental group also expressed professional goals. One student's goal was to be a radiologic technologist, and another wanted to be a dietetic technician; two students were majoring in computer science, and three in accounting. Finally, there was one liberal arts major.

We have more in-depth information on the educational backgrounds of the experimental groups from their educational background statements. All students described the transition to U.S. schools and colleges as difficult. They all identified English and the differences in the U.S. and Bangladeshi educational systems

as major impediments. Describing her prior educational experiences, Asia, one of the participants, explained why she found English formidable:

> For students like me who came from abroad, English language is quite diffi-cult. In Bangladesh, only one subject was in English while the other subjects were in Bengali [Bengali was the medium of instruction while English was taught as a subject]. English is not so prevalent in our country.

She reported that English was her weakest subject in school and, on a scale of 1–5, she rated her reading and writing both as 3 (good). Another student, Kamal, expressed similar concerns with English. He felt he was underprepared for the academic challenges of U.S. higher education. He complained that the schools he attended in Bangladesh "could not provide quality education. These schools did not have any facilities to offer sports and cultural events. As a result, the children remained unchallenged and could not reach their potential." He also reported English as his weakest subject in school. He rated his reading and writing as poor, at the bottom of the five-point scale. Alia, one of the two participants to attend an NYC high school, also described the transition from school to college as a chal-lenge because she believed she lacked the requisite skills and knowledge to be suc-cessful at college. She, however, claimed that English was her strongest subject in school and that math was her weakest. Like Asia, she rated her reading and writing in the middle of the scale, as good.

We can see from the questionnaire results that the Bengali control and experimental groups have no major background differences. In both groups, students came from a range of regions in Bangladesh. It is important to note that although the educational system in Bangladesh is centralized, the quality of education varies across the country (BANBEIS, 2010). Although most of the students completed high school in Bangladesh, one student in the Bengali con-trol group and two students in the experimental group attended high school in the United States. Thus, the students in both groups have a range of educational experiences. The students from both groups reported that they sometimes read and write in their spare time, and notably there was not a big difference in the literacy practices of the students in the Bengali control group and the experi-mental group.

Intervention Findings

Based on the questionnaire results, we can see that the Bengali control group and the experimental group have comparable backgrounds. In order to ensure that all three groups had comparable baseline academic literacy, we first compared the Bengali literacy skills of the Bengali control and experimental groups. The pre-test results indicated that the groups were not noticeably different in terms of Bengali literacy. We then compared the English literacy skills of all three groups. Again, we found that their baseline academic English proficiency was comparable (ACT

and CATW tests). Given that the students' literacy skills are similar, the success of the intervention was measured by comparing the ESL Exit Exam scores for their level. The Bengali LENS served as an additional post-test to measure improvement in Bengali reading among the experimental group.

ESL Exit Exam

Six out of eight students from the experimental group passed their ESL Exit Exam, and thus passed their course. Of the two who did not pass, one had irregular attendance (missed more than six classes in a 14-week semester), which may have contributed to her failing the writing test. Nevertheless, both of these students had shown improvement in their writing, albeit not enough to exit their level. Of the nine students in the Bengali control group, only three passed their course. This means that only three students had significant improvement in their writing and were able to pass the ESL Exit Exam. One of the nine students withdrew from the class. We see a very notable difference between the experimental group and Bengali control group in terms of pass rates.

We also compared the pass rates of the Bengali and the non-Bengali students in Ruhma's class and discovered that the pass rate was higher for the experimental group (74%) than for the regular students (64%); out of nineteen students in her class, six did not pass. Two of these six students were in the intervention and the remaining four were not. The students in Ruhma's ESL class all attended class for seven hours a week with Ruhma. The only difference between the non-Bengali and Bengali students in Ruhma's class was that each week two hours of instruction were in Bengali for the Bengali students. The non-Bengali students received the same number of instructional hours (nine hours total), but all instruction was in English and they did not receive any home language support.

The students who did receive home language support showed gains in their essay writing. At the beginning of the semester, the students expressed an anxiety about writing essays because they were unfamiliar with the English essay organization and feared their background knowledge on essay topics was limited. Not surprisingly, their essays were often written without a clear focus, as the sample introduction from Salma's essay demonstrates:

> We are human being. According to this we have different opinions. The earth is full of different people, different cultures, different religions. So that some people have the same opinions and some people have different cultures. Some times they are happy some times they are not happy.

The introduction above is poorly constructed to the point that it is difficult to pinpoint what the essay is about. After receiving intensive instruction on essay writing both in the Bengali intervention and English class and detailed critiques of her essays in both languages, Salma produced an essay that was tightly organized with a clearer focus in week six of the semester:

A recent New York Times article reported that cell phone use particularly texting has become an addiction among high school students which may result in harm to their physical and psychological health and have long–term consequences for our society. Some high schools collect students' cell phones at the beginning of the day. I think this is a good policy because students can devote their time to studies.

Ruhma saw clear improvement in all students from the experimental group. She found that the students were able to use Bengali as a resource in developing English literacy. When the same skills were addressed in both Bengali and English, the students made significant gains in academic reading and writing.

Bengali LENS Post-Test Results

The students in the experimental group not only improved in English but also in their Bengali. The post-test average score for the experimental group was 88%. See Figure 10.1 for the results comparing the pre-test and post-test scores of the Bengali LENS for the experimental group.

Seven of the students show gains in their Bengali literacy, with many improving substantially. One student (S6 in Figure 10.1) did not show improvement from

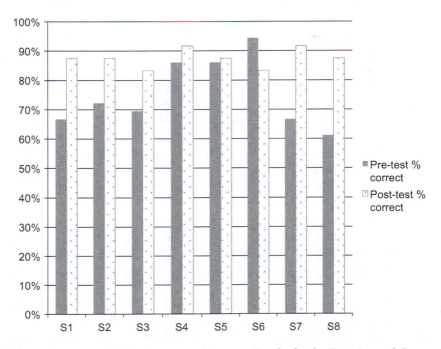

FIGURE 10.1 Bengali LENS Pre-test and Post-test Results for the Experimental Group

the pre- to post-test. This student missed the majority of the Bengali classes, so we would not expect to see growth. This same student did not pass the ESL Exit Exam. We see that the intervention led to significant improvements in Bengali reading.

Discussion of the Findings

Before the study, there was no data available specifically on the Bengali-speaking ESL population at LGCC. The study gave us a better understanding of the academic literacy skills and educational backgrounds of our Bengali-speaking students. Many of the students have relatively low Bengali literacy skills, and most finished high school in Bangladesh before arriving in the United States. This information shows us that although students are coming from high school in Bangladesh, they may not be ready to transition into college-level work in the United States. Due to their lower academic literacy skills in Bengali, many students struggle with both language and concepts in their English classes. Despite the small number of participating students, the semester-long intervention study reveals the usefulness of providing Bengali-speaking students with instruction in their home language. The comparison of the averages of pre- and post-tests for Bengali LENS shows a 13% gain.

Students who received L1 academic literacy instruction not only made significant gains in their L1 academic literacy but also excelled in English literacy. The experimental group had higher pass rates than both control groups. The difference in pass rates between the Bengali control group and the experimental group was quite surprising. The pass rate for the experimental group was 75% (6/8) and the pass rate for the control group was 33% (3/9). Finally, when we compared the Bengali students in Ruhma's class with the non-Bengali students, we also saw a difference in performance, with the Bengali-speakers outperforming their classmates who did not receive L1 instruction. Thus, our findings are aligned with the research of Cummins (2005), Lukes (2009), Shiotsu and Weir (2007), Thomas and Collier (2003), Van Gelderen, Schoonen, Stoel, de Glopper, and Hulstijn (2007), and others who discovered that L1 literacy practices do transfer to L2.

We have good evidence that our intervention helped the students who participated. They left with stronger Bengali and English literacy, and most of them went on to the next level of ESL. These results suggest that when students are encouraged to build on their home languages in the ESL classroom, they are acquiring academic literacy skills that will help them transition out of the ESL courses and into credit-bearing courses at the college. When asked how beneficial the intervention was to both their acquisition of academic Bengali and English, the participants expressed satisfaction. They shared with Ruhma that learning about new skills and information first in Bengali helped them acquire the skills faster and more thoroughly.

Although the intervention helped the students pass out of their ESL level, these students still have many transitions to make in the process of completing their educational goals, many of which require bachelor's degrees or higher. This is just a first step to help these multilingual students in their initial transition into academic English in the United States. We are hoping that some of the skills they learned in the intervention will be strengthened as they progress through college. Furthermore, these students now have higher literacy skills in both Bengali and English and view both languages as academic resources. We believe a view of their backgrounds through a deficit model will create disruptions for these students. We hope that validating their multilingual literacy practices will counter any negative perceptions of their limited English. When students feel they have valuable knowledge and backgrounds upon which they can build new information, they are less likely to succumb to disruptions based on perceptions of linguistic deficiency. For example, when students view their home language as part of their academic repertoire, even when peers or instructors view them as "less than," the students will be unaffected. On the other hand, students who do not view their home language as a resource will likely lose motivation when they are viewed as "less than." This would likely lead to more disruptions in education for these multilingual students in the United States.

As ESL instructors in a program with students who speak over 100 languages, we know that we cannot provide the same L1 instruction and support for all of our students as we did in this intervention. However, we believe the results from our study can still be of use in aiding students in their transition to and through our ESL program. Because we found that students who worked on their L1 literacy skills alongside ESL outperformed other students, we have started creating and implementing lessons that promote the use of students' languages in the classroom.

Although we do have preliminary evidence that home language instruction benefits ESL students, this study is only a small pilot. Our results appear to support the idea that building academic skills in the L1 benefits students as they are learning academic skills in the L2 (e.g., Cummins, 2009a; Lukes, 2009; Shiotsu & Weir, 2007). It could also be the case that forming a close community with other students, and having extra support from a faculty member who speaks their home language, could explain why the students in the intervention were so successful. Either way, bringing students' L1s into the classroom is beneficial to their development of academic literacy, which will aid in their transitions into and through college. This initial study provides foundational evidence for future research into programs that can support the academic needs of emergent bilinguals at the community college level.

Notes

1. This information was provided by LaGuardia Community College's Office of Institutional Research.
2. Pseudonyms are used.

3. All examples of student writing appear in their original form and have not been edited.
4. Only seven of the nine students in the Bengali control group completed the questionnaire.

Bibliography

American Association of Community Colleges. (2014). *Students at community colleges*. Community College Trends and Statistics. Retrieved from www.aacc.nche.edu/AboutCC/Trends/Pages/studentsatcommunitycolleges.aspx on November 15, 2014.

Asian American Federation. (2013). *Profile of New York City's Bangladeshi Americans: 2013 Edition*. Retrieved on May 20, 2015, from www.aafny.org/cic/briefs/bangladeshi2013.pdf

BANBEIS (Bangladesh Bureau of Educational Information and Statistics). (2010). Retrieved on November 15, 2014, from www.banbeis.gov.bd

Bernhardt, E. B., & Kamil, M. L. (1995). Interpreting relationships between L1 and L2 reading: Consolidating the linguistic threshold and the linguistic interdependence hypotheses. *Applied Linguistics, 16*, 15–34.

Bragg, D. D. (2011). Examining pathways to and through the community college for youth and adults. In J. C. Smart & M. B. Paulson (Eds.), *Higher education: Handbook of theory and research, volume 26* (pp. 355–393). New York: Springer.

Burt, M., & Peyton, J. (2003). *Reading and adult English language learners: The role of the first language*. Washington, DC: National Center for ESL Literacy Education.

Carrell, P. L. (1991). Second language reading: Reading ability or language proficiency? *Applied Linguistics, 12*, 159–179.

Collins, B. A. (2014). Dual language development of Latino children: Effect of instructional program type and the home and school language environment. *Early Childhood Research Quarterly, 29*, 389–397.

Condelli, L., Wrigley, H., Yoon, K., Cronen, S., & Seburn, M. (2003). *What works study for adult ESL literacy students*. Washington, DC: U.S. Department of Education.

Conway, K. M. (2009). Exploring persistence of immigrant and native students in an Urban Community College. *The Review of Higher Education, 32*, 321–352.

Cummins, J. (2005). Teaching for Cross-language Transfer in Dual Language Education: Possibilities and Pitfalls. *TESOL Symposium on Dual Language Education: Teaching and Learning in Two Languages in the EFL Setting*. Istanbul, Turkey: Bogazici University.

Cummins, J. (2009a). Literacy and English language learners: A shifting landscape for students, teachers, researchers and policy-makers. *Educational Researcher, 38,* 382–383.

Cummins, J. (2009b). Multilingualism in the English-language classroom: Pedagogical considerations. *TESOL Quarterly, 43*, 317–321.

Dickmeyer, N. (2014). *LaGuardia community college institutional profile*. Long Island City, NY: LaGuardia Community College, CUNY.

Klein, E., & Martohardjono, G. (2014). *Literacy Evaluation for Newcomer Students (LENS) [Assessment instrument]*. New York, NY: New York City Department of Education, Office of English Language Learners.

Lukes, M. (2009). We thought they had forgotten us: Research, policy and practice in the education of Latino immigrant adults. *Journal of Latinos and Education, 8*, 161–172.

Ramani, E., & Joseph, M. (2010). Promoting academic competence in two languages: A case study of a Bilingual BA degree (In English and Sesotho Sa Leboa) at the university of Limpopo. *EFL Journal, 1*, 33–59.

Shiotsu, T., & Weir, C. J. (2007). The relative significance of syntactic knowledge and vocabulary breadth in the prediction of reading comprehension test performance. *Language Testing, 24*, 99–128.

Teranishi, R. T., Suárez-Orozco, C., & Suárez-Orozco, M. (2011). Immigrants in community college: Toward greater knowledge and awareness. *The Future of Children, 21*(1), 153–169.

Thomas, W., & Collier, V. (2003). *A national study of school effectiveness for language minority students' long-term academic achievement.* Santa Cruz, CA: Center for Research on Education, Diversity & Excellence, University of California.

Van Gelderen, A., Schoonen, R., Stoel, R., de Glopper, K., & Hulstijn, J. (2007). Development of adolescent reading comprehension in language 1 and language 2: A longitudinal analysis of constituent components. *Journal of Educational Psychology, 99*, 477–491.

Yamashita, J. (1999). *Reading in a first and a foreign language: A study of reading comprehension in Japanese (the L1) and English (the L2).* Doctoral thesis, Lancaster University.

11

IMMIGRANT MOSAICS

Advancing Multilingual Education in Canadian Postsecondary Settings

Julia Kiernan

Introduction

Canada is a country founded with the basic understanding that all citizens are immigrants; correspondingly, multiculturalism and multilingualism are encouraged and promoted. However, there has not been an impetus for educators and policymakers in postsecondary settings to create programs that cultivate and maintain linguistic and cultural development for diverse learners. While Canadian federal and provincial language policy recognizes the importance of immigrant linguistic identities, there is no precedent to ensure that multilingual students work with and draw upon their diverse language resources as they move from K–12 to university education. This lack of attention to immigrant languages within educational settings, which are under federal and provincial jurisdiction, is particularly troubling given that 20% of Canadians identify with a mother tongue other than the official English (58% of population) and French (22% of population) (Statistics Canada, 2013).

This chapter will consider these sociopolitical ideologies in an examination of the language practices and policies that impact resident multilingual youths as they move from high school to Canadian postsecondary contexts. It considers the irony that these policies and practices seem to be out of sync with the practices and expectations around multilingual youths who enroll in writing courses in Canadian colleges and universities. By extending the current U.S. discussion concerning language practices among resident multilinguals into the domain of Canadian postsecondary education and national policy position, this chapter seeks to illustrate the specific circumstances of the linguistic landscape of Canada; the country's official language policies provide a useful site to consider the relationships between pluralist language policy and multilingual writing education.

Much of the research on multilingualism and education in Canada focuses on primary and secondary education, or Québécois francophone culture versus national French-English bilingualism. Minority language scholarship pertaining to resident multilinguals—such as the work of Wilson (2016, this volume)—is based almost exclusively within K–12 research (Bumsted, 2008; Cormier, Bourque, & Jolicoeur, 2014; Gentil, 2005; Hayday, 2005; Heller, 2007; Li, 2003; Lotherington, Holland, Sotoudeh, & Zentena, 2008; Mady & Carr, 2011; Potts & Moran, 2013). Research on the relationships between resident multilingual populations and postsecondary education has been limited, which is often due to the inclusion of minority language education in K–12 programs and not in postsecondary settings. In this chapter, "English only" or "French only" expectations in college writing classes ignore the reality that resident Canadian multilinguals are growing exponentially in relation to monolingual French- and English-speaking populations. The continued increase of resident multilinguals in classrooms across North America runs somewhat parallel to many teachers' anxiety of how to best engage these diverse learners. As a Canadian who has attended postsecondary institutions in both the United States and Canada, and who is now working in a U.S. university, the linguistic landscape of my home country cannot help but inform my teaching practices. This background has positioned me to consider how the similarities and differences between U.S. and Canadian writing classrooms can be explored in order to offer strategies that engage multilingual learners—regardless of their institutional location. That said, because multilingualism in Canada has been cultivated in such a unique way, this chapter builds out of the Canadian context, and considers how the cultivation of multilingualism within government policy can serve as a potential asset to students' knowledge-building and the development of critical thinking processes.

Writing Studies in Canada: A Writing-in-the-Disciplines Approach

In the United States, the response of composition research to immigrant growth in student populations, particularly studies concerned with language and globalization, has flourished. There has not been the same concern with writing and multilingualism in Canada—despite Canada's various national policies that promote and encourage multiculturalism and multilingualism. A primary reason for this is the nature of writing studies in Canada. If composition courses are offered within Canadian postsecondary institutions, they are generally electives. In undergraduate programs across the country, such as Memorial University of Newfoundland, students are most often required to complete two writing-intensive humanities courses; these courses span the disciplines and are found in departments ranging from history to philosophy to folklore. Moreover, what makes these courses "writing intensive" could simply be the completion of a research essay; students are often expected to produce university-level texts without writing-based instruction. In

such courses, the primary goal is to teach the discipline-specific subject matter, not writing. The primary difference between the two nations is that unlike in the United States, the majority of Canadian institutions do not recognize first-year writing or a universally required composition course as being useful to undergraduate students. Instead, writing instruction is offered through a writing-in-the-disciplines (WID) approach where students are taught to write in terms of their academic field. Ideologies that do not recognize the instruction of writing—via a course comparable to U.S. composition—as integral to postsecondary education continue to be maintained in many Canadian institutions of higher learning. Of the two models of writing instruction that have emerged, the first is a WID approach and positions the teaching of academic writing to prepare students to think critically in their field; the second is the more common, U.S. first-year-writing approach where students explore the fundamentals of effective writing via inquiry into process, organization, style, audience, and purpose.

Methodology

While descriptive in nature, this research is seated in theoretical analysis. A review of government legislation from both Canada and the United States will be used to compare and contrast the roles that languages play in social policy and public use, particularly in K–12 schools, the workplace, and college contexts. This gathering of data concerning student language demographics will ensure a more comprehensive understanding of the needs of Canadian resident multilinguals who enroll in postsecondary education. A qualitative, inductive approach is used to build upon current research concerning resident multilingual students, and in turn offers an analysis of Canadian policies on multilingualism. In describing multilingual students in terms of language politics, this research draws upon the work of a variety of scholars globally (Bhabha, 1996; Blommaert, Muyllaert, Huysmans, & Dyers, 2006; Canagarajah, 1994; Horner & Trimbur, 2002; Leung, Harris, & Rampton, 1997; Rassool, 2004; etc.), who have argued that if we are to fully understand and teach the complex linguistic practices of students, it is important to better understand who these students are.

The primary qualitative data collected comes from Census Canada and the language of federal policy; secondary qualitative data comes from the publications of Canadian language scholars, with particular attention to historical legislative documents. The theoretical analysis of these documents offers insight into the various ways student multilingualism exists within Canadian society. The focus on resident multilingual students seeks to enable a stronger understanding of this population in terms of one central issue: the analysis of the function of the Canadian Multiculturalism Act within education systems.

The focus of my analysis is to mark disparities between social practices and expectations, postsecondary education, and minority and multicultural language policy that positions a reimaging of contexts of writing instruction that better

align with the guidelines and expectations of government policy, particularly in terms of the globalized Canadian mosaic. In this sense, research into the writing practices of resident multilingual students pushes toward inquiry that is not only comparative, but seated in social action and recommendation for change (Lewin, 1946; McLaren, 2007).

Language Policy

In Canada, the designation *allophone Canadian*, which complements the anglophone-francophone labeling system, is used more widely than resident multilingual. An allophone speaker is a Canadian citizen whose first language is not English, French, or First Nations, but an immigrant or heritage language. Allophones are immigrants with plural language abilities, and may be bilingual, trilingual, or polyglot. Canadian multicultural policies differ from U.S. English-only agendas in that allophones are encouraged via official and legal channels to pursue cultural free choice (Li, 2003, p. 134), one of these choices being whether or not to maintain a heritage language in addition to one (or both) of Canada's official languages. Such multicultural initiatives shape Canadian identity in terms of diversity, and as such the image of Canada as a cultural mosaic is generally used when describing national identity. This concept holds that no other country in the world encompasses inhabitants from so many different backgrounds who exhibit strong loyalty toward Canada while still preserving their immigrant heritage. And, because Canada is geographically next to the United States, the mosaic is most often contrasted to the U.S. metaphor of a "melting pot," which is described as attempting to shape all citizens into a set mold—U.S. English-only legislation is one area of education that upholds this melting pot paradigm (Horner & Trimbur, 2002).

Central in Canada's promotion of itself as a cultural mosaic is the Canadian Multiculturalism Act, which was implemented as a response to radical changes in the nature of immigration to Canada during the second half of the twentieth century (Harrison, 1999, p. 307). During this period, the federal government recognized multicultural initiatives as integral to public policy, establishing the Canadian Consultative Council on Multiculturalism in 1973; amending multiculturalist policy into the Constitution Act in 1982 and later the Charter of Rights and Freedoms in 1988; as well as establishing the Canadian Multiculturalism Act in 1988 (Williams, 1996, p. 157). Conversely, at the same time in U.S. history, bills were being introduced that sought to amend the Constitution to declare English the official language of the United States, specifically the official English amendments of 1981 and 1984 (Piatt, 1992, p. 21). Moreover, while multilingualism and minority language rights, via multicultural policy, have become an integral part of Canadian identity, in the United States bills toward amendments or statutes concerning English-only (also known as official-English) initiatives have appeared in every Congress since the early eighties (Schildkraut, 2013, p. 13).

In the United States, two official English bills were introduced in the House of Representatives of the 108th Congress, and both were sent to committee: the National Language Act of 2003 (Schildkraut, 2013, p. 13) and the English Language Unity Act of 2005 (Congress.Gov, 2013). While neither has ever passed, both have been put regularly to each U.S. Congress since 2009 (Congress.Gov, 2013). What is most interesting about these bills, particularly in regard to Canadian policy, is their language of exclusion that seeks:

> To declare English as the official language of the United States, to establish a uniform English language rule for naturalization, and to avoid misconstructions of the English language texts of the laws . . . of the Constitution.
>
> *(Congress.Gov, 2013)*

In contrast, Canadian multiculturalism policy works to "preserve and enhance the use of languages other than English and French, while strengthening the status and use of the official languages of Canada" (Justice Laws, 2011), with specific mandates that "facilitate the acquisition, retention and use of all languages that contribute to the multicultural heritage of Canada" (Justice Laws, 2011).

Minority language rights within the Canadian multicultural policy are particularly noteworthy. In the examples above, we see inclusive, nurturing language choices, namely: "preserve," "enhance," "facilitate," and "retention." Whereas, in the U.S. policy, the language choices of "declare," "uniform," and "avoid" are more forceful, exclusionary, and singular. While to date, U.S. efforts to pass restrictive language laws have been unsuccessful at the federal level, such legislation within individual states has thrived. In 2013, twenty-eight of fifty U.S. states had declared English the official state language, and at least fifteen of the remaining states have debated such legislation in the past decade (Schildkraut, 2013, p. 16). In other words, 86% of U.S. governing state bodies have either employed or considered the employment of English-only practices that would serve to legitimize English and marginalize minority languages, or—put bluntly—the language practices of resident multilinguals. In contrast, Canadian provinces work to uphold federal multicultural and multilingual policy. In fact, a number of provinces with unique and centralized immigrant populations have established provincial policy that supports the education of allophone students in their heritage languages.

Nevertheless, these provincial policies remain contingent on the Canadian Multiculturalism Act, which established Canada as the first country to adopt an official multiculturalist policy, reaffirming multiculturalism as a fundamental characteristic of Canadian society. Educational practices and policies vary by province and are ultimately shaped by regional immigrations and, consequently, population dynamics. For instance, Canada's geographic boundaries are emphasized by school systems that teach province-specific curricula. The lack of federal influence on language policies in education, particularly in the case of allophone languages, has created a "hodgepodge of competing principles regarding language policy

at the federal and provincial levels" (MacMillian, 1998, p. 3). In certain regions, provincial governments have made efforts to address linguistic diversity, but in others these issues have been overlooked. Examples of provinces that have addressed cultural and linguistic diversity include New Brunswick and Saskatchewan. New Brunswick has been home to Chinese immigrants since the 1890s; in the mid-1970s this group formed the Chinese Cultural Association and with federal government assistance opened schools with oral and written instruction in Cantonese and Mandarin (Leavitt, 1998, p. 378). In Saskatchewan, there is a long tradition of Ukrainian ancestry, and Ukrainian is offered as a core language program in primary and secondary education. There is one Ukrainian bilingual (with English) school in the province, and until 1990 the federal government funded after-school and weekend language classes in Ukrainian (Denis, 1998, p. 439). The benefit of regionalized systems is that students learn languages that are usable in their daily lives, and in areas where specific immigrant populations are dense, such as Ukrainians in Saskatchewan and Chinese in New Brunswick, heritage language schooling is available to primary and secondary school students. However, the regionalization of education also limits the influences of federal multicultural policy in its lack of a national standard (Kiernan, 2014, p. 23).

Moreover, within Canadian provinces there are also regional linguistic boundaries; some cities and towns may be predominantly anglophone while others may be francophone or allophone. For example, in Ontario—one of two provinces with markedly high allophone populations (the other being British Columbia)—a variety of ethnolinguistic-specific pockets exist both inside Toronto and the Greater Toronto Area (GTA); in these areas multicultural initiatives by the government would be received much differently than in the city of St. John's, in the province of Newfoundland and Labrador, where the anglophone population exceeds 97%. In respect to education, a high level of linguistic diversity among citizens pushes federal policy into action. For instance, in Ontario the teaching of heritage languages throughout the public school system began in 1977, and now more than 60 languages are taught to more than 120,000 students as part of the regular school day (King, 1998, p. 409). Moreover, since 1988, heritage language instruction takes place if 25 or more parents in one school board request it (MacMillian, 1998, p. 200). Thus, in Canada the inclusion of minority allophone education appears to be more of a bottom-up rather than top-down scenario, where the mandates of the federal government may come into play, but only when requested.

Due to the flux of educational policies and immigrant populations provincially, it is difficult to speculate on the impacts of allophone students who move from K–12 settings, which are accepting of multilingualism and multiliteracies, to postsecondary monolingual environments. For instance, Wilson (2016, this volume) speaks to the preparation of adolescent resident multilinguals for postsecondary education. While there are regionally based studies, such as the work of Miner (2011) in the GTA, there is no current research or tracking system that follows the success rates of immigrant students who enroll in Canadian universities and

colleges. While Miner offers a snapshot of immigrant students in the GTA, we cannot hold the educational backgrounds of these students as normative due to the very divergence of immigrant populations and educational programs nationally. Due to the sheer diversity of linguistic backgrounds (Wilson, 2016, this volume), educational research concerning immigrant populations is often generalized. Finnie and Qui (2008) found that throughout postsecondary education "immigrant and visible minority students are less likely to switch [programs] and leave [programs] not only during the first year, but also in the following years" (p. 20), which is in direct contrast to monolingual, native-born students. Similarly, Adamuti-Trache and Hawkey (2009), in their research study on immigrant participation in postsecondary education, suggest only that immigrant populations have a number of diverse educational goals and barriers to these goals. Attention to the importance of linguistic and cultural awareness in these studies often remains vague due to a focus on either (1) discrete populations of immigrants, or (2) immigrants as a singular amalgamated population.

Language Negotiation in Canadian Contexts

In addition to varied educational policies, Canada further differs from the United States in that it exists as a country with two official languages, namely French and English. Yet—while encouraged—most citizens are not required to be competent and fluent in both. In Canada, because of the plurality of official languages, there is an acceptance of language negotiation in daily communications. It is typical for a person with knowledge in both official languages to use them interchangeably within sentences, particularly in speech. Language negotiation takes different forms including borrowings, blendings, and meshings, all of which are prevalent in Québécois French. However, the movement between French and English, while informing our understanding of allophone language speakers, does not explicitly speak to the language conflicts of resident multilinguals. As such, the benefit of French-English negotiation is essentially a reduction in stigma placed on immigrants who use similar strategies when moving between English (or French) and their home language(s) in Canadian society, particularly when compared to such linguistic patterns in countries that do not promote multilingualism and cultural pluralism.

The existence of a policy such as the Canadian Multiculturalism Act would suggest that language negotiation is a facet of all areas of Canadian society; however, students who attend postsecondary institutions in Canada are expected to practice monolingualism, or language segregation. For example, if they speak Hindi, or a combination of English and Hindi, outside of the university, they are expected to use the postsecondary lingua franca of English once they are seated in their classrooms. Pennycook (2008, p. 34) contends a central problem in such an expectation is its perception of language as a monolingual enterprise, especially in official situations like the classroom. Yet, the Canadian reality is

that language is fluid and boundless. As such, the predominance of language segregation in the classroom appears at odds with the Canadian Multiculturalism Act and, consequently, is an essential theme herein. Of importance is the juxtaposition between government legislatures that promotes language negotiation by recognizing:

> Our diversity is a national asset. Recent advances in technology have made international communications more important than ever. Canadians who speak many languages and understand many cultures make it easier for Canada to participate globally in areas of education, trade and diplomacy.
>
> *(Government of Canada, 2012)*

Still, provincial governments often fail to recognize the merits of developing a multilingual agenda within postsecondary curricula and feel no real pressure from the federal government to modify existing programs. This is a major educational oversight.

Postsecondary Education: Multilingualism Sequestered

In regard to postsecondary writing education, multilingual communicative strategies could be fostered in technical, professional, and business writing courses. To borrow from the Charter, Canadian educational institutions are expected to teach tenets of effective communication within a socially and culturally stimulating environment (Martel, 1991, p. 16). In Canadian postsecondary education, "effective communication" has historically been defined as academic discourse in standardized English; however, in these situations, academic institutions are concerned with students' ability to communicate within the academic community rather than larger society. The Canadian Multiculturalism Act, as stated above, supports and pushes toward "international communications" that participate "globally" in areas of technology, trade, and commerce. However, there remains no real call to action in federal legislation to incorporate multicultural and multilingual perspectives within postsecondary systems despite legislation that views "diversity [as] a national asset," in terms of "recent advances in technology [that] have made international communications" central to Canada's participation "globally in areas of education, trade and diplomacy" (Government of Canada, 2012). Moreover, as long as there is no pressure to consider the national agenda of linguistic and cultural pluralism within the classroom, multiculturalist policy will remain symbolic rather than tangible and usable.

Guillaume Gentil's (2005) study of student biliteracy in an English-medium university in francophone Québec reinforces the current project's conjecture that scholars in composition and writing have rarely attended to the struggles of multilingual postsecondary students who attempt to write in more than one language. Gentil (2005, p. 425) affirms that "much research on academic literacies in

university settings remains focused on the struggles of monolingual or multilingual writers to attain English-medium literacy," rather than investigating the ways in which multilingual literacies exist in postsecondary education. Gentil concludes that social forces should be taken into account if we are committed to empowering allophone Canadians to invest in their heritage languages. He suggests the creation of social conditions within educational systems that allow for multilingual sustainability, as well as engendering student awareness of said social conditions in terms of the consequences of students' own multilingual writing. This chapter responds to these suggestions, presuming that these social conditions are already in place, namely Canada's multicultural policies and public tolerance, and positions writing classrooms as an ideal site for engendering student awareness and encouraging multilingual dialogue.

Taking the current U.S. ideologies surrounding standardized English and reading them in terms of Canadian situations allows a better appreciation of what version of U.S. composition scholarship could play out in Canadian writing classrooms. In Canada, much like in the United States, the lingua franca of the university is standardized English.[1] However, Canadian allophone students' interaction with language in daily life is often much different than the realities that face similar populations of students in English-only America because of the acceptance of plural language ability and usage in Canadian federal policy. Still, this paper does not argue that Canadian postsecondary education does not favor standardized English as the language of choice globally, but instead that allophone students who are able to negotiate between English and immigrant languages are better situated to excel in the global marketplace. This claim is supported by the government's own mandates that position "diversity is a national asset," wherein "Canadians who speak many languages and understand many cultures make it easier for Canada to participate globally" (Government of Canada, 2012). Yet there exist few places in Canadian postsecondary education where linguistic learning outcomes, expectations, and practices consider the benefits of multilingual communicative practices. Moreover, even postsecondary institutions that are bilingual French-English such as the University of Ottawa/Université d'Ottawa, which identifies on its home page as "A crossroad of cultures and ideas/Au Carrefour des cultures et des ideés," teach subjects as "English only" or "French only." While we cannot be sure of the classroom practices of individual teachers and their approaches to linguistic negotiation, it would appear that this division and segregation of languages as discrete entities sits in opposition to Canadian language policy. Consequently, there is a failure of alignment between with federal policies that argue "advances in technology have made international communications more important than ever. Canadians who speak many languages and understand many cultures make it easier for Canada to participate globally in areas of education, trade and diplomacy" (Government of Canada, 2012) and the current state of postsecondary education in Canada.

Discussion and Recommendations

This chapter has sought to illustrate how the specific circumstances of the linguistic landscape of Canada, as well as the country's official language policies, provide a useful site to consider the divide between pluralist language policy and monolingual postsecondary writing education encountered by youths transitioning from high school to postsecondary education. As argued, multiculturalism and multilingualism are recognized politically as one of Canada's most sought-after renewable resources, where diversity functions to bridge world marketplaces, positioning young Canadians to excel in areas of global commerce, cultural exchange, and political dialogue (Williams, 1996, p. 164). Nonetheless, as students graduate from K–12 educational programs—where linguistic diversity is often recognized and fostered—and move into postsecondary learning environments, there is little to no inclusion of allophone language experiences in the classroom. This is problematic given that a central tenet of the Canadian Multiculturalism Act is the federal acknowledgement of the commodity of language—wherein the linguistic and social diversity of Canadians has become a form of human capital used by the government to promote the development of Canada as a veritable leader in global relations (Li, 2003, p. 142).

The Canadian Multiculturalism Act is a policy that argues multilingual communication as paramount to the success of the Canadian economy; the primary goals of writing programs in Canada are to prepare students to succeed in their chosen discipline. In concert, this research suggests that Canadian writing programs must shift to recognize and address the untapped globalized communicative assets available to resident multilinguals, which are particularly noteworthy in the disciplines of technology, professional, and business writing, as they are best suited to employ multilingualism as a resource. Canadian writing programs are a ready platform for this form of communicative education.

Note

1. However, there are a small number of postsecondary institutions that provide bilingual French-English education, as well as institutions within Québec and New Brunswick that are Standardized French.

Bibliography

Adamuti-Trache, M., & Hawkey, C. (2009). Canadian post-secondary graduate and further education: Who continues and why? *Canadian Council on Learning.* 2009.

Bhabha, H. (1996). Cultures in between. In S. Hall (Ed.), *Questions of cultural identity* (pp. 53–60). London: Sage.

Blommaert, J., Muyllaert, N., Huysmans, M., & Dyers, C. (2006). Peripheral normativity: Literacy and the production of locality in a South African township school. *Linguistics and education: An International Research Journal, 16*(4), 378–403.

Bumsted, J. M. (2008). *The peoples of Canada: A post-confederation history* (3rd Ed.). Oxford: Oxford UP.

Canagarajah, S. (1994). Professing multiculturalism: The politics of style in the contact zone. *College Composition and Communication, 45*(4), 442–458.

Canagarajah, S. (2002a). *Critical academic writing and multilingual students.* Ann Arbor: U of Michigan P.

Canagarajah, S. (2002b). Multilingual writers and the academic community: Towards a critical relationship. *Journal of English for Academic Purposes, 1*(1), 29–44.

Canagarajah, S. (2006a). Toward a writing pedagogy of shuttling between languages: Learning from multilingual writers. *College English, 68*(6), 589–604.

Canagarajah, S. (2006b). The place of world Englishes in composition: Pluralization continued. *College Composition and Communication, 57*(4), 586–619.

Congress.Gov. (2013). *English Language Unity Act of 2013.* Retrieved from www.congress.gov/bill/113th-congress/house-bill/997

Cormier, M., Bourque, J., & Jolicoeur, M. (2014). (Re)-introduction to French: Four education models to revitalise an endangered group in Eastern Canada. *International Journal of Bilingual Education and Bilingualism, 17*(2), 160–177.

Denis, W. (1998). Language in Saskatchewan: Anglo-hegemony maintained. In J. Edwards (Ed.), *Language in Canada* (pp. 425–442). Cambridge: Cambridge UP.

Finnie, R., & Qui, H. (2008). The patterns of persistence in post-secondary education in Canada: Evidence from the YITS-B dataset. In *MESA: Measuring the effectiveness of student aid* (pp. 1–89). Toronto: Canadian Education Project.

Gentil, G. (2005). Commitments to academic biliteracy: Case studies of Francophone university writers. *Written Communication, 22,* 421–471.

Government of Canada. (2012). *Canadian multiculturalism: An inclusive citizen.* Retrieved from www.cic.gc.ca/english/multiculturalism/citizenship.asp

Harrison, B. R. (1999). Intergenerational language learning. In S. S. Halli & L. Driedger (Eds.), *Immigrant Canada: Demographic, economic, and social challenges* (pp. 307–319). Toronto: U of Toronto P.

Hayday, M. (2005). *Bilingual today, united tomorrow: Official language in education and Canadian federalism.* Montreal: McGill-Queen's UP.

Heller, M. (2002). Globalization and the commodification of bilingualism in Canada. In D. Block & D. Cameron (Eds.), *Globalization and language teaching* (pp. 47–63). London: Routledge.

Heller, M. (2007). *Bilingualism: A social approach.* New York: Palgrave Macmillan.

Horner, B., & Trimbur, J. (2002). English only and U.S. college composition. *College Composition and Communication, 53*(4), 594–630.

Justice Laws Website. (2011). *Canadian Multiculturalism Act.* Retrieved from http://laws-lois.justice.gc.ca/eng/acts/C-18.7/page-1.html

Kiernan, J. E. (2014). An analysis of the Canadian mosaic: Language usage among immigrant post-secondary students. *World Journal of English Language, 4*(2), 21–29.

King, R. (1998). Language in Ontario. In J. Edwards (Ed.), *Language in Canada* (pp. 400–414). Cambridge: Cambridge UP.

Leavitt, R. M. (1998). Language in New Brunswick. In J. Edwards (Ed.), *Language in Canada* (pp. 373–384). Cambridge: Cambridge UP.

Leung, C., Harris, R., & Rampton, B. (1997). The idealized native speaker, reified ethnicities, and classroom realities. *TESOL Quarterly, 31,* 543–575.

Lewin, K. (1946). Action research and minority problems. *Journal of Social Issues, 2,* 34–46.

Li, P. S. (2003). *Destination Canada: Immigration debates & issues.* Don Mills: Oxford UP.

Lotherington, H., Holland, M., Sotoudeh, S., & Zentena, M. (2008). Project-based community language learning: Three narratives of multilingual story-telling in early childhood education. *Canadian Modern Language Review, 65*(1), 125–145.

Lu, M. (1994). Professing multiculturalism: The politics of style in the contact zone. *College Composition and Communication, 45*(4), 442–458.

MacMillian, C. M. (1998). *The practice of language rights in Canada.* Toronto: U of Toronto P.

Mady, C., & Carr, W. (2011). Immigrant perspectives on French learning in English-dominant Canadian communities. In C. Varcasia (Ed.), *Becoming multilingual: Language learning and language policy between attitudes and identities* (pp. 195–216). Bern, DE: Peter Lang.

Martel, A. (1991). *Official language minority education rights in Canada: From instruction to management.* Office of the Commissioner of Official Languages, Ottawa.

McLaren, P. (2007). *Life in schools: An introduction to critical pedagogy in the foundations of education* (5th Ed.). Boston, MA: Pearson Allyn & Bacon.

Miner, R. (2011). *GTA post-secondary access initiatives: Pointing the way to success.* Toronto: TD Bank Group.

Pennycook, A. (2008). English as a language always in translation. *European Journal of English Studies, 12*(1), 33–47.

Piatt, B. (1992). *Only English?: Law and language policy in the United States.* Albuquerque: U of New Mexico P.

Potts, D., & Moran, M. J. (2013). Mediating multilingual children's resources. *Language and Education, 27*(5), 451–468.

Rassool, N. (2004). Sustaining linguistic diversity within the global cultural economy: Issues of language rights and linguistic possibilities. *Comparative Education, 40*(2), 199–214.

Schildkraut, D. J. (2013). *Press "ONE" for English: Language policy, public opinion, and American identity.* Princeton: Princeton UP.

Statistics Canada. (2013). *Table 1: Population of immigrant mother tongue families, showing main languages comprising each family, Canada, 2011.* Retrieved from www12.statcan.gc.ca/census-recensement/2011/as-sa/98–314-x/2011003/tbl/tbl3_2–1-eng.cfm

Taylor, L. K. (2008). Of mother tongues and other tongues: The stakes of linguistically inclusive pedagogy in minority contexts. *Canadian Modern Language Review, 65*(1), 89–123.

Williams, C. H. (1996). Citizenship and minority cultures: Virile participants or dependant supplicants? In A. Lapierre, P. Smart, & P. Savard (Eds.), *Language, culture and values in Canada at the dawn of the 21st century* (pp. 155–182). Ottawa: Carleton UP.

PART III

Resident Multilinguals in First-Year Composition

Reimagining Faculty Development, Curriculum, and Administration

Part III explores how university writing and ESL programs can support resident ML writers as they move into higher education. Recent studies by Kanno and Kangas (2014) suggest that students may gain access into colleges and universities, but that does not necessarily guarantee their preparation or their success. Indeed, as noted in our introduction, the statistics on the attrition rates of linguistic minority youth at community and four-year colleges are troubling. But like Linda Adler-Kassner (2008), we believe that the work of scholars and administrators can be both strategic and idealistic (p. 7). With this belief in mind, the chapters in this section provide insights into how writing and ESL program administrators at the college-level might re-envision curriculum and program attributes to provide a stronger safety net for linguistic minority youth.

In Chapter 12, Patti Wojahn and her co-authors examine the challenges faced by resident multilingual writers in their first-year college composition courses. Their survey of first-year students at a Hispanic-Serving Institution along the U.S.-Mexico border collected data from students on what helped and hindered as they made the high school–college transition, particularly in terms of the first-year course. In particular, authors examine the experiences of resident ML students who *did not pass* the first-year course, comparing their responses with those of students who had passed. Wojahn et al. identify specific factors that students saw as interrupting actors, including academic language preparation, material conditions, access to textbooks and technology, exposure to English, attendance habits, and challenges with reading. Wojahn et al. recommend that more institutions need to learn about the needs and challenges that their linguistic minority students face, and then allocate funds and resources to help students to succeed. In the next chapter, Kimberly Harrison points to one of the challenges alluded to by Wojahn

et al.: faculty preparedness. Harrison notes that the retention of resident first-year multilingual students is an important priority for her Hispanic-Serving Institution. But without an ESL program and with writing faculty who had limited exposure to L2 writing theory and classroom practices, the first-year writing program did not serve the needs of these students as well as they could. To remedy this concern, Harrison describes an innovative grant-funded initiative, Project Gateway, aimed at strengthening the success of resident multilingual students through retention efforts, faculty awareness, and curricular changes. In this chapter, Harrison provides a rich description of the steps taken to provide a sustained and long-term professional development program for writing faculty, ending her chapter with recommendations for fellow program administrators striving to create successful programs that are responsive to the unique needs of resident students.

In Chapter 14, Randall Monty, Karen Holt, and Colin Charlton report on another innovative approach to provide a stronger network of support for resident multilingual writers in the context of first-year writing courses at an overwhelmingly Latino university on the U.S.-Mexico border. Monty et al. describe three initiatives developed by their FYC program: CompoCon, a series of program-wide workshops for all composition students; an embedded librarian initiative to broaden the networks of students; and the use of socially mediated classrooms that encouraged students to hack and create the spaces so that they met their needs. These initiatives, taken as a whole, aimed to facilitate collaboration, interaction, and investment among students and teachers. The authors sought to address concerns about low semester attendance and assignment completion by vulnerable resident ML students (Wojahn et al., this volume). Overall, the authors report that they were guided by goals to foster students' level of interaction, immersion into the campus and the course, and interventions that helped students to work through challenges. In Chapter 15, Tarez Graban reports on her work as a writing program administrator (WPA) and the efforts of her team to reframe a traditional FYC curriculum to embrace a more dialogic perspective on language and culture. Drawing on translingual approaches and L2 writing research, Graban reframed the FYC course toward a multilingual perspective. The revised curriculum shifted toward a paradigm that strove to build on students' strengths and multilingual competencies. In the end, Graban challenges readers by asking if working with resident ML writers is not only a question of bettering curriculum and teaching approaches, but also a question of "disrupting outmoded notions of fluency and identification."

In the concluding chapter to this volume, Ortmeier-Hooper, Dana Ferris, Margi Wald, Richard Lizotte, and Patricia Portanova consider the leadership roles of teachers and program administrators in these discussions. Within state colleges and universities, budgetary constraints at the state and federal level have meant fewer resources for programs that benefit first-generation and linguistic minority students while these institutions increasingly turn their eyes toward international students who are able to bring much-needed tuition revenue with the added benefit of diversifying student bodies. In this chapter, each author provides

a vignette about what he or she sees as the challenges and opportunities as colleges and universities move toward internationalization and an increased attention to international student recruitment. This final chapter calls administrators and teachers to action, urging them to identify "points of leverage" within institutions in order to facilitate more attention and opportunities for resident ML writers.

Bibliography

Adler-Kassner, L. (2008). *The Activist WPA: Changing Stories about Writing and Writers.* Logan: Utah State University Press.

Kanno, Y., & Kangas, S. E. N. (2014). "I'm Not Going to Be, Like, for the AP": English Language Learners' Limited Access to Advanced College-Preparatory Courses in High School. *American Educational Research Journal, 51*(5), 848–878.

12

WHEN THE FIRST LANGUAGE YOU USE IS NOT ENGLISH

Challenges of Language Minority College Composition Students

Patti Wojahn, Beth Brunk-Chavez, Kate Mangelsdorf, Mais Al-Khateeb, Karen Tellez-Trujillo, Laurie Churchill, and Cathilia Flores

Despite the fields of composition and second language writing evolving until quite recently as separate disciplines (Matsuda, 1999), researchers such as Braine (1996), Ferris (2009), Harklau, Losey, and Siegal (1999), Horner and Trimbur (2002), Matsuda (2006), and Silva, Leki, and Carson (1997) have continued a call for recognizing if not valuing the linguistic diversity in composition classrooms. Canagarajah (1999) wrote against what he described as "linguistic imperialism" and in 2013 argued for an orientation toward language in which *multilingualism*, as opposed to monolingualism, is perceived as the norm. Given the diverse linguistic makeup of the United States, this call makes great sense.

Although English is considered by many as the country's "official" language, with various groups arguing for English-only policies, the United States is and always has been a multilingual nation. According to the U.S. Census (2014), about 13% of those living in the United States are foreign born, and nearly 21% of the U.S. population speaks a language other than English in the home. This trend is particularly notable for young people. One in four young adults aged 18–34, or 17.9 million people, speaks a language other than English in the home. That number is up to one in three in states such as New Mexico, Texas, and New York, and as high as one in two in California.

Not surprisingly, at the U.S.-Mexico border where our study takes place, multilingualism is prevalent and highly visible. However, the benefits of multilingualism, such as increased cognitive development and greater metalinguistic awareness (García, 2009), are frequently erased due to educational, economic, and linguistic structures that disadvantage many multilingual school-aged students. Significantly, the prevalence of standard language ideologies, which stigmatize language-blending and privilege monolingual English speakers of the "standard" language,

separates multilingual children from their linguistically rich home environments and prevents them from drawing on their linguistic and cultural knowledge while in school (Mangelsdorf, 2010). As a result, students who transition into higher levels of schooling might not perceive their multilingual fluency as a resource to draw upon. Moreover, even at the border, the "myth of linguistic homogeneity" (Matsuda, 2006) is alive and well at institutions of higher education, where faculty members across campus too often assume that schooling has prepared students to write in "English" narrowly defined, a static English unwelcoming to linguistic diversity.

While scholarship has been published on academic, economic, social, and familial factors contributing to college students' persistence and success, few studies have asked students about their linguistic transitions in college-level writing classes. And despite Matsuda's (2006) advice that "all composition teachers need to reimagine the composition classroom as the multilingual space that it is, where the presence of language difference is the default" (p. 649), we still need to know more about students' educational experiences, attitudes, challenges, and strengths to avoid stereotyping them or making pedagogical changes based on hunches rather than data. Thus, we begin this study in the context of broader questions: As linguistically diverse students transition to higher education, what helps or hinders their progress? To what extent are the strengths and challenges of those for whom English is not a first language considered in higher education?

To explore such questions in a local context, we address characteristics of—as well as circumstances experienced by—domestic students for whom English is an additional language at New Mexico State University (NMSU), a land-grant and Hispanic-Serving Institution (HSI)[1] located near the U.S.-Mexico border. Challenges at HSIs have been treated elsewhere (see, for example, Garcia, 2012). Our survey-based study seeks to identify aspects that might interrupt or disrupt students' educational trajectory. We compare responses about obstacles faced in first-year composition from students whose first language was not English to those of students who had used English all of their lives. We also look at whether responses from language minority students who did *not* pass first-year composition provide different responses than do those who earned a top score in the course. Finally, we share strategies for supporting not just the growing number of U.S. students with a home language other than English, but also all students new to academic institutions.

Methods

To identify characteristics of NMSU students taking ENGL 111,[2] we conducted two surveys, one a survey eliciting open-ended, multiple-choice, and Likert responses. For the 4-point Likert scale, 1 equaled "Not at All," 2 designated "Occasionally," 3 indicated "Often," and 4 "Always." Students who earned an "A" along with the collective group of students who did not pass the class (leaving

the course with "D," "F," or "W" [the latter indicating that the student withdrew from the course]) were emailed a link to a 50-item online survey made available just after the semester in which they were enrolled in the course. The survey asked about students' backgrounds (e.g., when they began learning the English language, their eligibility for financial aid), their experiences in both high school and first-year composition (e.g., the extent to which reading or writing in English posed difficulties for them), and thoughts about their performance. We also sought to hear more about experiences *outside* of the classroom that might have helped or hindered their progress, such as transportation, access to the Internet from home, a sense of control over their grades (for more on this factor, see Dinther, Dochy, & Segers, 2011), finances, job or volunteer commitments, use of campus resources, and family and personal relationships (for more on this aspect related specifically to Latino students, see Torres & Solberg, 2001). The survey allowed us to hone in on distinctions based on linguistic diversity while preventing us from focusing only on student deficits.

Overall, 27% (164 of 601) of "A" students and 9% (20 of the 233) of "DFW" students completed the survey. Among these 184 respondents, 15% (27) reported a first language other than English. Among these 27 students, 20 left the course with an "A," while just 4 did not pass the class, a number too small to draw conclusions about.[3] We were interested in hearing whether transitioning between a home language (such as Spanish) and an academic language (such as academic English) might appear as a challenge, and the extent to which any challenges varied by grade in the first-year composition course. By using a high grade ("A") and the three non-passing grades ("DFW") as a framework, we attempt to extract what Yosso (2006) has called "the array of cultural knowledge, skills, abilities and contacts possessed by socially marginalized groups that often go unrecognized and unacknowledged" (p. 69). What patterns might we identify in responses from language minority students, and could those responses help us better understand strengths and needs of those who excelled in as opposed to those who did not pass ENGL 111?

To learn more specifically about students' use of languages other than English, we additionally canvassed all first-year composition courses in a given semester in a separate Language Background survey that students could complete in class. As we share the results, we will identify which survey we are discussing.

Survey Results: Language Minority Student Responses

So that we can better support U.S. multilingual students, our research is interested in the comparative experiences between U.S. students who reported learning English as a first language and those who used it for some but not all of their lives. Unless otherwise noted, for the results shared below, we conducted a 2 ("A" vs. "DFW") × 2 (1st Language English vs. Other) ANOVA to identify distinctions among the various groups who had responded using the scale of "1" indicating "Not at All" to "4" indicating "Always."

Before sharing differences[4] found by employing ANOVA, we begin with descriptive statistics on our demographic data to provide more context for the NMSU student population.

Students' Language Backgrounds

Contexts for Using Language Other Than English

In response to the Language Background survey, 22% (197 of the 895) of participants in non-international sections of first-year composition reported learning a first language other than English. To understand where these students employ their first language(s) as opposed to English, we asked about contexts of use. Table 12.1 indicates the extent to which students reported predominately using their initial language in various contexts.

As seen in Table 12.1, the most likely context in which students use a language other than English is when communicating with their parents, and a good share of the students use their first language for writing and reading at home, including reading for pleasure. Yet they used English almost exclusively when they read or write for school purposes. These data allow us to see a need for great facility in transitioning as audiences and contexts change, at times from moment to moment. Primarily reading and writing in English for school and primarily interacting in another language with parents and occasionally with friends or siblings can present challenges. But such experiences also provide opportunities to enhance rhetorical and other communicative abilities.

Strongest Language for Various Purposes

Among Language Background survey respondents reporting a first language other than English, only 64% reported English as their best language overall; just over

TABLE 12.1 Rates of Using a Language Other Than English among 197 Students Whose First Language Was Not English

Contexts for using language other than English	Percentage of students using a language other than English
Speaking with parents	80%
Speaking with siblings	37%
Writing/texting to friends	18%
Speaking with friends	15%
Reading for pleasure	14%
Reading and writing at home	11%
Reading and writing at school	3%

TABLE 12.2 Selection of Best Language for Various Purposes among Those Whose First Language Was Not English

	English	Spanish	Both	Other
Best language overall	64%	25%	7.5%	3.5%
Best language for speaking	51%	33%	10%	6%
Best language for reading	80%	7.5%	9%	3.5%
Best language for writing	79%	9%	9%	3%

half (51%) consider English their best language for speaking. However, the majority listed English as their best language for various purposes: 80% listed English as their best language for reading and 79% as best for writing. Table 12.2 lists additional percentages of respondents selecting various languages as their best for specific purposes.

Here we see what could be considered an obstacle for a number of students: finding one's best language for reading and writing to be English but one's best language for speaking another. Gaining facility for all of these purposes requires linguistic innovation and being rhetorically attuned. But might this situation also lead to challenges?

Challenges Experienced by Language Minority Students

In this section we note (1) general differences between those students whose home language was English as opposed to another language[5] and (2) differences between language minority students who earned an "A" vs. "DFW" in ENGL 111.

Access to Course Textbooks and Technologies

Costs of higher education include more than tuition. Textbook costs have continued to rise, and keeping up with technologies such as home computers, laptops, and other educational devices can cost a great deal. Economic realities in the U.S. reveal differential situations for those in different ethnic categories, a situation that was supported in our results. We were interested to learn whether students with different *linguistic* backgrounds report varied levels of accessing items contributing to college costs.

Access to Textbooks

Access to textbooks varied both by first language and by grade. With an average score close to "Always," students whose first language was English (m = 3.75, sd = .60) reported more access to textbooks than did language minority students

(m = 3.37, sd = .88), with an average score close to "Often" ($F_{(1,180)}$ = 8.14; p = .005). In addition, students who had earned an "A" reported more access (m = 3.73, sd = .62) than did students who did not pass the course (m = 3.40, sd = .88; $F_{(1,180)}$ = 5.84, p = .02). Notably, means for reporting regular access to text-books were similar for "A" students and for students whose *first language* was English; means for students who did not pass the course were lower, similar to those for students whose first language was *other than* English.

Access to Technologies

As the only first-year writing course, ENGL 111 is four credits rather than the three most other courses carry. However, just over a decade ago, the course was hybridized as one of the four contact hours was moved online for activities and discussions as well as assignment submissions, all of which currently occur on Canvas, a learning management system.

We often think that today's students are totally "wired," that they grew up not just with computers and the Internet but also with substantial experience in using computers to read, write, and interact. But do all students share similar experiences with technologies? When asked the extent to which they can readily access a computer, most students reported nearly always having access to a computer. There was no statistical difference in reported access to technology with respect to students' first language. Those whose first language was English averaged 3.73 (sd = .63), a score close to "Always," while the average for those whose first language was other than English, at 3.56 (sd = .75), a score just between "Often" and "Always," was similar. However, there was a significant difference with respect to reported technology access among those who earned an "A" (m = 3.76, sd = .60) and students who did not pass the course (m = 3.20, sd = .83; $F_{(1,180)}$ = 3.85; p = .05).

"Basic" Skills

Reading, writing, and arithmetic—and knowledge of the English language—are often considered educational staples in the United States. Yet not all students enrolling in institutions of higher education possess strengths in these areas. Our survey asked students about the extent to which they encountered challenges with reading, writing, and using the English language in their ENGL 111 course.

Reading

With respect to reading, we found a difference by first language: students whose first language was English (m = 1.36, sd = .73) reported less challenge with reading than did their counterparts whose first language was other than English (m = 1.85, sd = .91; $F_{(1,180)}$ = 7.42; p = .007). Although students among the latter category who did *not* pass the course averaged a rating above "occasionally" finding reading

for ENGL 111 challenging (m = 2.25, sd = 1.50), the number of students in this category was so low (4 students total) and the variation in responses so wide that we can make no claims about the latter result. With respect to challenges with reading, we were surprised to find no main effect for grade, that is, no mean differences between students who received an "A" (m = 1.42, sd = .80) as opposed to students who received a "DFW" (m = 1.60, sd = .88) in the course.

Writing

With respect to challenges with the writing assigned in ENGL 111, there were no significant differences overall by first language or grade group. The overall average for all respondents was 1.92 (sd = .95), close to the response of "Occasionally" experiencing challenges with writing. However, a custom hypothesis test allowed us to identify a difference among those whose first language was English by grade group ($F_{(1,179)}$ = 4.67, p = .032). More specifically, among students whose *first* language was English, those who did not pass the course reported a greater level of challenge with writing (m = 2.31, sd = .70) than did their counterparts who earned an "A" in the course (m = 1.79; sd = .90). Unfortunately, we did not have a large sample of students whose first language was other than English who did not pass the class to draw firm conclusions about distinctions among them. Twenty-three language minority students earned an "A" in the course and averaged a mean of 2.30 (sd = 1.06) (just above "Occasionally"). Just four participating students whose first language was other than English did not pass the course. Their average of 2.75 (sd = 1.50) approached the response of "Often" experiencing challenges with writing, indicating substantial challenges in writing for the course. But with so few students in this latter category (coupled with the great variability in responses among the 27 language minority students), the data we gathered are not usable for making claims about writing challenges among those whose first language was other than English.

English Language

When asked about the extent to which they experienced challenges with the English language, students not surprisingly differed based on first language. With respect to the extent to which they reported challenges with the English language, we found differences in challenge levels reported by students who had spoken English for all of their lives (m = 1.31, sd = .83, a score close to "Not at All") as opposed to challenge levels reported by language minority students (m = 1.92, sd = 1.06, a score close to "Occasionally"). This difference was significant ($F_{(1,179)}$ = 8.15; p = .005).

Academic Behaviors in First-Year Composition

We know that behaviors such as attending class regularly, completing homework on time, and submitting all work assigned contribute to success in first-year

composition courses. We wondered whether these behaviors differed among any groups of students.

Attendance

With respect to self-reported attendance, students overall differed by grade earned, with "A" students averaging 3.94 (sd = .29), a score very close to "Always," and students not passing the class averaging 2.85 (sd = .93), a score approaching "Often" ($F_{(1,180)}$ = 47.70; p < .001). A closer review of the data revealed an interesting finding among the group who did not pass the class: In contrast to their counterparts for whom English was a *first* language, students whose first language was *other than* English reported attending at quite high rates (m = 3.5; sd = .58), a score between "Often" and "Always." This rate was similar to that of the students overall who had earned an "A." In other words, in contrast to their first language counterparts, the *language minority* students who received "DFW" reported attending regularly, but they did not pass the course. Unfortunately, given that only four students were in the DFW category coupled with a first language other than English, we must, again, qualify this finding. We see this as a potential trend warranting further research with a larger pool of participants. Since attendance seemed a primary factor for first language students who didn't pass the class, more research is needed to identify specific factors at play among language minority students who do not pass the class.

Assignment Submission

We found no significant difference between the reported rates of submitting assignments between those whose first language was English or another language. The rate at which students completed and turned in assignments once again differed by grade. Students who earned an "A" reported submitting assignments nearly always (m = 3.90, sd = .41). In contrast, students not passing the course on average reported submitting assignments at a point between "Occasionally" and "Often" (m = 2.65, sd = .41). This difference was significant ($F_{(1,180)}$ = 54.89, p = .005).

Students who first learned to speak a language other than English provided some explanation for not submitting all assignments, most of which acknowledged, at least to an extent, their own role in this behavior. Several times, students reported not understanding an assignment but being reticent to ask for clarification. For instance, one "A" student for whom English was an additional language acknowledged: "Through out the entire semester I think I only missed one assignment and it was because I didn't know what to do and was embarrassed to ask my instructor (big mistake)."[6] In such explanations for not submitting work, students for whom English is an additional language in particular seem to be embarrassed by their lack of understanding of an assignment or strategy.

Accessing Resources

In responding to the Language Background survey, students whose first language was not English overall did not vary much with respect to their reports on accessing academic resources in comparison to counterparts for whom English was a first language. The Writing Center proved to be the resource students reported accessing most prevalently. Descriptive results revealed that 38% of students for whom English was an additional language reported visiting the Writing Center, compared to 23% of students whose first language was English. Students reported accessing other resources, such as visiting instructors during office hours, at quite similar rates. Given that the Writing Center serves as one of the only sites where domestic English language learners can access assistance related specifically to language, it clearly plays a critical role at our institution.

Language Minority Students' Thoughts about Writing Ability

When asked the extent to which they believed they were "good writers" and why, one "D"-earning student's comment was not surprising given that the student learned English as an additional language: "I'm still learning the basic stuff about the English language." A multilingual "A" student recognized writing in English as an accomplishment: "English being my third language, [I am a] good [writer]." Yet one "A" student who had a first language other than English acknowledged a challenge in articulating ideas because "there are words I don't know." Another "A" student whose first language was not English stated that when it comes to writing in English, "its still hard, even with my speaking I still make simple errors." Here we see students acknowledging the challenges they face when writing in a language that was not their first and, in particular, possessing differing facility in aspects of speaking as opposed to writing in English, their additional language (for further discussion of this phenomenon, see Cummins, 2000). We also see awareness that academic writing can extend the limits of their language backgrounds in ways they—but perhaps not their instructors—are well aware of.

Summary of Findings

When compared to their first language English peers, language minority students reported more challenges with reading and with using the English language. Qualitative explanations from language minority students included concerns about use of standard academic English. Correspondingly, a larger percentage reported visiting the Writing Center. Language minority students mentioned more challenge in gaining access to textbooks, which continue to rise in cost. The handful of language minority students surveyed who did *not* pass the class reported attending at the same levels as did students overall who earned an "A," but because of their small numbers, we cannot include this as a finding. Still, we want to mention the

possible trend among the small population of "DFW"-earning language minority students, who were more likely to differ from their "A"-earning counterparts as well as, in some cases, other "DFW"-earning students. Therefore, it is this subset of students—"DFW"-earning language minority—we suggest universities in general and writing programs in particular can research and consider more fully.

Given that these students are already showing commitment to attend class regularly, we are left with a number of questions: Can we learn more about why some students don't take advantage of resources such as the Writing Center, instructor conferences, textbooks, supplementary online course activities, and campus technology? Can the university do more to consider costs of textbooks, support students with the learning management system, provide more hours for computer labs, and advertise the purpose of office hours—strategies that would help all students, not just this cohort?

As our Language Background survey data revealed, at our institution, 22% of students in ENGL 111 (a course for *non*-international students) first learned a language other than English. Possessing facility in multiple languages is an asset that ENGL 111 and other courses can draw and build from. Despite the challenge of using academic English, "A" students whose first language was *not* English consistently provided ratings similar to those of their "A" counterparts who had learned English from the time they were born. We suspect we have much to learn from the "A" students whose first language was not English, specifically their strategies or habits of mind that can inform all students as well as suggestions for at-risk language minority counterparts.

Still, among the 22% indicating a language other than English as their first in the Languages Background survey, a majority listed English as their best language for reading and writing, but only half listed English as best for speaking. This finding supports the notion that rather than language users being "balanced bilinguals," or equally competent in all contexts, most bilinguals have "diverse and unequal experiences with each of the two languages" (García, 2009, p. 45). The language transitions that these students make on an everyday basis as they switch, in our institution, primarily from English to Spanish (and Spanglish) and back again indicates a kind of rhetorical sophistication that monolingual students might not possess. The rhetorical and linguistic transitioning performed by language minority students on a daily basis is impressive, indicating abilities that ideally can be tapped into—and shared among monolingual students—within writing classrooms and beyond.

Conclusions: Closing the Gaps

This study on the strengths and the challenges students face in first-year composition as they transition into higher education and between languages has implications for writing programs beyond the U.S.-Mexico border because, as Kanno and Harklau (2012) emphasize, language minority students are the "fastest

growing demographic subgroup in the U.S. educational system" (p. 1). Institutions of higher learning, particularly land-grant and public universities, admit students with a wide range of entry-level strengths, interests, and abilities. Yet we still can't answer the question of how to optimize learning experiences of diverse students in our writing courses at the institutional, programmatic, and course level.

To build on multilingual students' strengths and address their challenges, changes can be made at the institutional level. For example, a recent internal NMSU grant brought 15 campus entities together to discuss how English language learners, both international and domestic, are or are not taken into account in programs, offices, or departments across campus. This effort revealed that our institution has much work to do before we can more fully assess performance, persistence, needs, and completion rates of English language learners, many of whom are local, Hispanic, and/or first-generation college students—critical populations that we admit in large numbers and want to support. Additionally, institutions can gather more information about students' language backgrounds upon enrollment and elsewhere to plan and allocate resources accordingly. For instance, when data from the NMSU Writing Center revealed that one-third of its clients reported a language other than English, the center was awarded a new line: an associate director with expertise in second language writing.

Similarly, at a nearby institution, the University of Texas–El Paso (UTEP), surveys of entering students ask about their first and other languages. Such data have already allowed UTEP to track students for whom English is not a first language, providing institutional awareness of the substantial number who fit this category and the ability to plan programmatic approaches accordingly.

Institutional data gathering can lead to programmatic changes. For example, additional data at NMSU also supported our provost's recent decision to move two faculty who teach first-year composition for international students into the Department of English, home to "the" writing program. Previously, composition courses for U.S. residents and international students—and their instructors—were separated by departments. Because of the additional staff who are sharing their second language writing expertise, all instructors can now enjoy professional development and extended conversations about how to work effectively with linguistically diverse students in their classrooms, in the Writing Center, and beyond. Faculty and Writing Center tutors alike can participate in discussions on issues relating to multilingual students, such as second language acquisition and research on effectively responding to multilingual student writing. WPAs and instructors can encourage students to attend the Writing Center and also collaborate with writing centers to design specific language-related interventions for multilingual students (Brunk-Chavez et al., 2015). Moreover, we can continue to do more to prepare our graduate students and other instructors for today's realities of a growing multilingual population in their classrooms.

The small number of participating language minority students who did not pass the class reported less regular access to course textbooks, and when explanations

were provided, they were nearly all related to finances. While the university bookstore now offers textbook rentals as well as a temporary charge system allowing students to purchase their textbooks on credit until their financial aid check arrives, the writing program is making efforts to reduce costs as well. We place textbooks on reserve in the library; we've tried, though without success, using the less expensive online versions of textbooks; and we are seeking to reduce the number of required texts as well as seeking textbooks that cost less than those currently being used.

The results regarding challenges with reading, writing, and English language ability suggest that colleges and universities can do more to support students for whom English is an additional language. Support structures in place for international students as well as students studying languages *other than English* might provide effective models, such as a Language Laboratory, where students can use computers with multiple language dictionaries and links to software provided by publishers of textbooks used to teach the various languages. Students with first languages other than English could likely benefit from a listening lab for hearing English or taping themselves speaking English. Such students might also benefit from an "English Conversation Corner" where participants can practice the language among others interested in improving their language abilities.

At the course level, instructor preparation and attitude can improve the experiences of the growing number of U.S. resident students whose first language is other than English (Miller-Cochran, 2010). A crucial aspect of supporting students in a writing course is perceiving multilingualism as an asset rather than as a deficit. Jordan's (2009) study of multilingual writers in composition highlighted students' lexical competence, awareness of cultural contexts, and sensitivity to group dynamics. In her study of multilingual writers, Leonard (2014) also described their rhetorical attunement: they "hear something distinct in language. They hear cultural history, differences, politics, negotiations, 'mess'" (p. 243). In our study, multilingual students described the various domains in which they use Spanish and English—home, work, with friends and family, in school. Multilingual writers' constant transition between languages and cultures helps support this increased awareness of rhetorical and cultural complexity, an awareness that could benefit monolingual students as well.

To learn more about students earlier on in—and throughout—our classes, we can take advantage of a range of approaches. For instance, to learn more about students' language backgrounds and transitions entering college, we can ask students to write literacy narratives at the start of the semester (Ortmeier-Hooper, 2008; Sharma, 2015). We can promote our availability during office hours and through email so that students with questions are more likely to come forward without embarrassment, as some mentioned experiencing when they didn't understand an assignment. We can offer culturally relevant readings, give students opportunities to write in their home languages, and develop assignments in which students can draw on their cultural knowledge and skills (Ferris & Hedgcock, 2013). We can

avoid timed writing (which can disadvantage multilingual students), carefully scaffold projects, and use technology to deliver information in various modes (Goen, Porter, Swanson, & Vandommelen, 2002). As some students in the study suggested, instructors can be more "flexible," "understanding," and "less judgmental." Students also suggested that it would help if the instructor took more time to "let students know how they are doing in the course." At NMSU, for the first time, the provost is now insisting on midterm grades so students are more aware of how they are doing while there is still time to improve. These types of activities benefit all students, not just multilingual students.

At UTEP, awareness of linguistic strengths has already impacted the curriculum of the writing program, which has instructors encouraging students to write in Spanish or other home languages in their early drafts and to continue to use that language in later drafts when the rhetorical situation is appropriate (Brunk-Chavez & Fredricksen, 2008). Many instructors at UTEP are multilingual themselves, though this is primarily a fortunate accident of geography rather than an intentional practice.

Furthermore, WPAs need to invest time in collaborations between high schools and college to ensure smoother transitions for students. In general, instructors and WPAs need to see themselves as advocates for multilingual students in writing classes designed primarily for native English speakers (Brunk-Chavez et al., 2015; Ruecker, 2014). Most relevant to this study, we can advocate for better access to and students' awareness of the benefits of technology and textbooks, among other resources.

As the "CCCC Statement on Second Language Writing and Writers" (College Composition and Communication, 2009) states, we should "include second language perspectives in developing theories, designing studies, analyzing data, and discussing implications of studies." As our study indicates, by considering language as a factor rather than looking at broad characteristics of students, we are able to identify specific aspects that might challenge some populations more than others and address these challenges accordingly. Such considerations can also allow writing teachers to follow the CCCC statement's argument that we "take responsibility for the regular presence of second language writers in writing classes . . . and to develop instructional and administrative practices that are sensitive to their linguistic and cultural needs."

Similarly, such considerations can better position us to take up the call to identify and then optimize assets that language minority writers bring to our composition classroom, for instance, what Canagarajah (2006) describes as rhetorical creativity. Facility in multiple languages can, he explains, enable multilingual students to better "understand possibilities and constraints of competing traditions of writing" and draw from "multiple identities," working to "modify, resist, or reorient themselves" to match what writing contexts require (p. 602).

It will take work, but we can effect change, particularly if we seek to understand the academic, cultural, and linguistic transitions students make. In addition

to transitioning between high school and college, multilingual students transition between languages in their everyday lives. These linguistic transitions involve more than language—they involve resources, contexts, and identities. By optimizing multilingual students' strengths and identifying multilingual students' challenges in their writing classes, we can better support all as opposed to just some students in achieving their goals in higher education and beyond.

Notes

1. According to the U.S. Department of Education, HSIs are federally designated colleges and universities in which at least 25% of students are of Hispanic ancestry. Such institutions aim to provide access and opportunity to this "historically underserved population" given the federal funding for which this designation makes them eligible (Ruiz & Valverde, 2012). At NMSU, 47.3% of students recently listed their ethnicity as Hispanic (2012–2013 NMSU Quickfacts). Just 6.3% of students reported as international, with 33.6% of students overall reporting as white.
2. International students at NMSU take an alternative writing course focused more specifically on English language issues.
3. Although the sample size of the "A" group was much larger than was the "DFW" group, we used the analysis of variance (ANOVA) in SPSS to divide values by the number in the group to compare proportional variances by group size. Even when one group (e.g., the "A" group) is larger than the comparison group, they are standardized by dividing each variance from its own "n" in order to make them comparable. With the t-test, we employed Levene's test for equality of variances to learn whether the average variance for each group is significantly different. In that event, we use the "equal variances not assumed" line in the t-test results. In this line, SPSS adjusts the degrees of freedom for the t-test to account for this discrepancy in variances.
4. We use the threshold of $p < .05$ for defining "difference." In other words, when we report something as "different," it was statistically significant at that level.
5. Although we asked questions related to aspects outside of the classroom (such as transportation, job commitments, and personal relationships), we found no differences between average responses from those who listed English or another language as their first.
6. All students' responses are verbatim.

Bibliography

Braine, George. (1996). ESL students in first-year writing courses: ESL versus mainstream classes. *Journal of Second Language Writing, 5*(2), 91–107.

Brunk-Chavez, B., & Fredricksen, E. (2008). Predicting success: Increasing retention and pass rates in college composition. *WPA: Writing Program Administration, 32*(1), 76–96.

Brunk-Chavez, B., Mangelsdorf, K., Wojahn, P., Urzua-Beltran, A., Montoya, A., Thatcher, B., & Valentine, K. (2015). Exploring the context of U.S.-Mexican border writing programs. In David Martins (Ed.), *Transnational writing program administration* (pp. 138–159). Logan: Utah State University Press.

Canagarajah, A. S. (1999). *Resisting linguistic imperialism in English teaching: Oxford applied linguistics*. Oxford: Oxford University Press.

Canagarajah, A. S. (2006). Toward a writing pedagogy of shuttling between languages: Learning from multilingual writers. *College English, 68*(6), 589–604.

Canagarajah, A. S. (2013). *Translingual practice: Global Englishes and cosmopolitan relations.* London: Routledge.

College Composition and Communication. (2009). *CCCC statement on second language writers and writing.* Retrieved from www.ncte.org/cccc/resources/positions/secondlangwriting

Cummins, J. (2000). *Language, power, and pedagogy: Bilingual children in the crossfire.* Clevedon: Multilingual Matters.

Dinther, M. V., Dochy, F., & Segers, M. (2011). Factors affecting students' self efficacy in higher education. *Educational Research Review, 6,* 95–108.

Ferris, D. R. (2009). *Teaching college writing to diverse student populations.* The Michigan Series on Teaching Academic English in U.S. Post-Secondary Programs. Ann Arbor: University of Michigan Press ELT.

Ferris, D. R., & Hedgcock, J. (2013). *Teaching L2 composition: Purpose, process, and practice* (3rd ed.). New York: Routledge.

Garcia, H. S. (2012). Hispanic-serving institutions and the struggle for cognitive justice. *Journal of Latinos and Education, 11,* 195–200.

García, O. (2009). *Bilingual education in the 21st century: A global perspective.* Chichester, UK: Wiley-Blackwell.

Goen, S., Porter, P., Swanson, D., & Vandommelen, D. (2002). Working with generation 1.5 students and their teachers: ESL meets composition. *CATESOL Journal, 14*(1), 131–171.

Harklau, L., Losey, K. M., & Siegal, M. (1999). *Generation 1.5 meets college composition: Issues in the teaching of writing to U.S.-educated learners of ESL.* New York: Routledge.

Horner, B., NeCamp, S., & Donahue, C. (2011). Toward a multilingual composition scholarship: From English only to a translingual norm. *College Composition and Communication, 63*(2), 269–300.

Horner, B., & Trimbur, J. (2002). English only and U.S. college composition. *College Composition and Communication, 53*(4), 594–630.

Jordan, J. (2009). Second language users and emerging English designs. *College Composition and Communication, 61,* 310–329.

Kanno, Y., & Harklau, L. (2012). Linguistic minority students go to college: Introduction. In Y. Kanno & L. Harkau (Eds.), *Linguistic minority students go to college: Preparation, access, and persistence* (pp. 1–16). New York: Routledge.

Leonard, R. L. (2014). Multilingual writing as rhetorical attunement. *College English, 76,* 227–247.

Mangelsdorf, K. (2010). Spanglish as alternative discourse: Working against language demarcation. In B. Horner, M.-Z. Lu, & P. Matsuda (Eds.), *Cross-language relations in composition* (pp. 113–126). Carbondale: Southern Illinois University Press.

Matsuda, P. K. (1999). Composition studies and ESL writing: A disciplinary division of labor. *College Composition and Communication, 50,* 699–721.

Matsuda, P. K. (2006). The myth of linguistic homogeneity in U.S. college composition. *College English, 68,* 637–651.

Miller-Cochran, S. K. (2010). Language diversity and the responsibility of the WPA. In B. Horner, M.-Z. Lu, & P. Matsuda (Eds.), *Cross-language relations in composition* (pp. 212–220). Carbondale: Southern Illinois University Press.

New Mexico State University. (2013). *NMSU quickfacts.* Retrieved from http://oia.nmsu.edu/files/2013/04/2012QuickFact_NMSU.pdf

Ortmeier-Hooper, C. (2008). English might be my second language, but I'm not 'ESL'. *College Composition and Communication, 59,* 389–419.

Ruecker, T. (2014). Here they do this, there they do that: Latinas/Latinos writing across institutions. *College Composition and Communication, 66,* 91–118.

Ruiz, M., & Valverde, M. (2012). Transformative Hispanic-Serving Institutions: Realizing equity praxis through community connections and local solutions. *Journal of Latinos and Education, 11,* 189–194.

Sharma, G. (2015). Cultural schemas and pedagogical uses of literacy narratives: A reflection on my journey with reading and writing. *College Composition and Communication, 67,* 104–110.

Silva, T., Leki, I., & Carson, J. (1997). Broadening the perspective of mainstream composition studies: Some thoughts from the disciplinary margins. *Written Communication, 14*(3), 398–428.

Torres, J., & Solberg, V. S. (2001). Role of self-efficacy, stress, social integration and family support in Latino college student persistence and health. *Journal of Vocational Behavior, 59,* 53–63.

U.S. Census Bureau. (2014). *Quickfacts.* Retrieved from www.census.gov/quickfacts/table/EDU685213/00

Yosso, T. (2006). Whose culture has capital? A critical race theory discussion of community cultural wealth. *Race, Ethnicity, and Education, 8,* 69–91.

13

RE-ENVISIONING FACULTY DEVELOPMENT WHEN MULTILINGUALISM IS THE NEW NORM

Conversations on First-Year Writing at a Hispanic-Serving University

Kimberly Harrison

Florida International University (FIU), an urban, multi-campus, designated Hispanic-Serving Institution (HSI) in Miami serves over 50,000 students, of which 88% are classified as racial/ethnic minority. Hispanic students, in particular, comprise 63% of the university's student population. In our first-year writing classes, 57% of our students identify as resident ESL students, those whose home/first language is not English, who reside in the United States, and who have American K–12 experience.[1] While our writing classes are linguistically diverse, the training of most of our program faculty was not so diverse, the result of what Paul Kei Matsuda has described as the disciplinary division of labor (1999). Most of our writing faculty had not been exposed to L2 research that could inform classroom practice. Additionally, our department does not have an ESL program. The pedagogical norm in our mainstream writing classes was to apply best practices in teaching writing for a monolingual English-speaking audience.

In response to our context, we drafted a proposal for a professional development program for our writing faculty and teaching assistants with the goal of adapting our first-year curriculum to better serve our multilingual students.[2] We argued the need for training all of our writing instructors to understand research and best practices in working with multilingual writers. Our proposal outlined an ongoing program with visits by national consultants, a series of face-to-face in-house workshops, and the development of online training modules. Along with faculty training, we planned for curricular changes in the first-year writing classes to better meet the needs of our students. We also proposed adapting the teaching assistant training courses to incorporate throughout the curriculum readings, discussion, and practical activities focused on working with multilingual student writers. Such professional development and curricular changes only make

sense considering our city of Miami and our university, which ranks first among four-year colleges in the United States for the numbers of bachelor's and master's degrees awarded to Hispanic students.

Our proposal was included in our university's application for a Department of Education Title V grant, and in 2010, the university was awarded $500,000 with the goal of increasing graduation rates at HSIs.[3] Student retention is a concern at HSIs, as in general, HSI graduation rates are lower than those at non-HSI institutions. At FIU, the six-year graduation rate is at 53%, a relatively high percentage when compared with an average of 39% at U.S. HSIs (Núñez & Elizondo, 2012, p. 20). However, when compared to the state's flagship university, University of Florida, with its 89% graduation rate, it is clear that more could be done to assist our multicultural, multilingual, often first-generation-in-college students in their transition to the university and in their efforts to successful degree completion. The Title V grant proposal, entitled "Project Gateways," was an effort to do just that, with a key component of the proposal focused on first-year college writing, specifically on faculty development and, subsequently, course redesign to better meet the needs of our multilingual/resident ESL writers.

This chapter outlines our program's efforts to respond to the CCCC Statement on Second Language Writing and Writers (2001), which states, in part, that universities must "recognize and take responsibility for the regular presence of second language writers in writing classes, to understand their characteristics, and to develop instructional and administrative practices that are sensitive to their linguistic and cultural needs." Such reform in the first-year writing class is important for student retention. As Beatrice Mendez Newman argues, drawing on her experience as a writing program administrator at a Texas HSI, the composition classroom, with its relatively low enrollment and active learning pedagogy, figures "prominently in the HSI student's decision to persist or drop out, to cross the 'threshold' or to retreat from the institution" (2007, p. 23). At FIU, the first-semester writing class is a significant indicator of our students' likelihood for degree completion, as 50% of the students who fail their first composition course leave the university before their second year. As a large program, we offer over 300 classes during an academic year to around 8,000 students, and thus our curricular efforts are wide reaching. In this chapter, I will describe our faculty development program and then outline resulting changes in curricular design and in faculty awareness that multilingualism is our norm and that it is a rich resource for teaching college writing, not a challenge to be overcome.

Project Gateways: Theoretical Grounding

In planning our faculty development program and in re-envisioning our curriculum, we drew on two distinct bodies of scholarship: L2 writing and translingual writing. Most participating faculty, with professional affiliation primarily in composition studies, were initially influenced by the call from Bruce Horner,

Min-Zhan Lu, Jacqueline Jones Royster, and John Trimbur (2011) to "see difference in language not as a barrier to be overcome or as a problem to manage" but as a rhetorical resource (p. 303). Further research led us also to the fields of applied linguistics and education theory and to a body of scholarship focused on multiliteracies and the valuing of linguistic diversity.[4] This work provided theoretical cornerstones that inform Project Gateways. Generative concepts include, for example, a "difference-as-resource" perspective as opposed to a "difference-as-deficit" view (Canagarajah, 2002, p. 13) and code-meshing, a form of writing in which writers incorporate their own languages and varieties of English with dominant conventions in "rhetorically strategic ways" (Canagarajah, 2006, p. 598; Canagarajah, 2013, p. 40). Such attention to the valuing of linguistic diversity helped expand our ideas about and goals for mainstream writing courses in a Hispanic-Serving Institution.

Additionally, with experience in multilingual classrooms, we realized the need for knowledge and strategies that would help us better understand and meet the linguistic needs of our resident ESL writers. In wanting students to be empowered to make rhetorical choices, including whether or not to use standard English, their first language, or a variety of the languages and dialects spoken, we needed more understanding of language acquisition and L2 pedagogical tools. Such grounding would better prepare our faculty to assist students in using all of their language resources in rhetorically strategic ways. While acknowledging the tension in L2 and translingual scholarship, we have found them to work together productively to inform our professional development efforts and curricular interventions. Scholarship stemming from a translingual perspective has engaged and encouraged program faculty. On its own, however, it would not have led to the increased instructor knowledge about language acquisition and L2 pedagogical practices that our assessment indicates as empowering for our faculty.

Another helpful theoretical concept for our program, also bringing with it tension, is that of Universal Design principles. Focused on adapting pedagogical strategies to meet the needs of a diverse student audience, the concept of Universal Design for Learning (UDL) was developed by education researchers beginning in the mid-1980s. It builds on the Universal Design movement in architecture and product design that calls for "designs that from the outset accommodate the greatest variety of individuals" (Rose, Meyer, & Hitchcock, 2005, p. 3). UDL has been helpful in thinking about designing a mainstream writing course that meets the needs of both resident ESL and native English speakers by, for example, providing instructions for all activities both verbally and in writing and in choosing carefully academic vocabulary with the different educational histories of our students in mind. However, as the concept was initially affiliated with disability studies, it could imply that second language students have a deficit to overcome, an implication in opposition to a "difference-as-resource" perspective (Canagarajah, 2002, p. 13) and a valuing of linguistic diversity.

Mindful of these tensions, we began to think of moving from theory to practice and established the goals of

- Clarifying all course and assignment goals and reminding students of them often;
- Using those goals to drive all our lessons and assessments;
- Assessing the specific learning objectives we have set out to reach; and
- Building in flexibility and respect for the strengths of all students.

We also planned for opening up new options for students in our first-year writing classes by

- Tapping into the rich linguistic resources of our multilingual students;
- Inviting use of other languages in planning, writing drafts, consulting sources, and completing final projects when such a strategy suited the rhetorical context; and
- Including texts by or about multicultural and multilingual writers and writing in our reading assignments.

We agreed that our classroom practices should remove barriers for students by

- Demonstrating writing expectations concretely using a variety of multilingual models;
- Building in extra time for reading outside of class; and
- Using descriptive and strategic grammar approaches rather than prescriptive ones.

Faculty Development

With some consensus about our large goals, our faculty development program began formally in fall 2011. It consists of professional development workshops to serve full-time faculty, teaching assistants (TAs), and part-time faculty teaching the two sections of our first-year writing sequence (ENC 1101 and 1102); 10 online tutorial modules (built locally); an online resource bank for faculty; and a redesigned pedagogy course for first-semester TAs that includes attention to theory and practices of working with multilingual writers.

For our workshops, the grant has enabled us to invite nationally known scholars to work with our faculty to improve understanding of and instruction for multilingual writers. We have benefited from the expertise of both Paul Kei Matsuda and Dana Ferris. In addition to the workshops offered by our consultants, we have hosted since Fall 2011 three to four in-house workshops and reading groups a term, each offered on several different days and times to meet needs of various teaching schedules. While we offered program workshops prior to the grant, we

have since focused each one, at least in part, on working with multilingual writers. Most of these events are facilitated by the program coordinator whose position has been made possible through the grant. Of the three faculty to hold the coordinator position, two are multilingual writers themselves, and all are specialists, or emerging specialists, in multilingual writing. Workshop titles have included "Understanding Errors in Student Writing: Sources, Types, & Gravity," "Providing Effective Language-Focused Feedback to Student Writers," "Reading in the Composition Class," "How Response Systems Support Universal Design for Diverse Classes," "Treatment of Error in Multilingual Student Writing," "Toward a Translingual Approach to Writing Instruction in ENC 1101," and "Citation Behaviors of Second Language Students."

Our online modules were developed largely with our part-time faculty in mind. As most teach at multiple institutions, they do not have schedules that allow them to regularly attend face-to-face workshops. Examples of topics addressed in the online tutorials include "Understanding English Language Learner Populations at FIU and Nationwide," "Universal Design for Learning," "Approaches to Grammar in 'Ear Learner' Classrooms," and "Response Systems for All Student Writers." Each module provides readings, PowerPoint slides, materials from our consultants, multimedia components, and opportunities for reflective writing and assessment. Relatedly, our frequently used online teaching resource bank includes examples of assignments that support grant goals and readings that address issues of language diversity, multilingualism, and language/identity.

By Fall 2014, 100% of our full-time faculty had attended at least three training sessions for working with multilingual student writers. In that semester 94, or 67%, of our first-year writing courses were being taught with Project Gateways interventions. And 92% of the instructors who had participated in the professional development program believed the training had changed, either somewhat or quite a bit, their understanding of ELL students.[5]

Assessment Data

While as a faculty we worked together to formulate pedagogical goals in response to our grant activity, we did not specify how individual faculty would realize the shared goals. Therefore, implementation varies. In articulating the primary pedagogical changes seen as a result of our grant interventions, I draw on survey data from faculty participating in the grant effort, on faculty reflective writing produced as part of the online training modules, and on analysis of teaching materials. Survey data were collected from fall 2011 to summer 2015. Surveys have been conducted after each grant workshop, for a total of 32 surveys. These surveys consist of two multiple-choice questions and four open-ended ones. At the end of spring 2014, as we planned for the last year of the grant in 2014–2015, we conducted a survey of faculty to further gauge response to grant interventions, asking them eight multiple-choice questions and five open-ended ones. At the end

of spring 2015, the last semester of the grant cycle, we conducted a more in-depth survey with 25 multiple-choice questions, 18 of which allow options for additional comments. We also plan for follow-up interviews with participating faculty.

All surveys are conducted anonymously through Qualtrics, and survey response rate averages just over 50%. For the online modules, the number of responses to each online module varies. Part-time faculty receive a stipend for completing three modules each semester, and many complete them linearly, so those offered early in the sequence have more responses. In analyzing teaching materials, we collected pre- and post-grant intervention syllabi, assignment sheets, and class plans from six volunteer full-time faculty members. As the surveys are anonymous, when reporting their results, I vary use of pronouns to identify speakers. The module reflections are not anonymous, so I identify gendered pronouns and the institutional status of the writer, whether teaching assistant, full-time faculty, or part-time faculty.

Assessment Analysis and Discussion

Changes in Course Design and Daily Basic Practice

After grant interventions, faculty indicated increased and more intentional uses of strategies such as scaffolding of larger assignments, calling attention to learning goals/outcomes and grading criteria, encouraging reflection and metacognition, and not assuming a shared language about the academy and about writing, strategies shown to be especially useful to both international and resident ESL writers. While most instructors had used these teaching practices previously, they indicated a renewed understanding of their importance for our local audience. For example, while our program focused prior to the grant on encouraging instructors to use teaching-for-transfer strategies, grant interventions seemed to reinforce the need for metacognitive assignments to assist all, but especially our linguistically diverse students. Representatively, a full-time faculty member noted giving more attention to "returning sporadically to learning outcomes to address metacognition." Previously, she had discussed learning outcomes "only at the beginning and very end" of a writing project. Other examples of more intentional uses of pedagogical best practices include those related to scaffolding of large writing assignments. As one adjunct faculty wrote in her response to an online training module,

> In order to ensure that students are not overwhelmed with assignments I break them up. Scaffolding is a major factor in how students perceive the assignment. For the major research paper in ENC 1102, students follow a series of steps to get to the final product. After reading the material on Universal Design, I think it may be beneficial to my students for me to add a few more steps.

Another adjunct faculty member commented, "I think I will use scaffolding more purposefully."

Improving communication between instructor and students is another pedagogical goal often articulated by faculty as they make changes in their teaching practices to better serve our students. For some, this attention focuses on clarifying terminology used in writing assignments. As one adjunct instructor noted when reflecting on the materials in an online module,

> While discussing student writing I have assumed students had writing vocabulary they may well have lacked or did not understand well. . . . Maybe some were embarrassed to ask me what those terms meant. In the future, I will dedicate time to discussing those terms. That way I can ensure they understand them and give them more vocabulary to discuss their writing.

Similarly, another part-time faculty member reflected on a reading assignment she made in her first-year writing class, noting,

> What I had not considered when assigning this text was the extent to which my students may not understand the vocabulary. I started thinking about issues of vocabulary after a presentation by Dana Ferris this past January, but this module and response activity have made this a more present concern.

> She continued: Even more than issues of meaning of single words, though, students (and especially multilingual students) may not understand the contextual space in which [the author] is writing. They may not know . . . what it means to write an editorial for the *New York Times Magazine*.

In related efforts to improve teacher/student communication, a full-time instructor indicated her efforts to better ensure that students understood the written feedback on drafts. Drawing on a suggestion that Ferris made in a workshop held at FIU, she explained, "I am now asking my students to respond in writing to my feedback on their developing drafts. This way I can make sure they are reading and understanding my feedback." Further, to encourage better communication and understanding between student and instructor, a number of faculty reported assigning a survey or questionnaire at the beginning of term that asks students about their language history.

Instructors also reported providing more strategic attention to sentence-level issues and to teaching self-editing, placing emphasis on rhetorical editing strategies. The assumption of a monolingual English classroom can result in students not receiving support with sentence-level issues and/or it can result in what Carol Severino (1993) has called an "assimilationist" approach in which faculty expect English language learners to aim for written texts undistinguishable from those by native English speakers. The concept of "written accent" (Zawacki et al., 2007) that parallels the spoken accents so prevalent at our institution has been helpful for

faculty in understanding that linguistic difference does not always mean that an error has been made. With more awareness of the realities of multilingual writing classrooms, faculty have incorporated strategies as well as learned a vocabulary for more productively teaching English language learners in the mainstream classroom at an HSI. For example, they distinguish between what Ferris (2011) has termed "treatable" or rule-governed errors and "untreatable" ones that are "idiosyncratic" and not rule-governed, such as word choice (p. 36). Additionally, instructors noted benefits from focusing on patterns of error as opposed to individual "mistakes." In practical application, a number of faculty began asking students to "chart and keep track of their errors," to "identify patterns, marking them in different colors." They also commented on increasing conference time and on including more attention to sentence-level issues during conferences. Some also reported including "mini lessons" on common grammatical issues in class.

Changes in Attitude and Awareness

For a number of our faculty, particularly our monolingual instructors, learning more about language acquisition led to more understanding and changed practice in terms of responding to student writing and to respecting "accented" writing. In general, faculty indicated more comfort with the first-year writing classroom being one in which multiple languages are spoken, read, and written. Many noted a shift from thinking of the first-year writing class as a monolingual space to a space in which various languages mingle as students work to grow as writers and rhetors. As one instructor stated, "[I realize] the importance of underlining for students that our courses are . . . not 'English Only' courses." Another noted the impracticality of separating the writing classroom from Miami's multilingual reality. "I live in a bilingual house," he wrote, "so [this workshop] was a reminder to begin carrying more of this over to my classes [with] a more focused design." "I don't see my students' multilingualism as a weakness," another instructor observed.

In practice, this new comfort with a multilingual writing classroom plays out in various ways. Some instructors encourage students to brainstorm and freewrite in their first language if they think it helpful. A number of others ask students to speak their home languages in class when useful, and others, who are themselves multilingual, reported more comfort speaking to their students in a shared language other than English in class or during conferences. Still others explained that they invite, in the words of one instructor, "the use of both languages [in writing projects] when applicable."

Also, instructors appeared to gain empowerment along with their increasing awareness of the processes of English language learning and of multilingual pedagogical strategies. Understanding concepts such as "ear learner" and "eye learner" (Reid, 2006) and the different L2 writer subgroups (international, late-arriving, and early-arriving resident immigrants) (Ferris, 2009), for example, helps instructors better relate to their students and to the knowledge that they bring into the

classroom. "One simple thing I learned is to treat a Generation 1.5 student and a student who has come to the U.S. as an adult differently," one part-time instructor noted. "It's not that one would get more attention than the other," she explained, "it's that one student has different expectations than the other." Similarly, another part-time instructor drew on her new knowledge about "eye" and "ear" learners to better understand the errors in her students' papers. Such understanding meant a change in her attitude toward her students' work and a change in her respond-ing practices: "It was only until I started reading and learning from this module that I have now learned to appreciate that errors in word order are 'less teachable' issues, and therefore I am less frustrated by seeing this issue." Likewise, a monolin-gual part-time instructor responded to an online training module, indicating the importance of thinking deeply about the process of language learning:

> This . . . was a total revelation to me. . . . I remembered how I learned a 2nd language in high school and then college. The process was awful. I learned more of the language when I actually visited the country than in the classroom. What I can do is now be more sensitive to the process [of language learning]. Another thing I learned is that . . . hello—this takes time!

Changes in Course Content

In addition to changes in awareness and increased attention to daily classroom practices, faculty have made changes to the content of their first-year writing class-room. Instructors who identify their class as part of the Project Gateways initiative include the following statement on their syllabi:

> FIU recently received funding to strengthen its capacity to improve the aca-demic success of students whose first language is not English, and this class has been designated as a site for this work. In general, this course is just like any other ENC1101, with some added emphasis on multicultural contexts, audiences, and the choices we make as we write and read in college. We believe that these changes will help you to think more broadly about the languages and cultures in the Miami community. They will also bring an international flavor to much of what we do in the course and will support the campus global initiative.

The extent to which content shifts in response to grant initiatives varies, from inclusion of new readings that address multilingual realities and showcase the work of multilingual writers to a complete revision of the course to focus on multilingualism and negotiation across languages. Finding middle ground, some instructors incorporate one or two specific assignments that call for inquiry into language issues and difference.

For example, in the first-semester writing course (ENC 1101), a number of faculty now assign a literacy narrative project that encourages students to reflect on their language histories and to read the work of multilingual writers. One full-time faculty member described, "I have adjusted the opening essay of the semester to allow students to share about their language background." Also, an adjunct instructor noted, "Even though I include sample pieces from multicultural writers, and I have noticed that it really resonates with students, I think I could include even more. For next semester, I plan to incorporate a few more sample pieces in the literacy narrative assignment for ENC 1101." A full-time faculty member added an international component to a visual analysis assignment, explaining the benefits of asking students to select advertisements for analysis from their home country. By doing this, he intends to make the students "more comfortable" but also, for the class as a whole, to highlight writing for "multilingual audiences."

Others incorporate rhetorical analysis of texts that focus on language issues. "In the rhetorical analysis unit," one full-time instructor wrote, "all of the primary texts that students can analyze address issues of language or communication." Another requires an analysis of a text written by a multilingual writer or one with a focus on the topic of multilingual writing. Similarly, another full-time faculty member reported that for a synthesis essay assignment, "I provide optional readings of arguments on teaching 'Standard English' in college writing courses."

In the second-semester course (ENC 1102), which is research-based, faculty often either encourage or require research in language diversity. As one instructor noted, she tries "to make as many topics local to the Miami language/cultural communities represented in our class as possible." Another described a class that involved both student and teacher research on a single topic the entire semester. Along with the students, the instructor works "on my own project in parallel with the students that I can continually use as that example in class discussions." Her current research focus was on second language education in Miami public schools. And another full-time faculty member asks her students to explore "discourse practices in a discourse community of your choice."

As evidenced by instructor surveys, more attention is being paid throughout the first-year program to the needs and perspectives of our multilingual student writers. Monolingualism is certainly not our norm, and through our Project Gateways initiative, we have been able to create professional development opportunities to increase faculty awareness about the needs and realities of our diverse student writers and to improve strategies for better working with them. Our intentions are to follow up with faculty as we continue our professional development program through both surveys and interviews. Additionally, we plan to analyze data on student retention related to our Project Gateways efforts. We expect to see continued commitment to and benefits from targeting pedagogical approaches to our diverse student audience.

Conclusion

As more and more writing programs work to accommodate the increasing numbers of multilingual students in their classrooms, I close with an analysis of strengths and weaknesses of our four-year professional development and curricular reform effort, with the goal of assisting program directors and faculty embarking on a similar effort. Based on our experiences, I offer the following suggestions and observations.

Foreground Collaboration between L2 Specialists and Writing and Rhetoric Specialists

The Title V grant allowed us to appoint a half-time program coordinator to work with me as writing program director. Throughout the term of the grant, this position was held by a faculty member with second language writing expertise. Such expertise was essential as we planned workshops and reading groups and developed sample teaching materials. As we come to the end of the grant, we have proposed that the current grant coordinator continue in her administrative role to work with the WPA and oversee second language professional development, coordinating it with an overall professional development plan. This is a position that we now see as essential in order to "bridge the disciplinary divide" and to prepare our faculty and TAs to better work with multilingual students.

Recognize the Limitations of Training for Part-Time Faculty

Through the grant, we offered part-time faculty stipends of $150 to either attend three face-to-face workshops or to complete five online training modules. Yet, even with the stipends, participation by part-time faculty was lower than we expected. While the online modules were developed specifically with the goal of involving busy part-time faculty in training, only 32% completed five of the modules. It is possible that larger stipends could have led to more participation. However, what we have argued is the need not just for stipends but for conversion of part-time lines to full-time lines. The working conditions of many of our part-time faculty made investment in this professional development and curricular change difficult, if not impossible, even when training is offered online.

Create Spaces for Faculty to Share Ideas and Instructional Materials

As faculty began to make changes to course materials, they shared ideas through email, until we realized the need for an online space to collect these materials. We developed a course management system shell for faculty to share new ideas, strategies, and teaching materials related to Project Gateways. Initially, this shell was distinct from another one we had established for all first-year writing faculty and that included various teaching materials for ENC 1101 and 1102. However, as a

Project Gateways approach to first-year writing became more and more common, we merged the two shells. We also introduced a writing faculty listserv where faculty often discuss both theory and classroom practice. For us, having spaces for all faculty to share their new ideas encouraged collaboration, avoided a top-down approach to project goals, and generated a plethora of ideas and enthusiasm.

Encourage Faculty and Students to View the First-Year Writing Classes as "Writing and Rhetoric" Classes, Not as "English" Classes

While this applies only to programs housed in English departments, such a shift in terminology can assist in creating a classroom context in which multilingual students feel more comfortable practicing rhetorical strategies, in English and in other languages. It also encourages faculty to put aside a monolingual lens when thinking of their teaching assignment.

As we come to the end of our grant cycle, we remain committed to continuing the Project Gateways initiative and, on a broader scale, to encouraging that writing programs—especially at minority-serving but also at majority-serving universities—make efforts to bridge the disciplinary divide between mainstream writing and second language writing studies. Doing so in our context has invigorated our practices and empowered faculty to more expertly work with our student writers. It has also made the writing classroom a welcoming one in which language diversity is better understood and valued.

Notes

1. Terminology has been something we've grappled with. In the grant proposal, we used the term *Generation 1.5*, but we have shifted to what we think is a more nuanced distinction between international and resident ESL writers (Matsuda & Matsuda, 2009) while also using the term *multilingual* to refer to both categories of students (Ortmeier-Hooper, 2008).
2. As WPA, I worked with two other writing program associate directors, Cindy Chinelly and Michael Creeden, to draft our section of the grant proposal.
3. The Department of Education Title V Grant is offered through the Developing Hispanic-Serving Institutions (DHSI) Program. The grants assist HSIs in improving educational opportunities for Hispanic students.
4. See, for example, the work of Suresh Canagarajah (2002, 2006, 2013), Ofelia Garcia (2009), Sarah Benesch (1993), and the New London Group, Bill Cope and Mary Kalantzis (1999).
5. Response rate to the faculty survey was 66%.

Bibliography

Benesch, S. (1993). ESL, Ideology, and the politics of pragmatism. *TESOL Quarterly*, *27*(4), 705–717.

Canagarajah, A. S. (2002). *Critical academic writing and multilingual students*. Ann Arbor: University of Michigan Press.

Canagarajah, A. S. (2006). The place of world Englishes in composition: Pluralization continued. *College Composition and Communication, 57*(4), 586–619.

Canagarajah, A. S. (2013). Negotiating translingual literacy: An enactment. *Research in Teaching of English, 48*(1), 40–67.

Conference on College Composition and Communication. (2001, revised 2009). *CCCC statement on second language writers and writing.* Retrieved from ncte.org

Cope, B., & Kalantzis, M. (Eds.) (1999). *Multiliteracies: Literacy learning and the design of social futures.* New York: Routledge.

Ferris, D. (2009). *Teaching college writing to diverse student populations.* Ann Arbor: University of Michigan Press.

Ferris, D. (2011). *Treatment of error in second language student writing.* Ann Arbor: University of Michigan Press.

García, O. (2009). *Bilingual education in the 21st century: A global perspective.* Chichester, UK: Wiley-Blackwell.

Horner, B., Lu, M. Z., Royster, J. J., & Trimbur, J. (2011). Opinion: Language difference in writing—toward a translingual approach. *College English, 73*(3), 303–321.

Matsuda, P. K. (1999). Composition studies and ESL writing: A disciplinary division of labor. *College Composition and Communication, 50*(4), 699–721.

Matsuda, P. K., & Matsuda, A. (2009). The erasure of resident ESL writers. In M. Roberge, M. Siegal, & L. Harklau (Eds.), *Generation 1.5 in college composition: Teaching academic writing to U.S.-educated learners of ESL* (pp. 50–64). London: Routledge.

Newman, B. M. (2007). Teaching writing at Hispanic-serving institutions. In C. Kirklighter, D. Cardenas, & S. W. Murphy (Eds.), *Teaching writing with Latino/a students: Lessons learned at Hispanic-serving institutions* (pp. 17–36). Albany: State University of New York Press.

Norris, J. M., & Ortega, L. (2006). The value and practice of research synthesis for language learning and teaching. In J. M. Norris & L. Ortega (Eds.), Synthesizing research on language learning and teaching (pp. 3-50). Amsterdam: John Benjamins.

Núñez, A., & Elizondo, D. (2012). *Hispanic-serving institutions in the U.S. mainland and Puerto Rico: Organizational characteristics, institutional financial context, and graduation outcomes.* White Paper for HACU, 1–47.

Ortmeier-Hooper, C. (2008). English may be my second language, but I'm not 'ESL'. *College Composition and Communication, 59*(3), 389–419.

Reid, J. (2006). "Eye" learners and "ear" learners: Identifying the language needs of international student and U.S. resident writers. In P. K. Matsuda, M. Cox, J. Jordan, & C. Ortmeier-Hooper (Eds.), *Second-language writing in the composition classroom* (pp. 76–88). New York: Bedford/St. Martin's.

Rose, D. H., Meyer, A., & Hitchcock, C. (2005). *The universally designed classroom: Accessible curriculum and digital technologies.* Cambridge: Harvard Education Press.

Severino, Carol. (1993). The sociopolitical implications of response to second language and second dialect writing. *Journal of Second Language Writing, 2*(3), 181–201.

Zawacki, T. M., Hajabbasi, E., Habib, A., Antram, A., & Das, A. (2007). *Valuing written accents: Non-native students talk about identity, academic writing, and meeting teachers' expectations* (2nd ed.). Fairfax, VA: George Mason University Publication on Diversity.

14

TRANSITIONAL ACCESS AND INTEGRATED COMPLEXITY

Interconnecting People, Research, and Media for Transitional Writing Students

Randall Monty, Karen Holt, and Colin Charlton

> *And where does the newborn go from here? The net is vast and infinite.*
> Major Motoko Kusanagi, *Ghost in the Shell* (1995)

> *A sustainable building is not one that must last forever, but one that can easily adapt to change.*
> Peter Graham, *Environment Design Guide* (2003)

For any student, the transition to college is a *vast and infinite* network. For a student with a complex language background, the requisite compilation, negotiation, and construction of knowledge that takes place within the writing classroom can make the experience even more complex. In order to more effectively and affectively meet the diverse needs of transitioning students, a contextualized and systemic approach to program design is warranted.

In the writing program at the University of Texas–Pan American[1] (Writing Program, UTPA), the transitions of first-year multilingual students are supported via networks of interdisciplinary and interpersonal collaboration integrated throughout the program and course designs. In this chapter, we describe and critically reflect on three innovative pedagogical approaches that help multilingual students negotiate writing situations through interdisciplinary and interpersonal networks of collaboration.

Located in the Rio Grande Valley of South Texas, about half an hour's drive from the international border connecting Mexico and the United States, a significant portion of our student population self-identifies as Hispanic, comes from families below the national poverty line, and speaks more than one language (typically Spanish and English). In addition, UTPA serves many nontraditional students, including returning and first-time adult learners, full- and part-time workers, and

commuting students. As noted by Griffin and Minter (2013), these demographic groups have been increasingly represented in college writing classrooms.

Although we work at a single institution, we hope to articulate emergent themes and concepts applicable to a wider range of contexts, including postsecondary ESL and high school–college bridge programs. In this way, our ultimate focus is less on program and institutional specifics, and more on the theory built through our project. Put another way, we are mindful of the affordances brought about by our local context and, to a further extent, the region, but we do not assume that our situation is the *only* one that matters or to which our data could apply.

Our study took place in the context of English 1302: Rhetoric and Composition II, the second course in a two-part first-year writing sequence. The course's learning outcomes demarcate a complex network of student abilities related to reading, inquiry, and writing. In addition to building on the goals of English 1301, English 1302 specifically helps students to critically approach, conduct, report, and analyze their own scholarly research. As a team of teachers interested in how our multilingual students navigate these outcomes, though, the driving question became a simple articulation of *How?* How do we set this mix of activities into play? How can we foster productive experiences among invested people, research activities, and composing?

To answer these questions, we combined three initiatives to create a more cohesive and interactive experience for our students. Those initiatives were:

- The Composition Conference Series for Writing, Inquiry, and Student Engagement (CompoCon)—A three-part, program-wide workshop series that functioned as a program-wide group meeting for all 1302 students. In addition, instructors, administrators, and disciplinary and professional experts from outside Rhetoric and Composition participated in the conference.
- Embedded Librarians—Dedicated instructional librarians were paired with instructors to incorporate a research pedagogy into the course design and to assist students with the development of their research projects. The initiative was expanded to incorporate specialist librarians from outside institutions who similarly assisted students with research and project developments via social media networks.
- Socially Mediated Classroom—Mobile technologies, multimodal pedagogies, and social media were integrated into the English 1302 course design to facilitate collaborative interactions and create an ambient and hybrid class space.

Taken together, these initiatives helped the writing program foster the place *and* space for multilingual students to make equitable *and* epistemological transitions to college writing. Through these initiatives, we recognized that students were able to interact with, better understand, and even apply disciplinary, contextual, and technical expertise; understand and interact with the everyday curriculum of

composition and how it influences, and is influenced by, students' lived writing experiences; and hack and create institutionalized places and spaces that more effectively meet their individualized and collaborative inquiry needs.

Through a comprehensive methodology that included firsthand observations, analysis of student-created discourses, and students' written reflections, we collected useful data for recursively assessing our program and course designs. In addition, multilingual writers who attended high school in the United States were asked how each initiative met instructional objectives, prepared them to write at the college level, and revealed potential areas of need. These student reflections provided insights into how the interactions that took place led to increased levels of confidence and willingness to participate, as well as to anticipated transfers of writing skills to interdisciplinary and professional contexts.

We hope that the patterns of engagement we define allow colleagues at other institutions to reverse engineer our model in order to develop their own localized, interconnected networks based on students' lived experiences. Rather than say, "This is what we've done—isn't it cool?!" we want to say, "This is what we've learned from our students and resources, now YOU go create something cool!"

Scholarly Contexts

Building out of previous work with embedded undergraduate interns and guest instructor programs, we wanted to add people to writing classes and increase interactive opportunities for students. A brainstorming session mentioned Comic-Con, roundtable conference panels at the Council of Writing Program Administrators' summer conference, expertise, and pop-up kitchen culture. Emerging from that discussion and previous applications of Grego and Thompson's (2007) articulation of studio third space to developmental curricula, CompoCon emerged as an event to involve more student-not-my-teacher interactions (emphasizing adaptation), increase the visibility and everyday-ness of our work as writers (organizing a two-day, all-day open conference in the university's ballroom), and invite more real audiences and feedback loops into student research as it developed (fostering process and choice awareness). It was, and continues to be, a large-scale experiment in immersion and community building, but one in which we create a time and space while challenging students to drive the conversations.

Embedding librarians into composition classrooms is one way to effectively facilitate these interactions. Defined by Schumaker and Talley (2009) as "focusing on the needs of one or more specific groups, building relationships with these groups, developing a deep understanding of their work, and providing information services that are highly customized and targeted to their greatest needs" (p. 9), embedded librarianship is a continually evolving collaborative act adapted to the needs of particular communities.

As Hines (2013) noted, "in order for face-to-face embedding to work at its best, librarians must become fully involved in the activities of those with whom they are embedding." Thus, academic librarians have experimented with a variety of ways to embed themselves into the social fabric of their campus, ranging from participating in Twitter back-channel discussions to attending class lectures and teaching for-credit courses. In these ways, embedded librarianship has become a fluid framework that can be adapted into a multitude of contexts to create more information-literate students.

Likewise, over the past decade and a half, Composition Studies has proved quick at incorporating the use of emergent, computer-based technologies into the teaching of writing. As examples, Watkins (1999) argued that the use of hypertext writing can "emphasize learning as collective, rather than individual" (p. 393), while Alexander (2009) posited that, "[video] gaming involves complex use of multiple modes of writing and a need to develop a sense of how text and visuals interact" (p. 36). More recently, compositionists have looked for ways to augment classroom interactions through social media. Some have framed this mixture of social media and classroom spaces as leading to distraction (Baker, Lusk, & Neuhauser, 2012; Froese et al., 2012), or viewed by students as inauthentic (Meng-Fen, Hoffman, & Borengasser, 2013). Conversely, Junco, Heigerbert, and Loken (2011) have argued that integrating Twitter in the classroom experience "showed that students and faculty were both highly engaged in the learning process in ways that transcended traditional classroom activities" (p. 119), while Hsu, Ching, and Grabowski (2014) found that the contextualized use of microblogging and social media helped develop "a positive sense of community" among students (p. 752). Significantly, the critical use of mobile technology and social media can draw from students' own lived experiences and act as scaffolds upon those experiences in order to inform classroom practices (see also Garcia, 2012; Tessier, 2013).

As a means of both implementing and analyzing our initiatives, we subtly embraced Phelps's (1989) practice-theory-practice arc, as articulated by Huot (2002):

> A practitioner starts with a specific practice (the first P) that she is unhappy with. Her goal is to arrive at a practice (the last P in the arc) with which she is more comfortable. However, before she can really change her practice, she must also confront the practice on a theoretical level.
>
> *(p. 66)*

This subtle approach is less a rigid program than a way to allow for opportunities where specific themes emerge. In order to do this, an end-of-the-semester survey was used to contextualize in-class, observational data from the socially mediated classroom in accordance with the stated objectives and learning outcomes of the course.[2] This approach revealed the themes of Interactive Expertise, Everyday Curriculum, and Student-Hacked/Created Place and Space in our research, and it

in turn allowed us to emphasize the built theory, rather than the specifics of our local context.

Local Contexts

The survey study focused on a single English 1302 course section, scheduled during the spring 2014 semester. UTPA recorded a total enrollment of 18,774 undergraduate students. Roughly 3,500 were in their first year of college, 9,957 self-identified as first-generation[3] college students, 9,918 were primary speakers of a language other than English,[4] and 343 self-identified as residents of Mexico. As the courses in the first-year writing sequence were compulsory under the Texas Common Core, the demographics of the writing program mirrored those of the institution. During this semester, 1,527 students were enrolled in Rhetoric and Composition II course sections. The number also reveals an exigence for instruction specifically designed to meet the needs of transnational writing students: 119 in their first semester at UTPA, 893 self-identified as first-generation college students, 1,074 primary speakers of a language other than English, and 36 international students from Mexico. All of these students from our survey were able to participate in the CompoCon, and nearly half were served by the Embedded Librarian Initiative. Twenty-five students of this cohort were also enrolled in the Socially Mediated Classroom discussed here, although some other course sections did integrate multimodality, mobile composition, and social media.

In the class we focused on, roughly one-third of the students self-identified as "transnational," meaning they moved across the international border of Mexico and the United States during the course of the semester, either physically or in hybrid spaces (Monty, 2015). In addition, roughly two-thirds of the students self-identified as multilingual speakers. Although there was some crossover among these groups, there was no apparent or dependent correlation. In other words, some multilingual speakers did not consider themselves transnational, while some transnational students identified as monolingual English speakers. Furthermore, there was significant diversity throughout the class regarding demographic markers like competency, experiences, and confidence when speaking English; frequency and purpose of transnational movement; country where students attended high school; nationality; and ethnic, racial, and gender identification.

Integrated Initiatives

The negotiation of professional and expert networks is an ever-increasing challenge faced by first-year writing students. Across the disciplines, students are being invited to seek out and interact with professionals through first-person research and data collection, for instance with observations, interviews, surveys, and service learning projects. However, first-year writing students most frequently encounter professional expertise via the names listed underneath journal

article titles, removed from the actual sources of that expertise. For many of these students, these names are abstractions representing unknowable or unrelatable constructs and not actual people—author functions without actual authors. In this section, we will detail three initiatives integrated within the Writing Program at UTPA, all of which were designed to facilitate the transitions of first-year writing students. Along the way, we will highlight thematic concepts that unfolded over the course of the semester that we think demonstrated the unique and special ways that multilingual students embraced, challenged, modified, and hacked our program.

CompoCon

CompoCon takes students out of their comfort zones, and it helps freshmen come out of their shells. They are able to ask questions and the research mentors are able to answer in critical and thoughtful ways.

CompoCon Student Participant

CompoCon, the annual spring conference for English 1302 students, began as a way to address comparatively low semester attendance and assignment completion. The origins and structure of CompoCon (Charlton, 2014) were in response to a semester pattern, but we wanted to experiment across the writing program to sustainably engage writing teachers and students. Even with energetic and supportive writing and research instructors in the classroom, we saw many of our students losing the thread of their rhetoric and composition work due to increased familial responsibilities, increased coursework, freshman-year stresses, and an increased sense of cognitive dissonance. Furthermore, numerous class observations revealed concerns about single-instructor, single-student interactions, an arbitrary limitation that can result in inefficient and inconsistent instruction and assessment (Brunk-Chavez & Fourzan-Rice, 2013). It seemed a perfect storm for teacher burnout and student dependence, and the students who were not seeking out individualized attention were suffering.

Given that approximately 90% of our student population self-identifies as Hispanic, relationship building emerged as an important consideration for us. In a two-year ethnographic study on the student research process at Northeastern Illinois University, researchers noticed a trend among the Hispanic student participants. When asked who assisted them with their research process, it was usually someone they knew. Green (2012) noted that "students sought assistance from their instructor, their former high school teacher, a public librarian whom they had received help from before, peers in their class, and/or a sibling. Students rarely asked for help from someone based on their position" (p. 95).

In fact, it is quite possible that our multilingual students face two different and related binary identity pressures. They are struggling, as all freshmen, with becoming "college students" who belong in university learning situations. But success

for multilingual students is more complicated by the support systems that, in one sense, haunt them. At UTPA, for instance, there are a variety of culturally based initiatives that center on reengaging, privileging, or honoring students' Hispanic backgrounds. While intentions are good, the comparison of home culture to school culture, home language to school language, the classroom to the real world is damn near unavoidable. How can we combat those binary patterns and make identity a more fluid construct in terms of disciplinary or research expertise? Part of the answer lies in creating unavoidable access to people who can make an immediate difference in learning.

CompoCon provides students with opportunities to interact with experts from Rhetoric and Composition and other disciplines to pitch, discuss, and revise research questions, arguments, and public documents. This is the conference event as a multilingual rhizome (Deleuze & Guattari, 1987; Hagood, 2008), mixing disciplinary discourse communities with student projects on language and learning and setting a stage for understanding our language interactions as rhetorical (rather than as communal or gatekeeping). Introducing students to professional scholars supported immediate projects and introduced students to expert communities. Furthermore, face-to-face interactions at CompoCon provided students with opportunities to talk through their writing concerns, a practice that has a positive effect on writing anxiety (Corbett, 2007).

Embedded Librarians

> *My suggestion is to have [embedded librarians] keep coming to class. This helps students that are afraid to go and approach librarians on their own.*
>
> *English 1302 Student*

The Embedded Librarian Initiative was developed through a joint collaboration between librarians in the Reference & Instructional Services Department and instructors in the writing program in order to provide students with dedicated, localized support with their secondary research. Parallel to CompoCon, students received direct attention and assistance with their current projects and, more significantly, gained sponsored entry into the world of college-level research (Martin et al., 2012).

Where there are experts available to help with their research, students experience high levels of fear and anxiety (Mellon, 1986). These feelings hinder students from approaching librarians who are available at a variety of service points to help them navigate the world of university research. Underscoring this hesitancy is the student's belief that they should already know how to use the library. The vast majority of first-year students are transitioning from a one-room school library that can be easily browsed for research materials to a building with hundreds of thousands, if not millions, of books and a complex wayfinding structure. The simultaneous transition to a new space combined with a new set of expectations

for conducting college-level work can make the research process overwhelming for many students.

To address this need, positive relationship building was emphasized through the Embedded Librarian Initiative. Librarians were present from the beginning and worked with individual faculty throughout the semester to craft an embedded program that best supported and enhanced individual class structures. As examples, librarians led discussions about the research process, tweeted with students, contributed to class blogs, met with groups of students in personalized consultation sessions, attended student presentations, and participated in other contextually appropriate ways.

Instead of being a shadowy figure on the periphery of college research, the librarians were an integral part of the class and negotiated an in-between space as a co-teacher, research mentor, and life coach. These positive and frequent interactions with librarians helped to alleviate the students' anxiety about research (Kwon, 2008). As one student reflected, "Librarians did a very good job. I think librarians should be more involved because they always have great ideas!"

What became apparent in this initiative was the multiple roles that librarians could play, challenging existing binaries of what it means to do intellectual and individual work. Instead of creating a frame for *the* research process, embedded librarians saw real-time emergent inquiry and responded to it when students had a question that needed answering in a particular research process. Progress became something that instructors, students, and previously external experts could track and improve upon because there was a shared sense of project *development*.

Socially Mediated Classroom

I used Twitter to interact with professors that had more experience in writing than I did and they were asking me questions about how I was using Twitter as a writing medium in class.

English 1302 Student

The Socially Mediated Classroom integrated social media, multimodal pedagogies, and mobile writing into a reduced seat (or hybrid) class dynamic. Students were required to interact via a dedicated course wiki and over the social media network Twitter, while additionally they were invited to utilize their own preferred modes and networks as classroom spaces. Through each of these media, students remained in consistent contact and collaboration with the instructor and peers, were introduced to scholarship and scholars selected to create a context of reflexive use, and were integrated into a community of practice that valued participation and places of secondary research.[5] The Socially Mediated Classroom was designed to capitalize on emerging scholarly trends by supplementing conventional classroom interactions and augmenting students' lived mobile writing practices with social media and multimodal pedagogies in order to create an equitable and empowering classroom space for multilingual learners (Hsu, Ching, & Grabowski, 2014).

Initially, students who were less familiar with the Twitter format (all students reported they had heard of it, although not all were active users) admitted to having feelings of consternation regarding this mode of class interaction, thoughts that reflected Romberger's (2013) warning that student anxiety can be compounded when interactions take place via a digital discourse community. As the semester progressed, however, students began to more naturally integrate social media and mobile use into the everyday of their coursework to, among other tasks, send private messages and email, disseminate public messages, share content with classmates, geotag themselves and peers participating in events like small group meetings and CompoCon, and upload content to hybrid spaces—all of which are activities that "count" as writing (Wolff, 2013). Therefore, through the Socially Mediated Classroom, students continued to be students no matter where they were, and the traditional understanding of classroom spaces was replaced by a new ambient reality where students interacted with their instructors, peers, disciplinary experts, and course content through a consistent hybridity.

Importantly, this shift of classroom space was not solely an instructor-imposed change, but a natural extension of students' lived experiences. As a result, it was largely endorsed and enforced by students themselves. Students stayed in constant contact with their instructor throughout the day via traditional (email) and emergent (Twitter direct messaging) modes, while automated email notifications of wiki updates and geotagging allowed students to passively and actively remind their peers that classwork was being done. In addition, students introduced mobile social applications like Vine, Instagram, and Snapchat to build community, share content, compose invention drafts of their research methodologies, and expand classroom space.

Connecting the previous initiatives, students tweeted with a global team of librarians to workshop their research questions, an approach that afforded students direct personal attention while also allowing them to choose a mentor who closely aligned with their research agenda. During CompoCon, students composed selfies with their professional collaborators, at once recording their participation and tacitly announcing their equal place within the scholarly community. Recalling what Lasorsa, Lewis, and Holton (2012) described as "omnipresent, often fragmented, and a collective effort involving the audience," students reported that these types of social media interactions led to reduced fear and increased confidence in their work (p. 20).

One of our goals was to encourage transitioning students to interact with the everyday world around them through the lens of their composition curricula. The plugged-in nature of the contemporary composition class, supported by the lived mobile and digital realities of twenty-first century students, has resulted in necessary expansions of classroom space and place, which in turn has led to a shift in the expectations that instructors have of their students' engagement with their class and coursework. For students engaged in the sorts of interconnections discussed here, the ambiance of mobile and online writing marks the everyday

curriculum of composition work a logical extension of their lived writing practices.

Fostering Student Interactions, Immersions, and Interventions

Through our experiences with and analyses of the three initiatives described here, three conceptual themes emerged: the value of interactive expertise, the presence of an everyday curriculum, and the intuitive ways that students hacked/created academic space. In this section, we will articulate these themes and begin scaffolding a theory from them.

Interactive Expertise

At CompoCon, students were introduced to experts, individually or while grouped with their peers, through informal settings of inverted privilege. For example, when students workshopped their ideas with a librarian, the librarian was the resident expert on research, but the student's peers also contributed search tips, tips for relieving anxiety, ideas on how to structure their essays, potential avenues for exploration, and a general support for each other's work.

What resulted from these mediations was a student-created community of knowledge sharing. That type of community can emerge outside of a formal space, but an event like CompoCon connects the potential for student-student interaction to mentor-student interaction in the same space or discursive field, making those discussions and developments part of the same conference discussion.

Everyday Curriculum

When we name the "everyday curriculum" of first-year composition, we are talking about the ways the various aspects of composition work, intersect with, and are influenced by students' lived writing practices (Mailloux, 2006). We are also referring to the ways those lived writing practices recursively inform the work done in the composition classroom, both in terms of day-to-day action as well as with programmatic functions (Rowsell, 2013). For transitioning multilingual writing students, these literacies are at once multilingual and multimodal: students can be fluent in different languages (at our institution, those languages are typically English and Spanish), as well as in a variety of modes of composition. As others have noted, students from these demographic groups are more likely to use mobile devices when compared to other groups (Lee, Elkasabi, & Streja, 2012), but their reasons for adoption and rates of use are varied (Ruecker, 2012).

Critical to these sorts of negotiations is the expertise that students bring with them to the writing classroom. Naydan (2013) noted that students' multiliteracy "exists in everyday reality and by default" and that the expectation of this expertise is "always

already present in the twenty-first century" (p. 1). Taken together, the identification of contemporary student writers is revealed as one that represents multiple discourse communities while requiring multiliterate ways of interacting with the world.

Hacked/Created Space

This lived reality has permeated college composition classrooms, as composition instructors have increasingly incorporated multimodal, online, and mobile components into their pedagogies (Griffin & Minter, 2013). Overall, however, contrary to instructors' awareness of students' increasing digital literacies as well as the modes used to practice those literacies, *less than 1%* of higher education faculty incorporated social media into their classes or assignments (Meng-Fen, Hoffman, & Borengasser, 2013).

Due to the increasing availability of mobile computing devices such as phones, tablets, and laptops, mobile writing—the writing work done in spaces not traditionally coded as "academic" or "institutional"—has become normalized for transitioning students. In most cases, students aren't told to do their writing work in these nontraditional spaces, but as academic work increasingly becomes the everyday, transnational students have proved able to successfully hack assigned spaces and create new spaces through their lived mobile writing practices. These savvy moves allowed students to challenge and diffuse the power inherent in traditional institutional structures, which led to more comfortable and effectual learning opportunities. Initiatives like CompoCon, the Embedded Librarian, and the Socially Mediated Classroom were designed to encourage and invite student hacking and creation, wherein transitioning students used social media spaces to overcome animosities and anxieties often associated with first-year writing classes.

Concluding Thoughts and Suggestions

In this chapter, we talked about three initiatives at work within our Writing Program—CompoCon, Embedded Librarians, and the Socially Mediated Classroom— that helped to meet the unique developmental needs of transitional, multilingual students. Our initial analyses suggest these approaches have created a positive environment for transitional students. Here are some takeaways for teachers and program coordinators.

Think of the types of additive events you and your program can support. Deficiency models of how students think, learn, behave, and engage knowledge and people are, if not on their way out as tenacious paradigms at our institutions of higher learning, at least under close scrutiny. Some writing program administrators, writing instructors, and instructional librarians who are interested in learning about real student processes and hearing actual student voices while engaged in struggles to make connections/knowledge are trying new ways to engage students and faculty and an even wider range of experts. One way to frame this idea of engagement is the event. The important element to an accessible and sustainable event is that

it happens when students are available—during class time. Both our embedded librarians and our conference series, not to mention the amount of online interactions in the mediated classroom, depended on in-class integration. Learning better processes requires enactment and additive events that bring more voices to the mix and more opportunities for feedback, both to mirror our multilingual students' realities and foreground the need to become more fluid at rhetorical language awareness, use, and practice on real audiences.

Think of the types of materials you can collaboratively create. The professional development/planning meetings shared by the Writing Program and our librarians did more to concretize a relationship and a vision than any number of regular calls to act because of this or that crisis. The payoff is learning a shorthand for the instructors of our multilingual students, one that can help us act on student need more immediately and avoid a simple shuffling of students from one area of expertise to the next. The Embedded Librarian Initiative literally grew out of such a meeting, and it could not have developed as it did without the participants' desire to understand how each of our "disciplines" learned and sought to teach.

Think of the processes that your students seem to struggle with the most. We're not suggesting that every student struggle can be solved by throwing three different processes/people at them. What we are saying is that immersion can create a context in which the multilingual student wants to experiment with a new discourse, a new train of thought, a new peer group, or a new set of available sources. And once anyone has a project that can frame a language acquisition purpose, instructors are better able to address language/cultural/affective issues, because addressing them is a signal of progress toward research and composition rather than a sign of lack on the student's part.

A shared characteristic we have recognized among the transitioning students at our institution, an observation that has proved consistent with disciplinary conversations as well as in our experiences at other schools, is students' need and desire to be taught *how to make the transition to college writing.* By highlighting the interconnected theories that emerged from these initiatives, we believe that we demonstrated how these elements can be transferred and adapted to meet the needs of transitioning students in other contexts. Through guided access to the networks of higher education, transitional multilingual students are able to more conscientiously cultivate their networked selves, authoritatively establish their own places within the academy, expand institutionalized spaces where writing work gets done, and initiate the place and space for multilingual students to make safer and more equitable transitions to college.

Notes

1. As of the fall 2015 semester, UTPA has been joined with the University of Texas at Brownsville to form the University of Texas Rio Grande Valley.
2. These course-specific surveys were keyed to student learning outcomes focused on the students' understandings of audience, purpose, and form in their writing.

3. Information only available for students who submitted a Free Application for Federal Student Aid (FAFSA).
4. Information not submitted by all students; obtained from Texas Common Application.
5. For example, students read Jorge Gomez's (2013) "On Tweeting in the Classroom," and then, over Twitter, engaged the author in a discussion of the article. In doing so, students were able to directly apply the concepts of their reading in engaged practice.

Bibliography

Alexander, J. (2009). Gaming, student literacies, and the composition classroom: Some possibilities for transformation. *College Composition and Communication, 61*(1), 35–63.

Baker, W. M., Lusk, E. J., & Neuhauser, K. L. (2012). On the use of cell phones and other electronic devices in the classroom: Evidence from a survey of faculty and students. *Journal of Education for Business, 87*(5), 275–289.

Brunk-Chavez, B., & Fourzan-Rice, J. (2013). The evolution of digital writing assessment in action: Integrated programmatic assessment. In H. A. McKee & D. N. DeVoss (Eds.), *Digital writing assessment & evaluation*. Logan, UT: Computers and Composition Digital Press/Utah State University Press. Retrieved from http://ccdigitalpress.org/dwae

Charlton, C. (2014). The weight of curious space: Rhetorical events, hackerspace, and emergent multimodal assessment. *Computers and Composition, 31*, 29–42.

Corbett, S. (2007). The give and take of tutoring on location. *Praxis: A Writing Center Journal, 4*(2), n.p.

Deleuze, G., & Guattari, F. (1987). *A thousand plateaus: Capitalism and schizophrenia.* Minneapolis, MN: University of Minnesota Press.

Froese, A. D., Carpenter, C. N., Inman, D. A., Schooley, J. R., Barnes, R. B., Brecht, P. W., & Chacon, J. D. (2012). Effects of classroom cell phone use on expected and actual learning. *College Student Journal, 46*(2), 323–332.

Garcia, A. (2012). 'Like reading' and literacy challenges in a digital age. *English Journal, 101*(6), 93–96.

Gomez, J. (2013). *On tweeting in the classroom.* Inside Academic Technologies. Retrieved November 30, 2013, from http://inside.at.utep.edu/?p=1560

Graham, P. (2003). Building Ecology: First principles for a sustainable built environment. Oxford UK: Blackwell Publishing.

Green, D. (2012). Supporting the academic success of Hispanic students. In L. M. Duke & A. D. Asher (Eds.), *College libraries and student culture: What we now know* (pp. 87–108). Chicago: American Library Association.

Grego, R. C., & Thompson, N. S. (2007). *Teaching/writing in thirdspaces: The studio approach.* Carbondale, IL: Southern Illinois University Press.

Griffin, J., & Minter, D. (2013). The rise of the online writing classroom: Reflecting on the material conditions of college composition teaching. *College Composition and Communication, 65*(1), 140–161.

Hagood, M. C. (2008). Mapping a rhizome of 21st century language arts: Travel plans for research and practice. *Language Arts, 87*(1), 39–48.

Hines, S. S. (2013). A brief history of embedded librarianship. In A. L. Daugherty & M. F. Russo (Eds.), *Embedded librarianship: What every academic librarian should know* (pp. 1–12). Santa Barbara, CA: ABC-CLIO.

Hsu, Y., Ching, Y., & Grabowski, B. L. (2014). Web 2.0 applications and practices for learning through collaboration. In M. Spector, M. D. Merrill, J. Elen, & M. J. Bishop (Eds.), *Handbook of research on educational communications and technology* (pp. 747–758). New York, NY: Springer Science+Business Media.

Hsu, Y-C, Ching, Y-H, Grabowski, B. Web 2.0 applications and practices for learning through collaboration. In Spector M. Merrill MD & Elen J. Bishop MJ (Eds.) *Handbook of research on educational communications and technology (4th ed.)* (pp. 747-758). New York, NY: Springer.

Huot, B. (2002). Toward a new discourse of assessment for the college writing classroom. *College English, 65*(2), 163–180.

Junco, R., Heigerbert, G., & Loken, E. (2011). The effect of Twitter on college student engagement and grades. *Journal of Computer Assisted Learning, 27*(2), 119–132.

Kwon, N. (2008). A mixed-methods investigation of the relationship between critical thinking and library anxiety among undergraduate students in their information search process. *College and Research Libraries, 69*(2), 117–131.

Lasorsa, D. C., Lewis, S. C., & Holton, A. E. (2012). Normalizing Twitter: Journalism practice in an emerging communication space. *Journalism Studies, 13*(1), 19–36.

Lee, S., Elkasabi, M., & Streja, L. (2012). Increasing cell phone usage among Hispanics: Implications for telephone surveys. *American Journal of Public Health, 102*(6), 19–24.

Mailloux, S. (2006). Places in time: The inns and outhouses of rhetoric. *Quarterly Journal of Speech, 92*(1), 53–68.

Martin, J. A., Reaume, K., Reeves, E. M., & Wright, R. D. (2012). Relationship building with students and instructors of ESL: Bridging the gap for library instruction and services. *Reference Services Review, 40*(3), 352–367.

Mellon, C. (1986). Library anxiety: A grounded theory and its development. *College and Research Libraries, 47*(2), 160–165.

Meng-Fen, G. L., Hoffman, E. S., & Borengasser, C. (2013). Is social media too social for class? A case study of Twitter use. *TechTrends, 57*(2), 39–45.

Monty, R. (2015). Everyday borders of transnational students: Composing place and space with mobile technology, social media, and multimodality. *Computers and Composition, 38*, 126–139.

Naydan, L. M. (2013). Just writing center work in the digital age: De facto multiliteracy centers in dialogue with questions of social justice. *Praxis: A Writing Center Journal, 11*(1), n.p.

Oshii, M. (1995). *Ghost in the shell.* Tokyo: Production I.G.

Phelps, L. W. (1989). Images of student writing: The deep structure of teacher response. In Chris M. Anson (Ed.), *Writing and response: Theory, practice, and research* (pp. 37–67). Urbana, IL: NCTE.

Romberger, J. (2013). Multimodality, and evidence: How the treasure house of rhetoric is being digitally renovated. In Tracy Bowen & Carl Whithaus (Eds.), *Multimodal Literacies and Emerging Genres* (pp. 204-222). Pittsburgh, PA: University of Pittsburgh Press.

Rowsell, J. (2013). *Working with multimodality: Rethinking literacy in a digital age.* New York, NY: Routledge.

Ruecker, T. (2012). Exploring the digital divide on the U.S.-Mexico border through literacy narratives. *Computers and Composition, 29*(3), 239–253.

Schumaker, D. & Talley, M. (2009). *Models of embedded librarianship final report.* New York, NY: Special Libraries Association. Available at http://www.sla.org/pdfs/Embedded LibrarianshipFinalRptRev.pdf

Tessier, J. (2013). Student impressions of academic cell phone use in the classroom. *Journal of College Science Teaching, 43*(1), 25–29.

Watkins, J. R. (1999). Hypertextual border crossing: Students and teachers, texts and contexts. *Computers and Composition, 16*(3), 383–394.

Wolff, W. I. (2013). Interactivity and the invisible: What counts as writing in the age of web 2.0. *Computers and Composition, 30*(3), 211–225.

15

TEACHING MULTILINGUALISM, TEACHING IDENTIFICATION

Embracing Resident Multilingualism as a Curricular Paradigm

Tarez Samra Graban

Institutional Context

Prior to 2012, the multilingual student population at Indiana University reflected similar trends to those of other nonurban, public flagship universities across the midwestern region of the United States: its largest enrollments consisted of students with Asian, Arabic, and Indo-Aryan linguistic heritages (University-wide, 2015). Most of these students were identified as "ESL" and tracked through the registrar by their visa/immigration status, and the resident multilingual population (generally smaller than the international student population) went largely untracked. Resident multilinguals were identified through a frustrating pattern of adding and dropping the "basic" and "regular" first-year composition courses, or because of mismatched expectations among instructors and students, sometimes sidelined with complaints about plagiarism and attrition. Even on a campus that prided itself on recognizing the heterogeneity of second language acquisition (SLA) students' needs, the majority of language support structures served to buoy the experiences of foreign students. In my role as coordinator of multilingual composition from 2007–2012, I sought to include resident multilingual students in these support structures, and to help trouble students' linguistic identifications for first-year composition (FYC) even more (Demont-Heinrich, 2010; Ortmeier-Hooper, 2008; Spack, 1997).

As coordinator, I oversaw approximately 25 sections of first-year composition, specially designated for students whose core educational backgrounds occurred in languages other than English, accommodating students who were not "language-dominant" in English while providing them with an equivalent FYC experience to native English speakers (NES), and to do so on a campus that historically did not see resident multilingualism as an integral part of its academic mission. Well aware

of the moral, ethical, and pedagogical complexities of such a course, I consulted with the Intensive English Program on campus to determine whether it was possible to justify *fluency* as a curricular outcome for first-year composition, without precluding a commitment to multilingualism or to process pedagogy. My concern was motivated by three questions: How can we intervene in students' multilingual processes without identifying "resident multilinguals" as a discrete group of learners (Ferris, 2009)? How can we achieve this without implying a separation between students' second language acquisition (SLA) and their acquisition of what gets typically labeled as more "critical knowledge"? And how can a curricular orientation that is identified as "multilingual" help promote *both* students' attainment of English fluency *and* the transformation of U.S.-based pedagogy, without merely "adapting" U.S.-centric perspectives for non-native use?

This chapter describes the resulting layered and sequenced FYC curriculum—ENG W131ML.[1] The "layering" occurs in how various sets of goals operated on the course simultaneously: critical, rhetorical, discursive, and linguistic. Teaching methodologies included face-to-face conferences with electronic markup integrated into each phase of the sequence, embedded library instruction through team-taught workshops, and visual literacy components and multimodal invention strategies integrated through all units of the course. ENG W131ML was intended to facilitate the transition to college for a wide range of students by merging the goals of academic literacy development with rhetorical identification (Ortmeier-Hooper, 2010; Pedersen, 2010), where the "self" is not fixed, but discursively fluid (Fraiberg, 2010; Ortega & Carson, 2010; Oullette, 2008).

Theoretical Justification

There were three productive challenges to contend with in this work. First, concurrent with the renovation of ENG W131ML, the Intensive English Program revised its language placement exam and curriculum, resulting in a sequence of eight-week modules that presented an integrated-skills approach to academic literacy (Ewert, 2011, p. 7). Students' performance on the placement exam resulted in a series of recommendations for certain modules prior to or alongside eligibility for FYC, yet there was no way to systematically track or recommend resident multilingual learners for either language placement or enrollment in the modules, except on an individual basis. Second, students initially identified as needing linguistic support were—by the time they completed the required modules—often more prepared discursively, critically, and rhetorically than their resident multilingual peers. Finally, because various schools within the university had separate direct and general admission requirements, even the most linguistically homogenous group of students presented multiple placement needs, with some being identified as needing extensive work in English comprehension and conversation, and others being identified as writing at near-native fluency, depending on how they were assessed through the IEP.

As a result, greater cohesion among all of these programs (FYC, multilingual FYC, and IEP) ultimately contributed to a more complex spread of students' discursive competencies, making "multilingual" a more nuanced classification on campus than the FYC curriculum could support. Students' academic profiles comprised a constellation of factors now made more visible by this new curricular paradigm—including their professionalization experiences between secondary and postsecondary education, and the gaps between their language preparation and language performance. While such a redistribution of competencies is not unusual for a campus of this size, it became programmatically and institutionally preserved, complicating students' linguistic and academic identifications beyond the static "native/non-native" or "resident/foreign" labels that had previously been applied. ENG W131ML responded to this situation by recouping "multilingual" as a textual identification—one that develops over time and is realized through critical reflection. Thus, redefining fluency as a curricular goal became necessary as I learned more about students' pathways into the course,[2] and as I sought to align the sequenced curriculum *both* with recently revised FYC outcomes *and* with recently revised language placement practices of the Intensive English Program.

My own language background—and that of the teachers I trained—was insufficient to recognize the kinds of intricate discursive shifting that occurs in writers with strong metacognition (Matsuda, 2014, p. 482), nor could we know with certainty that our students were very aware of their own cognitive ability to shift between discourses. As a result, I aligned the course with Leki's (1992) sequenced writing project and with various negotiation pedagogies already theorized for L2 writing,[3] which did not assume that all students proceeded developmentally through the sequence at the same pace. For example, some students began the course understanding the multivocal nature of academic writing, but negotiating various assumptions about what Standard Academic English (SAE) tends to treat unreflectively as stock terms (e.g., "coherence," "claim," "perspective," "voice," "originality," etc.). To help root out the resident multilingual identification of many students on campus, the course presented fluency as the developmental practice that coincided with students' negotiation of these terms.

FYC Curriculum and Goals

ENG W131ML promoted textual identification not as an expertise to be arrived at, but as a coming-into-being by attending to how gaps between texts, perspectives, and experiences could help students invent a context for writing. The curriculum included four units, each one guided by a discursive "move" (Swales, 1981; Swales, 1990)[4] reflecting a critical action that students could not only understand as an academic English value, but also learn to problematize—to experience as a potential "contact zone" in the construction of academic discourse: *self-positioning* according to modality or culture; *complicating* perspectives; *negotiating* dissonance; and *offering* a critical position. Together, these metaphorical contact zones enabled

a set of discursive attitudes that built rhetorical, linguistic, and academic fluency, and that mapped onto stated information literacy and critical thinking goals undergirding the university's FYC curriculum. The final project—a critical argument with repurposed genre—was intended to bridge students' learned discursive capacities in FYC with other critical capacities they might encounter in more advanced writing. The redesigned course ultimately promoted several intellectual values identified by Matsuda (2014) as fueling translingualism (p. 479). It also promoted a meshing of students' multilingual behaviors much like Jordan (2012) describes, characterized by dialogic learning (p. 43), and bordering on "intercultural" in terms of the kinds of communicative competence it raises (p. 119). In justifying this curricular paradigm, I had to define our "common communicative arena" (Canagarajah, 2013; Molina, 2011), and to manage students' and instructors' expectations of the codes and purposes this new arena entailed. Moreover, I had to do so without reinforcing the false distinctions between expert and inexpert, or resource and deficit, that multilingual writing pedagogy has been working against. The goal of ENG W131ML was to not let language difference or cultural identification become unquestioned phenomena, but rather to employ them as *critical methods*.

To prevent linguistic and cultural differences from becoming commonplace "topics" for students to examine, each instructor selected a set of keystone readings around which to base his or her course, often striking a balance between language practice and language study, on themes ranging from authorship to censorship to institutional discourse. Students interacted with these keystone readings, combining and recombining them into "lens" relationships that, in turn, determined the moves they needed for organizing their writing—for example, *contradicting* a claim, *forwarding* another writer's claim even if they disagreed with it, *narrating* a series of events so as to clear up a potential misunderstanding, *explaining* a metaphor in order to illustrate an indescribable concept, or *speaking on behalf* of one writer who is using data from another writer's academic research in order to make an extra-academic claim. There was no finite list of relationships that could be generated from these exigent re/combinations of sources. Even as they grappled with the re/combinations, students were observing that linguistic markers, pragmatic strategies, and cohesion devices all occurred as patterns in these other texts. Furthermore, students observed that *discursive function* is as much an aspect of the *reader* and of the *reader's context* as it is the *writer's*. Finally, students also worked with sources that they cumulatively gathered over the semester—sometimes selecting from the "library" of texts already vetted by the instructor—allowing them multiple opportunities to use and reuse the authors' concepts as a way of gaining topical and lexical fluency on a question of their choosing.[5]

Overall, ENG W131ML sought to productively engage difference without reengaging monolingual assumptions—in fact, to reclaim *multilingualism* as a critically reflective term for composition programs that are in flux, catering to a student population whose own multilingual identifications are unstable, varied,

and complex. It sought to respond to the multilingual realities of the Indiana University campus by relying on learning methodologies based in three core principles: (1) linguistic and discursive "shuttling" (Canagarajah, 2002a, 2006); (2) a renewed commitment to interlanguage (Kutz, 1986; Tardy & Swales, 2008); and (3) "language salience" (Shuck, 2010).

First Core Principle: Understanding Shuttling as Language Negotiation

I introduced this curriculum to new instructors through Canagarajah's "shuttling" model of language negotiation (2006), which depends upon our observation of what happens (or what can possibly happen) when multilingual writers move between cultural expectations of those languages while writing professional genres. Whereas for Canagarajah *moving between* is seen in how the advanced writer strives to achieve moves in one task that resemble rhetorical priorities expressed in other writing tasks (p. 595), for our course *moving between* was seen in how novice writers positioned themselves as being informed or misinformed by language difference. The tensions between textual practices and linguistic beliefs became a critical methodology for ENG W131ML (Matsuda & Matsuda, 2010; Tardy, 2011).

The curriculum's appropriation of "negotiation" did not merely encourage students to treat language and culture as fixed positions, reinforce the belief that writers move naturally between an L1 and L2 located on distant trajectories, or celebrate the coping strategies of multilingual learners. Rather, it served as a critical orientation for instructors and students alike, enabling both to witness how a writer's multiple trajectories are always at work as the writer negotiates critical moves in a project of his or her own design. The notion of capitalizing on students' reflective versatility, rather than only measuring their stability in terms of specific linguistic forms or cultural competencies, informed our curriculum in very specific ways. The inquiry project sequentially built a set of discursive attitudes (attitudes toward sources and tasks) that in turn enabled students to develop expertise over a variety of genres by achieving four critical moves. As students moved through the sequence, they performed writing tasks in ways that were motivated by what they understood about negotiating multiple discourses, languages, texts, and textual practices. The inquiry project also involves students in the reflection and articulation of micro- and macroscopic levels of writing activity—for example, reflecting on their efforts at lexicon building, on their conscious and unconscious revision strategies, on the feedback their instructor provided during and after conferences, and on difficulties they had developing their question.

Most importantly, students invented a context for writing that was not necessarily grounded in the same assumptions as those of their instructors or their peers. They became aware of three contexts that were constantly in flux: the ongoing history of their question; their reader's probable knowledge of the questions; and

their own past history or present interest in it, often made more complex by a resident multilingual student's multiple academic experiences. For example, one student's project initially questioned the causes of Internet addiction among his peers, but developed into a more nuanced discussion by noting the problems with defining "addiction" according to actual practices, when those practices are motivated by evolving communicative needs. In a final reflective letter, he explained that the evolution of his research question from cause to definition was inspired in part by his positioning as an ESL student in a U.S. secondary school, where he often acquired knowledge of phenomena through definitions. Another student framed his multilingualism narrative with an analysis of Patrick Corrigan's "The Bard Does Twitter" cartoon (http://corrigan.ca/april5-09.htm), challenging the idea that the use of gadgets diminishes literacy. In this image, William Shakespeare is caricaturized as a pervasive innovator of technologized language, something the student argues cannot be dismissed as a backward move in evolutions of literacy, but also something that the student claims to realize based on his own charge to understand language as *diversity* through ENG W131ML.

Instructors of the course also found unique ways to invent contexts for writing by asking students to describe their closeness to or distance from certain languages. One instructor, Lane Rogers, asked students to compose their literacy narratives in Google Maps so as to illustrate the beliefs, ideologies, or experiences that contributed to their understanding of what it means to be "multilingual." Students mapped locations where they experienced various or conflicting definitions of that term, locations where they experienced written communication in intense ways, and locations where they experienced what they might now recognize as resistance to the themes or metaphors running through Richard Rodriguez's "Scholarship Boy" or Gerald Graff's "Disliking Books," two keystone essays in their instructor's syllabus. In short, the curriculum positioned both students and instructors as active negotiators of institutional and extra-institutional attitudes toward academic discourse.

Second Core Principle: Recognizing Students' Interlanguage

Because ENG W131ML promoted linguistic alongside rhetorical development, the writing sequence had to provide multiple opportunities for instructors to witness and engage with a student's "interlanguage" (Kutz, 1986). Kutz has suggested using this term to describe contact zones between practices, perceptions, and beliefs about what writers of all levels can do, thereby challenging the dichotomy between actual and perceived fluency and suggesting a pedagogy that recognizes a productive relationship between what has been taught so far and what the learner knows and can do at any given point in time (p. 45). ENG W131ML attempted to elide this actual-perceived dichotomy by considering "interlanguage" in much the same way as Ortega and Carson (2010) define "linguistic competence"—as a demonstration of how micro- and macro-contexts *help reveal students' embeddedness*

in their language tasks. Thus, I embedded feedback mechanisms throughout all four units of the course, enabling students to build knowledge about the lexicon we used to invent, reflect on, and evaluate their writing—to see them as connected knowledges. For example, while instructors found diverse ways to offer peer review—some combining in- and out-of-class peer response techniques—all instructors ensured that the language guiding their peer review materials echoed the language used to describe major assignments and looked ahead to the language of our evaluation rubrics, when rubrics were used. That same lexicon was employed during face-to-face conferencing through a combination of direct and indirect feedback (Ferris, 2009, p. 19). Ideally, our evaluative comments on past assignments foregrounded what students would do in the next genre since, in a sequenced project, it is not uncommon for students to be more linguistically accurate in some genres than in others. Linking feedback mechanisms together helped students and instructors to keep the longer view in mind, and to realize the usefulness of critical reflection in moving toward accuracy.

More recently, Tardy and Swales (2008) have argued that interlanguage helps us to rethink form and coherence as shaping forces in students' writing, and this is something we observed throughout the course. The lynchpin to ENG W131ML was the face-to-face conference that occurred between the first and final draft in each unit, along with the preparation we asked students to do prior to and following the conference, both of which were aided by electronic markup strategies that instructors and students completed together. Once in each unit (twice, if students demonstrated significant linguistic difficulty), instructors met with students over a desktop or laptop computer, having done a minimal markup of the student's writing in advance (often color-coding their highlighting), and having articulated a brief list of concerns from the assignment sheet, the peer review sheet, or the evaluation rubric. During the conference session, instructors gave students an opportunity to explain how they addressed the assignment and how they worked toward the goals implicated in the assignment's lexicon, such as "organization" or "coherence" or "development" or "style." Using tracked changes and commenting features, they marked up selected areas of the composition, showing areas of difficulty so as to begin addressing them together. Students could take notes (in any language), and instructors could address a student's evolving concerns by responding to individual queries or misunderstandings about the more abstract aspects of each assignment (e.g., "What does it mean to use this image as a lens onto another image?" "What's the difference between developing and supporting?" etc.), or by sharing strategies for initiating discussion (e.g., "What are you trying to say here?" "What I think you're trying to say is . . ."), using full sentences to articulate their comments, and modeling certain discourse practices. At the end of the session or shortly after, instructors could then email the collaboratively marked-up draft back to the student or transfer it to the student on a mobile device. Students could reflect further on how their knowledge of the lexicon shifted or changed between drafts by writing brief revision plans in which they synthesized peer

review feedback, conferencing feedback, and instructor feedback on the previous assignment.

Just as one overarching goal of the course was to give students time to turn assignment language into critical vocabulary *as dictated by the contexts they co-constructed*, the overarching goal of these conferences was to give students an opportunity to converse about their own writing and to understand how that conversation led to revision in both immediate and long-term ways, treating linguistic and rhetorical development as shared concerns (Canagarajah, 2002b; Foster, 2006). In addition to conferencing, a series of short assignments—some alphanumeric, most multimodal—were designed not only for students to practice the discursive strategy underlying each major assignment, but also to provide intermediary opportunities for instructors to deliver feedback that students could take up in their final reflections. Together, all of these mechanisms promoted a *prospective* rather than a *retrospective* relationship between what the writer had been taught so far and how the writer would proceed through the sequence.

Throughout this process, the pressure on instructors to mark student writing in ways that would stave off others' judgment never went away. This pressure stemmed in part from instructors' perceptions that faculty members in the department expected them to be able to eradicate error, but it also stemmed from instructors' genuine puzzlement about how their pedagogy could give more attention to students' language. Yet our goal was not 100% accuracy in the students' final drafts, but to see marked improvement in things we and the students together identified as needing improvement, as well as their conscious understanding of how they attained it. While error analysis was not an explicit focus of the course, the course's organization provided opportunities for students and instructors together to build hypotheses about students' own usage patterns. Specific grammatical constructions and citation conventions were rarely (if ever) taught as discrete units of knowledge through repetitive drills or quizzes. Instead, aspects of grammar were taught as micro-scale examples of macro-level concerns, generally in response to what two or more students would query about as they tried to master the specific communicative moves or discursive goals of an assignment, and often as a set of rhetorical choices for the writer to make. In sum, our instruction strived to help students continually renegotiate their identification as both individual and social language users in a fairly dynamic context.

Third Core Principle: Language Salience

Ideologically, ENG W131ML foregrounded the ways in which writers as individuals and groups could learn English writing as it is found in other global contexts (Canagarajah, 2002a; Fraiberg, 2010), as well as their own language inheritances, expertise, and affiliations (Shuck, 2010). Throughout the course, I was interested in observing students' linguistic and attitudinal competencies on a developmental trajectory that moved, as students negotiated multiple and changing competencies

over the course of a single assignment—academic, linguistic, and compositional, and not always in parallel fashion (Hyland, 2003; Ortmeier-Hooper, 2010, p. 19).[6] Such a developmental trajectory emphasizes *writing* as doing, *identities* as forming and being contested, and *ideas* as not being owned or originated but possessed, remembered, forgotten, or circulated (Oullette, 2008). It draws on both social and academic discourses, and both informal and formal means of expression, considering a single interaction with language as a series of active and participatory alignments and realignments. And it balances group with individual instruction, involving closer associations to the kinds of remixing and mashing processes that characterize multimodality (Fraiberg, 2010). Students' developmental trajectories throughout ENG W131ML were situated in ideological assumptions, familial contexts, gendered practices, and immediate as well as past educational backgrounds—all of which have histories, and all of which account for additional subsets of contextual factors that become more or less salient as writers negotiate various discourses in which they participate (Shuck, 2010, p. 119).

Shuck (2010) observes that, throughout this kind of composing, a student's salient language identity is nascent: "neither unified nor stable nor a singular entity to be arrived at only once, but rather shift[ing] in relation to multiple layers of context" (p. 118). Furthermore, when writers "shuttle" in the context of an FYC sequence, instructors can witness their immediate and self-positioning among overlapping—sometimes conflicting—contexts and cultures (Pedersen, 2010), connecting past with present educational experiences. For example, one student repurposed her final critical argument into an advice letter fictitiously written by Amy Tan (of "Mother Tongue"), yet forwarding the claims in James Baldwin's "If Black English Isn't a Language," in order to address the concerns of one of the authors whom Tan cites in her essay. The fictitious Tan commiserated with this author about the simultaneous importance and difficulty of negotiating a new language-learning environment when one's own multilingual development was not always fluid or comfortable at home.

In sum, ENG W131ML promoted a set of learning trajectories that demonstrated how what writers do either supports or disrupts instructors' expectations of what they *can* do. Students mastered literacy conventions in response to the demands created by the textual situations they initiated. While these demands often matched with the conventions instructors wished them to learn, it is significant that these demands were not motivated by beliefs about what the student must overcome. Instructors had to consider their own role in maintaining or rejecting their preconceptions about fluency and expertise. As a result, students would ideally realize the process of working with texts as a *process of identification*, rather than an arrival at a particular linguistic identification, or a way of accessing a specific community. Ideally, instructors would begin to reexamine how the labels we have historically applied to resident multilingual writers tend to overlook the constellation of factors that influence how they learn in our classroom and continue to learn beyond it (Cox, Jordan, Ortmeier-Hooper, & Schwartz, 2010).

Critical Reflection

In 2011, Horner, Lu, Royster, and Trimbur argued for more attention to language difference, not less—taking up Canagarajah's (2002b) notion of language difference as a resource that functions "expressively, rhetorically, [and] communicatively" (Horner, Lu, Royster, & Trimbur, 2011, p. 303). They further encouraged readers to recognize the "linguistic heterogeneity of all users of language both within the United States and globally" (p. 305). At the same time, Horner et al. remain critical of those notions of multilingualism that indirectly establish hierarchies between multi- and "true" bilingual students (p. 285), opting for *translingualism* as a more productive curricular paradigm. I agree, yet I still find in *multilingualism* a practically and metaphorically useful term for the ability to critically question those linguistic and discursive differences that can lead to necessary complications of student writers' identifications.

To help students understand "difference" as a generative concept, ENG W131ML challenged them to consider the tensions between various beliefs or attitudes about language as *critical orientations*—lenses through which they could investigate other questions—rather than as stock issues or stock identifications. Conversely, instructors were not using "multilingualism" to promote or reify difference for the exchange of linguistic capital, but as a critical perspective to inform the other intellectual processes driving the course. Thus, *fluency* was achieved through understanding *discursive attitudes*, and through being ready to employ them in genre situations where they might be required. Moreover, such an approach is possible when multilingualism is understood as always operating in conjunction with a writer's discursive attitudes (Kang, 2010; Rhee, 2010)—one's positioning toward certain discursive tasks—and not merely one's positioning as a purveyor or broker of multiple discourses.

However, over several years of course revision, I observed three major challenges in its enactment. First, students' individuated sense of "shuttling" often got lost as they settled into a perceived homogeneous existence as "just one of many" ethnically Indian, South Korean, or Chinese students at a large American university. As a result, instructors found themselves having to convince students to inhabit negotiation gaps more consciously as they progressed through the writing sequence. Second, I often had to remind instructors to accept this negotiation pedagogy as a journey toward multiple fluencies, rather than an evasion of fluency altogether (Matsuda & Matsuda, 2010). And finally, although the curriculum encouraged students to embrace the richness of a single linguistic interaction through critical reflection, their reflections often fell short of our expectations because we asked for only one mode of reflection—alphanumeric—when in fact our resident multilingual learners needed more flexible modes through which to reflect.

These challenges signal a need for more discussion and re-imagination of how "fluency" can be valued and measured in a multimodal multilingual world. As a result of my work with ENG W131ML over five years, I argue that an FYC

curriculum can make fluency its goal when it is aligned with a set of outcomes that integrate the trajectories of writing development, rhetorical identification, and language learning, rather than a set of beliefs about language difference or change.

Notes

1. I developed the curriculum from 2007–2009 after extensive consultation with past and present instructors, SLA specialists, librarians, and the campus writing center. From 2009–2011, I invited instructors to customize the course into various "approaches," each keyed to a different textbook, and some of which are reflected in examples throughout this chapter. Instructors of the course included myself and graduate students in the English master's and doctoral programs at Indiana University, many of whom had an interest in working with international or bilingual students, or had taught at least one semester of FYC before.
2. Some pathways were determined by mandatory language testing, while others were determined by the entrance requirements of their professional or academic schools—for example, business or music.
3. The sequenced writing approach provides a fuller context for multilingual writers who may not share U.S.-centric assumptions of text, claim, coherence, discourse, authorship, or genre. Investigating and developing an individual research question with more nuance allows instructors to combine classroom instruction with individual learning, and to mix academic with social and cultural goals.
4. "Moves" pedagogy emphasizes that most genres are comprised of sets of "moves" that support larger discursive aims as well as smaller linguistic ones. I borrow the concept primarily from research conducted by Connor (2000), Johns (2007), and Swales and Feak (2003), as well as other scholars interested in analyzing the distinct parts of genres for semantic units that carry rhetorical function. A "move" in academic writing refers to any textual action that has a particular communication objective related to the goals of the text itself (e.g., salutation, self-promotion, inquiry, appeal, etc.).
5. Source building was one principal way to allow students the constant language input and language information we knew they needed in order to build rhetorical knowledge. Reusing sources that they selected for different rhetorical tasks also provided students with a discursive repetition that supports topical and lexical fluency (i.e., learning to employ key terms or key phrases with more confidence in each assignment), and learning to re-see the terms on later assignments. Measuring the available English vocabulary of L2 writers is definitional at best, not to mention variant upon the specific rhetorical or linguistic measures that certain testing instruments employ (Biber & Gray, 2013).
6. Hyland (2003) devises a sliding developmental scale that shows how a language learner's attitude toward knowledge affects, and is affected by, various learning approaches and strategies.

Bibliography

Biber, D., & Gray, B. (2013). *Discourse characteristics of writing and speaking task types on the TOEFL IBT® test: A lexico-grammatical analysis.* ETS/TOEFL.
Canagarajah, A. S. (2002a). *A geopolitics of academic writing.* Pittsburgh, PA: University of Pittsburgh Press.

Canagarajah, A. S. (2002b). *Critical academic writing and multilingual students*. Ann Arbor, MI: University of Michigan Press.

Canagarajah, A. S. (2006). Toward a writing pedagogy of shuttling between languages: Learning from multilingual writers. *College English, 68*(6), 588–604.

Canagarajah, A. S. (2010). A rhetoric of shuttling between languages. In Bruce Horner, Min-Zhan Lu, & Paul Kei Matsuda (Eds.), *Cross-language relations in composition* (pp. 158–179). Carbondale, IL: Southern Illinois University Press.

Canagarajah, A. S. (2013). *Translingual practice: Global Englishes and cosmopolitan relations*. London: Routledge.

Connor, U. (2000). *Variation in rhetorical moves in grant proposals of U.S. humanists and scientists*. Text 20, no. 1: 1–28. Retrieved from IUPUI ScholarWorks. http://hdl.handle.net/1805/2663

Cox, M., Jordan, J., Ortmeier-Hooper, C., & Schwartz, G. G. (Eds.) (2010). *Reinventing identities in second language writing* (pp. xv–xxviii). Urbana, IL: National Council of Teachers of English.

Demont-Heinrich, C. (2010). Forum: Linguistically privileged and cursed? American university students and the global hegemony of English. *World Englishes, 29*(2), 281–298.

Ewert, D. E. (2011). ESL curriculum revision: Shifting paradigms for success. *Journal of Basic Writing, 30*(1), 5–33.

Ferris, D. (2009). *Teaching college writing to diverse student populations*. Ann Arbor, MI: University of Michigan Press.

Foster, D. (2006). *Writing with authority: Students' roles as writers in cross-national perspective*. Carbondale: Southern Illinois University Press.

Fraiberg, S. (2010). Composition 2.0: Toward a multilingual and multimodal framework. *College Composition and Communication, 62*(1), 100–126.

Horner, B., Lu, M-Z., Royster, J. J., & Trimbur, J. (2011). Opinion: Language difference in writing: Toward a translingual approach. *College English, 73*(3), 303–321.

Hyland, K. (2003). *Second language writing*. Cambridge: Cambridge University Press.

Johns, A. M. (2007). *Characterizing and teaching genre (An On-going quest)*. Paper delivered at AAAL Conference, April 24, Costa Mesa, CA.

Jordan, J. (2012). *Redesigning composition for multilingual realities*. Urbana, IL: CCCC/NCTE.

Kang, H. (2010). Negotiation of identities in a multilingual setting: Korean generation 1.5 in email writing. In M. Cox, J. Jordan, C. Ortmeier-Hooper, & G. G. Schwartz (Eds.), *Reinventing identities in second language writing* (pp. 296–302). Urbana, IL: National Council of Teachers of English.

Kutz, E. (1986). Between students' language and academic discourse: Interlanguage as middle ground. *College English, 48*(4), 385–396.

Leki, I. (1992). Building expertise through sequenced writing assignments. *TESOL Journal, 1*(2), 19–23.

Matsuda, A., & Matsuda, P. K. (2010). World Englishes and the teaching of writing. *TESOL Quarterly, 44*(2), 369–374.

Matsuda, P. K. (2014). The lure of translingual writing. *PMLA, 129*(3), 478–483.

Molina, C. (2011). Curricular insights into translingualism as a communicative competence. *Journal of Language Teaching & Research, 2*(6), 1244–1251.

Ortega, L., & Carson, J. (2010). Multicompetence, social context, and L2 writing research praxis. In T. Silva & P. Matsuda (Eds.), *Practicing theory in second language writing* (pp. 48–71). West Lafayette, IN: Parlor Press.

Ortmeier-Hooper, C. (2008). English may be my second language, but I'm not 'ESL'. *College Composition and Communication, 59*(3), 389–419.

Ortmeier-Hooper, C. (2010). The shifting nature of identity: Social identity, L2 writers, and high school. In M. Cox, J. Jordan, C. Ortmeier-Hooper, & G. G. Schwartz (Eds.), *Reinventing identities in second language writing* (pp. 5–28). Urbana, IL: National Council of Teachers of English.

Oullette, M. (2008). Weaving strands of writer identity: Self as author and NNES "plagiarist". *Journal of Second Language Writing, 17,* 255–273.

Pedersen, A.-M. (2010). Negotiating cultural identities through language: Academic English in Jordan. *College Composition and Communication, 62*(2), 283–310.

Rhee, E. H. (2010). Collision and negotiation of my identities in the TESOL graduate program. In M. Cox, J. Jordan, C. Ortmeier-Hooper, & G. G. Schwartz (Eds.), *Reinventing identities in second language writing* (pp. 96–103). Urbana, IL: National Council of Teachers of English.

Shuck, G. (2010). Language identity, agency, and context: The shifting meanings of multilingual. In M. Cox, J. Jordan, C. Ortmeier-Hooper, & G. G. Schwartz (Eds.), *Reinventing identities in second language writing* (pp. 117–138). Urbana, IL: National Council of Teachers of English.

Spack, Ruth. (1997). Forum: The rhetorical construction of multilingual students. *TESOL Quarterly, 31*(4), 765–774.

Swales, J. (1981). *Aspects of article introductions.* Birmingham, UK: University of Aston, Language Studies Unit.

Swales, J. (1990). *Genre analysis.* Cambridge: Cambridge University Press.

Swales, J., & Feak, C. B. (2003). *Academic writing for graduate students: Essential tasks and skills* (2nd ed.). Ann Arbor: University of Michigan Press/ELT.

Tardy, C. M. (2011). Enacting and transforming local language policies. *College Composition and Communication, 62*(4), 634–661.

Tardy, C. & Swales, J. (2008). Form, text organization, genre, coherence, and cohesion. In C. Bazerman (Ed.), *Handbook of research on writing: History, society, school, individual, text* (pp. 565-581). New York, NY: Lawrence Erlbaum.

University-wide enrollment trends. *iStart.* Retrieved on May 1, 2015, from https://istart. iu.edu/dashboard/index.cfm?graph=studentEnrollmentTrends&CFID=30414&CFTO KEN=26899305&isLoaded=yes

Zawacki, T. M., & Cox, M., (Eds.) (2014). *WAC and second-language writers: Research towards linguistically and culturally inclusive programs and practices.* Perspectives on Writing. Fort Collins, Colorado: The WAC Clearinghouse and Parlor Press. Retrieved from http://wac.colostate.edu/books/l2/

16

INTERNATIONALIZATION AND THE PLACE OF RESIDENT ML STUDENTS

Identifying Points of Leverage and Advocacy

Christina Ortmeier-Hooper, Dana Ferris, Richard Lizotte, Patricia Portanova, and Margi Wald

> *Most U.S. border universities allow only officially classified international students to enroll in ESL courses, while students who have progressed through the US school system must enroll in "mainstream" writing courses, regardless of their English language abilities or rhetorical and cultural backgrounds.*
>
> (Brunk-Chavez et al., 2015)

> *Composition journals and conferences have increasingly embraced international issues. . . . Yet, there are far fewer discussions of how these issues relate to broader institutional missions and strategies.*
>
> (Tardy, 2015, p. 259)

Resident multilingual students are often difficult to track or identify when they enter college; they do not arrive to campus indicating previous participation in ELL or bilingual programs. In contrast to international students who are tracked through TOEFL scores, visas, and international student counts, SAT scores do not reveal multilingual writers. Some resident students are happy to be freed from labels like ELL (Ortmeier-Hooper, 2008). But the lack of labels can also lead to a lack of accountability (by institutions and writing programs) and a lack of funding for support and services. It can also steer students who may still struggle with writing in a second or third language away from effective academic support. Invisibility can propagate issues of access, academic achievement, and inequity for resident multilingual students.

As teachers and administrators, we are alarmed by the low numbers of English language learners reaching higher education, as well as their attrition rates.

Adler-Kassner (2008) reminds us that we need "to be aware of the ideologies associated with the frames currently shaping discussions about education (and writing)" (p. 88). In encouraging WPAs to take activist stances, Adler-Kassner asks: "What stories do we want to change?" She notes that we often have more power to shape conversations on our campuses than we realize. We agree. In this chapter, writing teachers and administrators—working at community colleges and state universities—consider how their institutions frame forays into internationalization. Specifically, we ask: How do internationalization trends shape our programs, our interests, and the place of resident multilingual writers on campus?

Here, we share vignettes on institutional visions, resources, and programs that impact the visibility and success of resident multilingual students on our campuses. These stories of alliances and points of leverage show attempts to better serve resident multilingual writers, as well as where our institutions still fall short. The vignettes hold as many questions as answers, and we hope that these gaps provide impetus for further reflection, conversations, and research.

Five-Year Roller Coaster: Our Expendable, Marginalized, Strategic(?) Resident Multilinguals at UC Davis

Dana Ferris

In the spring of 2010, our campus was in the throes of a recession-fueled budget crisis, and one of the programs they looked to cut was the excellent, decades-old ESL writing program, then housed in the Linguistics Department, which for years had served resident multilingual undergraduates who needed extra language and writing support. Thanks to the efforts of several ESL professionals and the intervention of the university chancellor, the ESL program barely escaped the ax that year. Within a year, the conversation had abruptly changed. Like many other large state universities around the United States, UCD had made the decision to quickly and dramatically increase its recruitment and admission of international undergraduates as a way to boost revenue and address budget challenges. It was immediately apparent to those of us working directly with multilingual students that there was both a challenge and an opportunity before us.

The challenge, of course, was and is to suddenly adjust (and quickly expand) a program that for decades had focused almost exclusively on the needs of resident multilingual students to one that served a much more mixed population of resident and international students. (In 2010, there were about 50 new international freshmen who needed testing and ESL support courses. For fall 2015, we are placing nearly 1,000.) The instructors were not prepared for this transition, and the placement mechanisms and curriculum that had been working well needed some major reconsideration. In 2013, a very rapid decision was made to move the ESL classes to the University Writing Program and put them under my direction. Over the past two years, the instructors and I have raced through the process of creating a new placement process and redesigning the curriculum from the ground up.

We have struggled and are still grappling with the complexity of the drasti-cally changed student population. Practically overnight, resident multilingual students went from being the vast majority in our classes to a small minority. The teachers do find that some (not all) of their needs are different from those of the now-majority international population and are not entirely sure how to support all of the students in the same classroom. We are still pondering whether some separate sections of our classes for resident, U.S.-educated multilinguals might be appropriate.

Despite the challenges, the dramatic expansion in international student admis-sions has provided greater opportunities to serve *all* multilingual students on our campus. The administration has been willing to invest significant resources into our program—far more than the shoestring that the Linguistics Department was forced to operate on as recently as five years ago. Further, UCD has recently been designated a Hispanic-Serving Institution, and the responsibilities and resources that accompany this status will provide an additional argument for continuing to support our large and vibrant resident multilingual population.

Five years ago, UCD was ready to accept the financially driven and even Darwin-istic argument that resident multilinguals didn't need (or deserve) any extra campus support during their undergraduate studies. Now, due to the (also financially driven) initiative to quickly expand the international student population, language and writing support for multilingual students—both resident and international—is the strongest it has ever been in the history of our campus. Though the changes and the complexity have led to *some* growing pains, we are working through the challenges, and we are definitely better off than we were in 2010.

Acceleration, Integration, and Motivation

Richard Lizotte and Patricia Portanova

> i fell more comfortable reading and writing in Spanish . . . when i came to this country I fell that it was the worst thing that could happen to me because i don't know a perfect English and i think everyone would make fun about me.

This quote, from a student enrolled in a non-credit-bearing course entitled Read-ing, Writing, and Reasoning, reflects the anxieties that many of our students feel as they navigate postsecondary education while continuing to learn English. As both a community college with an urban campus in Lawrence, Massachusetts, and the only federally recognized Hispanic-Serving Institution in the state of Massachusetts, a significant portion of our student population at Northern Essex Community College includes resident multilingual student writers. Our Hispanic population has increased from 23% in the fall of 2008 to 37% in the fall of 2015 and, just recently, Northern Essex signed a historic articulation and transfer agree-ment with the public university system of the Dominican Republic, which may result in a greater influx of international, non-resident multilingual students.

Like many community colleges, support for multilingual student writers is shared between departments. English for Speakers of Other Languages (ESOL) and developmental reading and writing courses are housed in the Department of Academic Preparation, while composition courses are overseen by the English Department. Eight years ago, the Writing and Reading Alignment Team (WRAT) was created to increase collaboration between departments, resulting in stronger alignment among ESOL, developmental writing, and composition faculty.

Our multilingual students bring unique perspectives and experiences to the classroom, but working with this population is not without challenges. Some resident multilingual students struggle to see themselves as college students. Many ESOL and first-year writing courses are taught largely by adjunct faculty, making it difficult to create professional development opportunities to ensure curricular changes are enacted in the classroom. It is also difficult to track student success once they leave ESOL courses. Many students at the college avoid first-year writing courses in the first three years after demonstrating eligibility to take the course, and many English language learners (ELLs) are in this group.

However, there is a great deal of institutional support for multilingual students—a student success center to which students may be referred for personal and academic counseling, and tutorial labs where they can get help with reading and writing. ESOL instructors collectively norm and evaluate the writing and listening/speaking abilities of each other's students to assure a fair assessment. Students with college-level abilities in reading, writing, and critical thinking are placed in an accelerated learning program (ALP) in which English skills are strengthened in a separate course at the same time as English Composition I skills are learned. Developmental writing and reading courses also have accelerated courses that can reduce time to degree further for ELLs.

As an institution, our current assessment projects are creating opportunities for faculty across the curriculum to understand the unique challenges of language learners. A recent project by the Writing and Reading Alignment Team evaluated the use of sources by ELL, developmental, and English Composition I students to gauge the development of how well they research and integrate sources into their writing. Faculty members in the Academic ESOL Curriculum have developed a rubric based partly on the rubrics for developmental writing and English Composition I to judge ELL readiness for college-level writing. They are currently studying whether the use of this rubric has resulted in greater success for ELL students in other courses at the college, as well as looking at the question of how to make instruction in English grammar and mechanics more efficient and effective by determining which content needs the greatest focus and how this content needs to be taught.

We realize that our attempts at integration and acceleration of instruction will fail to be successful unless we attend to increasing the motivation of students, which for millennial and ELL students requires personalization of instruction in the classroom and embedding instruction in a plan for their future. Such personalization, we hope, supports and encourages students who feel less comfortable reading in English and worry about speaking "perfect English."

Lost and Found—and Lost Again? Long-Term Immigrant Students in the Age of the International Student Influx

Margi Wald

When I moved from Tennessee to California in the late 1990s, I had worked with—and had been trained to work with—international students only. While I had become increasingly aware of the immigrant populations in Tennessee, my professional life changed once I joined a community of scholars and teachers serving, studying, and sharing best teaching practices for long-term immigrant college students. We wanted to learn more about the strengths of and challenges faced by this diverse group of students we encountered in first-year composition classrooms. We also worked with our non-ESL colleagues to help them understand these strengths and needs—to help them understand the unique qualities of students betwixt and between cultures, languages, and the college classifications of developmental, ESL, and "regular" composition.

Jump ahead 10 years. Economic recession and declining contributions of the state government, at least in California, led to a drastic change in demographics (see Ferris, this chapter). For years, in first-year composition classrooms on public university campuses like mine, the international ESL freshman population had been so small that no separate first-year ESL composition track existed. Recently, however, these classrooms have been, in the words of some instructors, "flooded" with ESL students. To be fair to my colleagues, they did not sign on to teach international ESL composition, and these compositionists do not necessarily have ESL training. Many have spent years working with multilingual writers, and with TESL-trained colleagues like me to serve these writers, but the linguistic needs of the international students currently in their classes can differ significantly from the population instructors now feel "ready" to serve. Their attention and professional development discussions have been redirected from serving long-term immigrants (and their instructors) to serving recent arrival ESL students in FYC and in pre-FYC courses.

One concern, among many, is that the group we worked so hard to support, to make visible, will once again become invisible, their potential contributions and challenges overshadowed by instructors' attempts to serve international students. While all this has been said before, it is worth repeating here, and now:

- As SLW specialists, we need to keep this group in the foreground when planning lessons, crafting syllabi, and choosing texts—and help our L1 colleagues to do the same.
- We need to remind our SLW colleagues to continue to engage in research and curricular development with this group in mind. (It is interesting to note that, at a recent symposium on second language academic writing, there were no sessions focusing on resident multilingual writers despite the number of students fitting this category that live in the host country.)

- Given the mixed populations in our developmental and first-year composition classes, we need to focus on aspects of academic language instruction that both international and resident multilingual writers can benefit from. And we need to remember to present this instruction in perhaps more traditional ways for international students but also in inductive, metalanguage-free ways that speak to long-term immigrants.

- We must not forego oral-into-written practice in the classroom. Such activities can be difficult for international students but, if not in our small classes, where will international students get practice in a safe environment? And it is this type of practice that truly bolsters many resident multilingual students' writing development.

- Finally, in class, we need to remember to view resident multilingual student writers as assets, as experts, as resources given their highly developed repertoire of oral language; their knowledge of American culture and the U.S. educational system; and their awareness of socioeconomic, ethnic, and linguistic diversity within the United States—all items that international students want to learn more about.

Recently, the pendulum has swung back to a focus on international ESL students in first-year and developmental composition. But the first mission of public universities like the one I work in is to serve our resident students, many of whom in my state are multilingual. Let's not lose sight of them.

Combatting Silos: Making Resident Multilinguals Visible

Christina Ortmeier-Hooper

Across my campus, discourse on internationalization and transnationalism abounds. But our resident multilingual students are rarely mentioned. As the state's flagship institution, the University of New Hampshire includes this tenet in its 2010 strategic plan: to pursue "expanded global reach through foreign student enrollments, study-abroad programs, faculty exchanges, visiting scholars, and arts and cultural programs." The goal was envisioned on two fronts: (1) more international students, and (2) a more internationalized curriculum, more study abroad opportunities, and more diverse faculty recruitment. UNH aims to increase international students to over 12% by 2020. Although New Hampshire is often seen as rural and homogenous, the last 20 years have brought increasing numbers of linguistically and culturally diverse residents to the state. Cities and towns serve as refugee resettlement communities and secondary migration hotspots for Latino families and students originally from the Dominican Republic, Mexico, and countries in Central America. Some cities have resident multilingual populations that represent over 60 languages. Yet these student continue to be less visible on our campus despite efforts toward more global knowledge and diversity. As the WPA for our first-year writing program, I wondered how UNH's strategic plans, program statements, and organizational structures might be contributing to the "invisibility" of resident multilinguals on the campus.

In many ways, campus resources are set up for division. International students are seen as part of the internationalization plan, but resident multilingual students are more defined by diversity, inclusion, and multiculturalism. Institutional plans for resident multilingual students fall predominantly under UNH's target for "inclusive excellence," which is represented by the Community, Equity, and Diversity Office and far removed from international student affairs. These divisions mean that resources and funding for the resident and international multilingual students are distinct and provided by different programs. There is little overlap. Programs and resources for inclusion and multicultural students include the Connect program for minority, first-generation college students, the federally funded Upward Bound program, and the Office of Multicultural Student Affairs (OMSA). International students are assisted by the international program office, the ESL Institute, and the for-profit recruitment program. The programs assisting international students have recently grown exponentially, hiring scores of full-time staff members. In contrast, programs aiding resident multilingual students have faced state and federal budget cuts and are staffed by two to five assistants and a few undergraduate tutors. More subtly, programs focused on international students highlight multilingualism and transnational identities as strengths and resources, while discourse on resident students highlights their first-generation college status and financial need. Their multilingualism is rarely mentioned.

The differences in resources are troubling, and they are reflective of trends at other institutions as well. I believe, however, that there are also opportunities for WPAs to actively insert immigrant and resident bilingual students into the more dominant internationalization interests and discussions. At my institution, this has led me to think about the points of leverage, provided by goals of internationalization, that might be extended to resident multilingual students. Thus far, these points of leverage include:

- *Renewed interest in learning how to better teach multilingual writers.* International students have led faculty to be more open to professional development for their work with multilingual writers, whatever their backgrounds.
- *New publication opportunities for multilingual students.* ESL instructors started a journal, *International Voices*, dedicated to the voices of multilingual students. Further, there are concerted efforts to include multilingual writers in the annual FYC publication of student writing.
- *Recruitment of multilingual tutors.* Our writing center recruits U.S. resident multilingual tutors, recognizing the range of linguistic and rhetorical competencies that these tutors bring to the center as border-crossers and expert cross-language negotiators.
- *More upper-level, multilingual-friendly, culturally responsive writing courses.* There is demand (and institutional support) for upper-level, multilingual-friendly writing courses. We now offer themed composition courses on writing for global audiences, cross-cultural storytelling, and transnationalism that attract students from a variety of linguistic backgrounds.

But there is still more work to be done. From my vantage point, I see a drop-off in the number of resident ML students pursuing ESL support or working with ESL-trained staff. Multilingual sections of FYC have become predominantly the domain of only international students. The hiring of a large ESL staff has brought a higher level of expertise to our campus, but it has also led to complacency, since "the ESL teachers will handle it." Institutional silos continue to exist, due in part to how strategic plans outline and allocate resources. Stakeholders working with the different groups of multilingual students—resident and international—do not meet or see one another as potential allies. As the director of composition, I am a common point of contact for many stakeholders, because all students participate in the first-year writing program. As such, I've started using my position to connect these resources and individuals. We've established summer sections of FYC for Upward Bound students and hired teachers with L2 training. I am integrating the multicultural and first-generation programs more visibly into our training for FYC and ESL staff and TAs. The goal is to build long-term alliances, visibility, and accessible support for *all* of our multilingual, transnational students—not just the ones studying from abroad.

These are not new struggles; I have been making similar arguments about the visibility of resident multilinguals for over a decade. I draw inspiration and energy from my ongoing research with immigrant teenagers in local schools. When these teens tell me about their college ambitions and aspirations for the future, they remind me why this kind of critical engagement at the college level needs to continue. As my colleagues in this chapter and I all contend, keeping the voices and situations of linguistically diverse students—from our own states and regions—on the radar screens of colleagues and administrators is one way that writing teachers and program administrators can start to change the story of resident multilinguals in higher education.

Bibliography

Adler-Kassner, L. (2008). *The Activist WPA: Changing Stories about Writing and Writers.* Logan: Utah State University Press.

Brunk-Chavez, B., Mangelsdorf, K., Wojahn, P., Urzua-Beltran, A., Montoya, O., Thatcher, B., & Valentine, K. (2015). Exploring the contexts of US–Mexican border writing programs. In D. S. Martins (Ed.), *Transnational Writing Program Administration* (pp. 138–160). Boulder: University Press of Colorado.

Ortmeier-Hooper, C. (2008). English may be my second language, but I'm not 'ESL'. *College Composition and Communication, 59*(3), 389–419.

Tardy, C. M. (2015). Discourses of internationalization and diversity in US universities and writing programs. In D. S. Martins (Ed.), *Transnational Writing Program Administration* (pp. 243–262). Boulder: University Press of Colorado.

CONTRIBUTORS

Mais Al-Khateeb is a PhD student in the Rhetoric Professional Communication program at New Mexico State University and currently working as a writing program coordinator in the English Department. She has taught first-year composition, writing in the humanities and social sciences, and English for multilingual learners. Her research interests include transnational feminist rhetorics, critical body studies, queer/disability rhetorics, theories of performativity and identity, and multilingual writing.

Beth Brunk-Chavez is the Interim Dean of Extended University at the University of Texas at El Paso. She is also an Associate Professor of Rhetoric and Writing Studies and directed the First-Year Composition program for five years. Brunk-Chavez has research interests in teaching with technology, writing with technology, and writing program administration. In 2013, she was named to the University of Texas System Academy of Distinguished Teachers.

Colin Charlton is an Associate Professor of Rhetoric, Composition, and Literacy Studies at the University of Texas Rio Grande Valley. His areas of interest include the intersections of rhetoric, technology, and invention; writing program administration; high school-college transitions; and the integration of student voices into writing studies. He has published in *Computers and Composition*, is co-author of *GenAdmin: Theorizing Writing Program Administration in the 21st Century* (Parlor Press, CWPA 2012 book of the year), and has recently developed an iBook, *College Transitions: Integrated Reading, Inquiry, and Writing*.

Ruhma Choudhury is an Associate Professor in the Department of Education and Language Acquisition at LaGuardia Community College, the City University of

New York. Her research interests include language policy, teacher education, and critical approaches to language learning. Her most recent publication "Raising Bilingual and Bicultural Bangladeshi-American Children in New York City: Perspectives from Educators and parents in a Bengali Community Program" appeared in *Bilingual Community Education and Multilingualism: Beyond Heritage Languages in a Global City.*

Laurie Churchill has taught a range of writing and literature courses for the English Department at NMSU. Prior to joining the department in Fall 2010, she worked for the office of the Vice President for Research assisting faculty with grant proposal development, contributed to the accreditation reports for the university (2007–2008) and the College of Education (2008–2010), and served as Project Coordinator and Director for a National Science Foundation grant (2001–2007). Her publications include *Women Writing Latin: From Roman Antiquity to Early Modern Europe* (Routledge, 2002).

Genevieve García de Müeller is an Assistant Professor at the University of Texas Rio Grande Valley. Her work focuses on civil rights rhetoric and multilingual composition. She has held positions on the UNM Writing Across Communities Alliance, the Council for Writing Program Administrators Diversity Task Force, and is the founder and chair of the CWPA People of Color Caucus.

Luciana C. de Oliveira is an Associate Professor in the Department of Teaching and Learning in the School of Education and Human Development at the University of Miami, Florida. Her research focuses on issues related to teaching English language learners (ELLs) at the K–12 level, including the role of language in learning the content areas and teacher education, advocacy, and social justice. Her work has appeared in *Teachers College Record, Journal of Teacher Education, TESOL Journal, Journal of Second Language Writing*, among others. She is an elected board member for the TESOL International Association (2013–2016).

Dana Ferris is a Professor in the University Writing Program at the University of California at Davis. She directs a large writing program for multilingual undergraduates, including both international and resident multilingual students. Her research has focused on response to student writing, error correction, and understanding the needs of L2 writers and readers, especially in postsecondary contexts. She is the author or co-author of eight books and over 50 articles or chapters, and she is the editor-in-chief of the new *Journal of Response to Writing.*

Cathilia M. Flores is currently pursuing a doctorate in Rhetoric and Professional Communication at New Mexico State University. Her research focuses on the relationship between writing-to-learn strategies and the cognitive factors involved in successful learning. As a doctoral student, she has taught first-year and scientific

writing courses and participated on a research team examining factors that affect student performance. Flores is also a professional program evaluator and is currently teaching public health program evaluation at NMSU.

Leigh Garrison-Fletcher is an Assistant Professor of ESL and Linguistics in the Department of Education and Language Acquisition at LaGuardia Community College, the City University of New York. She received her PhD in Linguistics from the Graduate Center, the City University of New York, where she focused on second language acquisition. Her research interests include the role of the native language in second language learning, the acquisition of second language literacy, and the assessment of bilingual students.

Betsy Gilliland is an Assistant Professor in the Department of Second Language Studies at the University of Hawai'i, Manoa. Her research addresses second language, adolescent, and academic literacies of high school students and their teachers. Betsy co-authored a book (published in 2016) on assessment and accountability for secondary-level English learners in the Principles in Practice series published by NCTE. She has presented at AERA, AAAL, CCCC, TESOL, and the Symposium on Second Language Writing.

Tarez Samra Graban is an Assistant Professor of English at Florida State University. From 2002 to 2007, she taught academic writing and oral English proficiency to international graduate students at Purdue University. From 2007 to 2012, she coordinated Multilingual FYC at Indiana University, training TAs and forming partnerships with Second Language Studies, English Language Instruction, university libraries, and the campus writing center. She has presented on this work at the MLA, CCCC, and IWAC conferences.

Kimberly Harrison is a Professor of English and Director of the Writing and Rhetoric and Writing Across the Curriculum programs at Florida International University, a Hispanic-serving institution in Miami that ranks first in the nation for awarding bachelor's and master's degrees to Hispanic students. Her research interests are in women's rhetoric and in writing program administration. Her most recent book is *The Rhetoric of Rebel Women: Civil War Diaries and Confederate Persuasion* (SIUP, Studies in Rhetorics and Feminisms, 2013).

Sarah Henderson Lee is an Assistant Professor of English at Minnesota State University, Mankato, where she teaches in the MA TESL program and supervises graduate teaching assistants. Her teaching and research interest areas include second language literacy, language socialization, world Englishes, critical pedagogy, and TESL teacher education. Most recently she has co-edited a special issue of *TESOL Journal* titled *Critical Perspectives on World Englishes* and presented her work at AAAL, SSLW, and TESOL.

Karen Holt is the former Head of Reference and Instructional Services at the University of Texas–Pan American. Her research interests include information literacy, technology, and entrepreneurship in libraries. She has presented on these topics at the International Federation of Library Associations Camp in Finland and the World Library and Information Congress in France as well as at the annual meeting of the Texas Library Association. Karen was selected as an Emerging Leader by the American Library Association in 2012 for her early-career contributions to the library profession.

Amanda K. Kibler is an Assistant Professor of English Education at the University of Virginia's Curry School of Education. Her research interests include adolescent second language writing, bilingualism, ethnography, discourse analysis, and the impact of standards-based reform on ethno-linguistically diverse populations. Her work has been published in *Modern Language Journal, TESOL Quarterly, Linguistics and Education*, and the *Journal of Second Language Writing*, among others.

Julia Kiernan is an Assistant Professor at Kettering University. Her scholarship is intimately tied to her teaching experiences, and is seated in action research. Through focusing on transnational experiences, she strives to create learning spaces where students are encouraged to recognize the globalization of audience and the range of cultures and languages with which writing must be able to engage. Julia's current research is centralized within these ideologies, and considers topics of translation, translingualism, and technical writing.

Richard Lizotte is Professor of English as a Second Language at Northern Essex Community College where he teaches courses in reading, writing, and listening/speaking to English Language Learners. His research interests focus on tailoring modes of instruction for bilingual and monolingual English learners. He has presented his research at TESOL conferences and at the Conference for Innovation in the Community College. He has been an accreditor for the national accreditation agency for ESL programs and was elected to be a commissioner for this agency for the 2016–2018 term.

Kate Mangelsdorf has directed a number of writing programs at the University of Texas at El Paso (UTEP), including First-Year Composition and the University Writing Center. Her research has focused in large part on multilingual writers, including classroom-based research on peer reviews and more theoretical pieces on language ideologies. Currently she directs the Rhetoric and Writing Studies and English Education programs at UTEP.

Randall W. Monty is an Assistant Professor of Rhetoric, Composition, and Literacy Studies at the University of Texas Rio Grande Valley. His scholarly interests include writing center studies, multimodal composition, border studies, and

Critical Discourse Studies. His book *The Writing Center as Cultural and Interdisci-plinary Contact Zone* is forthcoming from Palgrave Macmillan. In the meantime, he can often be found collaborating with his students in Technical Writing and Rhetoric and Composition classes.

Christina Ortmeier-Hooper is an Associate Professor and Director of Composi-tion at the University of New Hampshire. Her research areas include writing stud-ies, school-university collaborations, writing teacher education, and immigrant adolescent literacy. Christina has edited three previous collections on second lan-guage writing, including *Reinventing Identities in Second Language Writing* (NCTE Press, 2010 with Michelle Cox, Jay Jordan, and Gwen Gray Schwartz). Her work has also been published in *English Journal, TESOL Journal*, the *Journal of Second Language Writing*, and *College Composition and Communication*. Her monograph *The ELL Writer: Moving Beyond Basics in the Secondary Classroom* (Teachers College Press, 2013) documents the writing experiences of adolescent second-language students in US schools.

Patricia Portanova is Assistant Professor of English at Northern Essex Commu-nity College where she teaches courses in writing and communication. She has research interests in cognition and writing, civic engagement, multilingual writ-ing, and cross-cultural communication. She has presented her research at CCCC, NCTE, and IWCA. She has previously served as chair of the Northeast Writing Across the Curriculum Consortium and currently co-chairs the CCCC Cogni-tion and Writing Special Interest Group.

Todd Ruecker is an Assistant Professor of English at the University of New Mexico. His work focuses on the transitions of multilingual writers from high school to college. He has published articles in a variety of journals, including *TESOL Quarterly, College Composition and Communication, Journal of Hispanic Higher Education, Critical Inquiry in Language Studies*, and *Writing Program Administration*. He recently published his first book, *Transiciones: Latina and Latino Students Writing in High School and College*.

Karen R. Tellez-Trujillo is a PhD student in the English Department at New Mexico State University. She joined her cohort at NMSU in 2014 after earning a Bachelor of Arts with honors in Rhetoric and Professional Communication, a Bachelor of Arts in Women's Studies, and a Master of Arts in English with an emphasis in Rhetoric, Digital Media, and Professional Communication from NMSU. She is associated with the National Writing Project as a fellow of the Borderlands Writing Project and Writing Across the Curriculum at New Mexico State University.

Margi Wald is a lecturer and Director of the Summer ESL program in UC Berkeley's College Writing Programs and a co-editor of *The CATESOL Journal*

(with Mark Roberge). Publications include *Exploring Options in Academic Writing* (with Jan Frodesen, Michigan ELT) and *Teaching U.S.-Educated Multilingual Writers* (with Mark Roberge and Kay Losey, Michigan ELT). Her scholarly interests include corpus-based materials development and academic literacy development among immigrant and international students.

Shauna Wight is an Assistant Professor of English at Southeast Missouri State University, where she teaches courses in English education, composition, and TESOL. Her research interests focus on programs and initiatives that help underrepresented students and their teachers bridge high school and college literacies.

Jennifer Shade Wilson is the Director of the Center for Written, Oral, and Visual Communication (CWOVC) at Rice University. She holds a PhD in second language literacy from OISE/University of Toronto, as well as an MA in applied linguistics and a BA in English literature. Jennifer has worked in the field of literacy education for more than 20 years, teaching university-level academic writing, high school English, and community-based ESL. Her research interests include adolescent literacy, college composition, and second-language writing.

Patti Wojahn recently concluded her seventh year as Writing Program Administrator (WPA) at New Mexico State University, where she works in the Rhetoric and Professional Communication program. As WPA, she explored characteristics of successful and less successful students in composition courses; students' access to computers and the internet within the local, impoverished area; first-year students' research practices; as well as language preferences and practices among first-year students.

INDEX

Page numbers in italics indicate figures and tables.

academic purposes, writing) 17, 21, 70
academic tracking 9; divisions 123; usage 118
academic writing: LM access 118; practices 29, 59
accelerated learning program (ALP) 232
administration, reimagining 169
adolescent literacy 66–7
advocacy, points (identification) 229
allophone Canadian, designation 160
annual yearly progress (AYP) 7
assignment language, vocabulary conversion 223
assimilationist approach 195–6
at-risk high school students: literacy development (study) 65–6; P2E development 67

basic skills, requirement 143, 178
Benchmark Assignments (BAs), usage 24–5, 29
Bengali LENS test *144*, 152–3
Bengali-speaking ML writers, transition 143–4
bilingual, bilingualism: bilingual-certified teachers, shortage 84; Bilingual Education Act (1968) 37; bilingual literacy sponsors 106; bilingual students, ghetto-ization 9; bilingual texts, usage (writing sponsor role) 107–8; biliteracies: continua, media (scripts) 58–9; defining

51; biliterate context continua 55; macro power-weighted end 54; English proficiency, emphasis 8; French-English bilingualism 158
Brandt, Deborah 95, 99, 100, 101, 112, 113, 114, 118

Camino a La Universidad (Lumina Foundation report) 131
Canada: contexts, language negotiation 163–4; government legislation, impact 159; language, fluidity 163–4; language policy 160–3; linguistic diversity, addressing 162; multicultural policy 161; postsecondary education, multilingualism (sequestration) 164–5; regional linguistic boundaries 162; writing studies, writing-in-the-disciplines approach 158–9
Canadian Multiculturalism Act 159, 160; policy 163–4, 166; provincial policies 161–2
Canadian postsecondary settings, ML education (advancing) 157; discussion/recommendations 166; methodology 159–60
Canagarajah, A. Suresh 58, 159, 173, 18, 191, 200, 219–20, 223, 225
CCCC Statement on Second Language Writers and Writing 128, 190

Census Bureau data 144; Census Canada data, usage 159; Current Population Survey (CPS) data 130; city/town demographics 7

classrooms: class size, impact 7

College Assistance Migrant Program (CAMP), usage 6

college composition: college-bound courses/tracks, transition 73–4; college composition, emphases 30–1; college English, curricular discontinuities 21; college writing classes, English only/French only expectations 158; course content, changes 197–8; course design, changes 194–6; discontinuities 32; technologies, access 177, 178; textbooks, access 177–8

Common Core State Standards (CCSS) 2, 36; argument text 39–41; CCSS focus 43–4; details 41; development, criteria 38; development, impact 8; ELA usage 39; expectation 42; genres, developmental trajectory/learner pathway 45; national curriculum establishment, intention (absence) 38; NCLB, relationship 18; student outcomes 41–2; text types 39–41; writing usage 39–42

Communities of Practice (CoP): application 119–20; classroom CoPs, focus 127; CoP framework 118; shared practices 127

community college: advantages 11; Bengali-speaking ML writers transition 143–4; Bengali literacy assessment 146–7; context 146; curriculum 147–9English as a second language (ESL) exit exam 151–2; English literacy measures 147; Hispanic-serving institution, 231–2; intervention findings 151–3; Literacy Evaluation for Newcomer Students (LENS) 146–7, 231–2

contact zone 58, 218

context of biliteracy (COB) model, power relations 52

curriculum: community college, Bengali-speaking ML writers (transition) 147–8; discontinuities 9; everyday curriculum 205, 211–12; ideologies, conflict 24–6; large-scale curricular decisions, district level occurrence 32–3; narrowing 9; paradigm, embracing 216; reimagining 169; writing across 55–6

Deferred Action for Childhood Arrivals (DACA) 130; IYJL guide 138; qualification, undocumented person requirements 132

desegregation, impact 117

Development Relief and Education of Alien Minors (DREAM) Act 96, 110; activist websites, genres (usage) 135; historical background 131–3; proposal 131–2; renaming 132; state-level DREAM Act 112; undocumented immigrants (U.S. context) 131–3

difference-as-deficit view 191

difference-as-resource perspective 191

difference, generative concept 225

discourse: analysis (Lamb) 134; levels, impact 23–4; limitation 56; modes 42–3; process discourse 27; skills discourse 25; student-created discourses, analysis 204

dissonance, negotiation 218

Development Relief and Education of Alien Minors (DREAM) Act activists: actions 133; analysis, three-tier system 133; assistance 133; characteristics 133; digital resources/genres, analysis 135–8; migrant calls 136–8; migrant guides 138; migrant narratives 135–6; online resources, rhetorical power 130; strategies 133; study/methods 133–5; websites/online resources 133–4; writing strategies 130–1

ear learner concept 196–7

ecological model 86–7

Embedded Librarian initiative, 208–9

English as a second language (ESL): credit-bearing courses, ESL courses (bridge) 145; curricular discontinuities 21; exit exam 151–2; LGCC ESL Program 146; re-becoming, stigma 102; writing curricula, discontinuities 21

English for Speakers of Other Languages (ESOL) 232

English language arts (ELA) 21; Common Core State Standards, impact 39; curricula, consideration 24–5; writing curricula, discontinuities 21

English language learners (ELLs) 5; assimilationist approach 195–6; classes, classification, increase 82; classroom, dependency (creation) 58; classroom, safe space/ghetto 57–8; definitions, acknowledgment (failure) 7; invisibility 9;

rural/small-town high school examples
82; student costs, support 85; students,
literacy learning experiences 86;
writing instruction/assessment, CCSS
implications 18, 36
English language learning processes
196–7
English literacy measures (Bengali-
speaking ML writers) 147
English-medium university, student
biliteracy (study) 164–5
English only: English only/French
only expectations, 158; writing
expectations 158
English writing, support (solicitation) 106
explanatory text 39–40
eye learner concept 196–7

faculty development 192–3; assessment
analysis/discussion 194–8; assessment
data 193–4; attitude/awareness, changes
196–7; course content, changes 197–8;
course design, changes 194–6; daily basic
practice, changes 194–6; faculty students,
writing/rhetoric class perspective
(encouragement) 200; L2 specialists,
writing/rhetoric specialists, foreground
collaboration 199; online training
materials, adjunct faculty response 195;
online training module, adjunct faculty
response 194; part-time faculty, training
limitations (recognition) 199;
re-envisioning 189; reimagining 169
faculty space (creation), ideas/instructional
materials (sharing) 199–200
familismo (value) 10
Ferris, Dana 170, 173, 184, 192, 195, 196,
217, 222, 229, 230, 233
financial sponsorship, public sources 104
first language, English (absence) 173; other
language usage rates *176*
first language students: reading, differences
178–9; writing, challenges 179
First Nations, language 160
first-year composition (FYC): academic
behaviors 179–80; courses, ESL students
(participation) 233; eligibility 217;
linguistic identification 216; multilingual
section, example 31; resident ML
students, presence 169
first-year writing: class reading assignment,
part-time faculty member perspective
195; enrollment data, analysis 85–6;

faculty students, writing/rhetoric class
perspective (encouragement) 200
first-year writing (Hispanic-serving
university) 189; assessment analysis/
discussion 194–8; assessment data
193–4; attitude/awareness, changes
196–7; course content, changes 197–8;
course design, changes 194–6; daily
basic practice, changes 194–6; faculty
development 192–3; goals 192; ideas/
instructional materials, faculty sharing
199–200; L2 specialists, writing/rhetoric
specialists, foreground collaboration 199;
part-time faculty, training limitations
(recognition) 199; Project Gateways,
theoretical grounding 190–2
fluency: achievement 225; valuation/
measurement process 225–6
*Framework for Success in Postsecondary
Writing* 42
French only writing expectations 158
friend relationships, importance 68–9

Generation 1.5, term (usage) 4, 197, 200
genre: genre-appropriate texts, analysis
25; genre-based approach 18; genre
families 43
Gentil, Guillaume 101, 113, 158, 164, 165
governmental sponsorship, impact 111
grade-level academic tasks, student
preparation 22–23

hacked space 205, 212
"Hanging in the Balance" (NCLR) 136
Harklau, Linda 1–3, 5–10, 22, 56, 57, 96,
102, 117, 118, 128, 173, 182
higher education: options, reduction
10–11; socioliterate interactions/support
73–6
high schools *see also* secondary schools:
at-risk high school students, literacy
development (study) 65–6; COB
model, power relations *52*; colleges,
discontinuities 31; Communities of
Practice (CoP) framework, application
119–20; contextualization 50; data
collection/analysis 51; feedback
inconsistencies 52–6; graduation
ambition, example 90–1; high school-
to-transition 74; inbound trajectories,
example 123–5; ML writers 17;
participation trajectories, contrast
121–3; peers, interaction 126; resident

ML writers, forced representation 56–7; writing challenge imbalance 54–5; writing instruction/practices 52–6; writing, non-English-related general education courses 53; writing practices, distinctions 53–4
Hispanic-Serving Institution (HSI) 169, 174; designation 189; first-year writing 189, 231–2
home language literacy skills, importance 145
Horner, Bruce 159, 160, 173, 190, 225

identification: process 224; teaching 216; core principles 220–6; courses, placement 31; ELL classification, increase 82; FYC curriculum/goals 218–26; institutional context 216–7; language salience 223–4; placement practices 106; shuttling, understanding (language negotiation) 220–1; student interlanguage, recognition 221–3; theoretical justification 217–8
identity: anti-writing identity 113; formation, process 121–2
immigrant: experience 56–7; mosaics 157; number, increase 143
Immigrant Youth Justice League (IYJL) 134, 137; DACA guide 138
inbound trajectories 123–5
in-class peer response techniques 222
in-class test preparation 104–5
in-class writing tasks, frustration 106–7
individual-level sponsorships 113
individual sponsors 111; role 111–12
informational text 39–40
in-school literacy practices, out-of-school literacy practices, bridge 57
in-school writing, importance 57
institutional sponsorship, impact 111
institutions (literacy sponsor examples) 100instructor, students (communication improvement) 195
integration 231–2
Intensive English Program (IEP) 217–28
interlanguage: commitment 220; consideration 221–2
internationalization 2, 171, 229–30, 234–5
international student influx, long-term immigrant students (challenges) 233–4
Internet access, limitation 107

Kanno, Yasko 1–3, 5, 6, 10, 11, 22, 96, 101, 117, 169, 182

L1 writing teachers, ML student awareness 3
L2 literacy, acquisition (facilitation) 144
L2 specialists, writing/rhetoric specialists, foreground collaboration 199
L2 writing teachers, ML student awareness 3
language: academic proficiency, transfer 145; acquisition, subtractive bilingualism (trade inequality) 58–9; best language, selection 177; critical orientations 225; development, elements 50; expectations 42; learning, purposes 71–2; negotiation (Canada) 163–4; negotiation, shuttling (understanding) 220–1; policy (Canada) 160–3; practices/policies, examination 157; primary language skills, preservation 59; salience 220, 223–4; skills, ranking 7–8; socialization framework 50; spoken language, application 41–2; strongest language, identification 176–7; student interlanguage, recognition 221–3; students, language backgrounds 176–7; surface aspects 145; usage, contexts 176
language minority college composition students: assignment submission 180; attendance 180; basic skills, requirement 178; best language, selection 177; challenges 173, 177–81; course technologies, access 177, 178; course textbooks, access 177–8; English language, challenges 179; findings, summary 181–2; first-year composition, academic behaviors 179–80; gaps, closing 182–6; language backgrounds 176–7; methods 174–5; other language usage rates 176; reading, differences 178–9; resources, access 181; responses, survey results 175–81; writing ability, student perspectives 181; writing, challenges 179
learning: collective, emphasis 205; opportunities, limitations 21–2; Universal Design for Learning (UDL), development 191
legislation: Bilingual Education Act (1968) 37; government legislation, impact 159
legitimate peripheral participation (LPP) 119; opportunities 122, 124; possibilities 127

Leki, Ilona 1; 7, 49, 64–5, 77, 173, 218
leverage points, identification 229, 235–6
librarians, embedding 208–9
limited English proficient (LEP) 5; term, usage 7
linguistic competence 221–2
linguistic diversity, addressing 162
linguistic homogeneity, myth 174
linguistic imperialism 173
linguistic minorities (LMs) 5, 117; academic writing access 118; participants, demographic profiles *120*; study 120–1
Linguistic Minority Students Go to College (Kanno/Harklau) 2
linguistic shuttling 220literacy: autonomous perspective 26; development 64–5; instruction, influences 91–2; literacy-based research 118–19; narrative project (FIU) 198; skill basis 17–18
Literacy Evaluation for Newcomer Students (LENS) 146–7
literacy sponsors: definition 100; examples 100–1; impact 99–100; postsecondary transitions (resident multilingual writers) *103*; promises/limitations 99; role 100–1
literacy sponsorship: understanding 100–1; Upward Bound (UB) example 117
long-term immigrant students, challenges 233–4
Lu, Min-Zhan 191, 225

mainstream English, curricular discontinuities 21
Matsuda, Paul Kei 1, 8, 173, 174, 189, 192, 218, 219, 220, 225
melting pot, U.S. metaphor 160
migrants: calls 136–8; guides 138; narratives 135–6; students, geographic crossover 131–2
Migration Policy Institute (MPI) report 130
monolingual literacy sponsors 106
motivation 231–2
multilingualism: acceptance 162–3; assessment analysis/discussion 194–8; assessment data 193–4; attitude/awareness, changes 196–7; course design, changes 194–6; daily basic practice, changes 194–6; faculty development 192–3; faculty students, writing/rhetoric class perspective (encouragement) 200;

goals 192; ideas/instructional materials, faculty sharing 199–200; L2 specialists, writing/rhetoric specialists, foreground collaboration 199; new norm, faculty development (re-envisioning) 189; part-time faculty, training limitations (recognition) 199; prevalence 173–4; Project Gateways, theoretical grounding 190–2; reclamation 219–20; sequestration 164–5; usage, instructor perspective 225
multilingualism, teaching 216; advancing multilingual (ML) education 157; audience, 198; core principles 220–6; FYC curriculum/goals 218–26; institutional context 216–7; language salience 223–4; pedagogical strategies, processes 196–7; shuttling, understanding (language negotiation) 220–1; student interlanguage, recognition 221–3; theoretical justification 217–8
multilingual (ML) students: academic tracking 9; acceleration/integration/motivation 231–2; curriculum, narrowing 8; ESL courses, usage 32; experiences 5–6; family responsibilities 10; higher education, socioliterate interactions/support 73–7; high school experiences, scholarship (limitation) 22; learning opportunities, limitations 21–2; research 18–19; resident ML students, attention 5–6; social networks, composition 68–9; social networks, contacts (domain percentages) *69*; social networks/support (role) 63; social networks, usage (reasons) 64–5; social networks, writing (impact) 69–72;teacher preparedness 8–9; UC Davis, expendable/marginalized/strategic resident ML students 230–1; work responsibilities 9–10; writing activities (percentages) *70*; writing process familiarity, teacher assumption 29–30; writing/social realities 6–10; writing, social support 72–3
multiliteracies: acceptance 162–3; defining 51

narrative text 39–40
National Assessment of Education Progress (NAEP) 37–8
National Council of La Raza (NCLR) 134

National Council of Teachers of English 42
national education legislation: English
Language Unity Act (2005) 161; impact
8; National Defense Authorization
Act, DADT inclusion 132; National
Language Act (2003) 161
National Governors Association Center
for Best Practices (NGA), CCSS
development 36
National Writing Project 42
native English speakers (NES), FYC
experience 216–17
negative social support, presence 76
negotiation, curriculum appropriation 220
New Literacies Studies (NLS), perspective
23, 32
No Child Left Behind (NCLB) 7, 8;
impact 84–5; institutionalized standards
37; trends 18

online training materials, adjunct faculty
response 194, 195
out-of-school literacy practices, 69;
bridging to in-school literacy practices
57, 69; out-of-school writing, computer
creation/sharing 105

Partnership for Assessment of Readiness for
College and Careers (PARCC) 92
part-time faculty: member perspective,
first-year writing class reading
assignment 195; training limitations,
recognition 199
Pathways to Education (P2E) 65–7;
personnel, interaction 75; tutor,
experience 74
peer relationships, saliency 127–8;
contribution of peer cohorts 124;
identification 123–4; impact of peer
dynamics, 117;
Pell Grants 9, 11
placement: courses 3; placement practices
106
postsecondary education: English learner
nonparticipation 3; multilingualism,
sequestration 1645; pursuit, goal 75;
transitions into, 103
power relationships 51, *52, 55*
pre-college outreach programs: literacy-
based research 118–19; potentials/
limitations 118–19
primary language skills, preservation 59
Project Gateways 170; initiative, usage 198;
theoretical grounding 190–2

reading 7; efficiency skills *67*
Reading/English Language Arts, content
standards (student performance) 37
remedial writing course, usage 106
resident multilingualism, curricular
paradigm (embracing) 216
resident multilingual (ML) students
(resident multilinguals): academic
tracking 9; attention 1; community
college advantages 11; curriculum,
narrowing 8; family responsibilities
10; first-year composition 169; higher
education, options (reduction) 10–11;
identification, absence 217; place,
internationalization 229; poverty 9;
teacher preparedness 8–9; visibility
234–6; work responsibilities 9–10
resident multilingual (ML) writers: forced
representations 56–7; literacy sponsors
(postsecondary transitions) *103*;
secondary curriculum 49; transitions,
sponsorship perspective 101–2
resident multilingual (ML) youths
(postsecondary schooling transitions),
literacy sponsors (promises/limitations)
99; alternative sponsorship 111–12;
cases 104–5; counter-sponsorship
108–11; discussion 112–15; findings
104–12; implications 114–15; matches,
cases 104, 105–8; mismatches, cases
104, 108–11; participants, settings *102*;
sponsorships, facilitation 105–8; study/
data collection/analysis 102–4
rural high schools: administrative
turnover 84; assessments/standards
movements 85; call to action 91–3;
challenges 83; discussion 91–3; English
language learners 82; funding shifts 85;
information/challenges 84–93; linguistic
diversity 82–3; preliminary findings
85–7; schools/students, examples
87–91; staff turnover 84; supplementary
educational services 84–5; teachers 84

secondary schools *see also* high schools:
COB model, power relations *52*;
contextualization 50; culture,
assimilation 90; data collection/
analysis 51; domain 69, 72; feedback
inconsistencies 52–6; NCLB, impact
84–5; performance 7; research
18–19; resident ML writers, forced
representation 56–7; students, cliques
123; writing challenge imbalance 54–5;

writing instruction/practices 52–6; writing, non-English-related general education courses 53; writing practices, distinctions 53–4

secondary curriculum, resident ML writers: COB model, power relations 52; conceptual framework 50; data collection/analysis 51; feedback inconsistencies 52–6; findings/discussion 52–9; forced representations 56–7; participants 50; postmethod approach 49; study, contextualization 50; writing instructions/practices 52–6

second language acquisition (SLA) 216–17

second language literacy (development), home language literacy skills (importance) 145

second language writing (SLW): contexts 65; specialists, awareness 233

Severino, Carol 195

short essay topics 27–33; college composition, emphases 30–1; college/high school discontinuities 31; discussion 31–3; Transitions, Senior Lit class (discontinuities) 29–30

shuttling: sense 225; understanding 220–1

silos, combatting 234–6

short-term amnesty 132

Silva, Tony 1, 7, 8, 49, 173

small-town high schools see rural high schools

social networks: composition 68–9; contacts, domain percentages 69; domain 68; domain percentage 72; protocol 68; role 63; usage, reasons 64–5

social relationships, impact 65

social support: importance 75–6; negative social support, presence 76; role 63; social network, domain percentage 72; usage, reasons 64–5

sponsors 95; bilingual literacy sponsors 106; corralling 112; counter-sponsors 101; literacy sponsors 99–101; matrix, creation 103; monolingual literacy sponsors 106; range 105–6

sponsorship: alternative 111–12; counter-sponsorship 108–11; facilitation 105–8; financial sponsorship, public sources 104; mis-matches 104; perspective 101–2

Standard Academic English (SAE) 218

standardized English/reading, U.S. ideologies 165

Standards Based Assessment (SBA) 88–9, 91

standards movements, impact 8; see also Common Core State Standards, No Child Left Behind

STAR test 89

state funding, impact 7

Student Adjustment Act 132

Student Parent Support Workers (SPSWs) 75

students: academic success 64–5; at-risk high school students, literacy development (study) 65–6; biliteracy, study 164–5; cliques 123; cohesive/interactive experience, creation (initiatives) 203; college and career ready 42; divisions (creation), tracking (impact) 123; ELL classification, increase 82; future plans, discussion 75–6; instructors, communication improvement 195; interactions/immersions/interventions, fostering 211–12; interlanguage, recognition 221–3; language minority college composition students, challenges 173; long-term immigrant students, challenges 233–4; multilingual (ML) students 5–10; reflective versatility, capitalization 220; self-identification 206; social networks, composition 68–9; student-created discourses, analysis 204; student-hacked/created place 205; undocumented students, exclusion 137; written reflections 204

subtractive bilingualism, language acquisition (trade inequality) 58–9

supplementary educational services (SESs), provision (requirement) 85–6

support, institutional: composition classrooms, librarians (embedding) 204; Composition Conference Series for Writing, Inquiry, and Student Engagement (CompoCon) 170, 203, 204, 207–8

teachers: preparedness 7, 8–9; TESOL-certified/bilingual-certified teachers, shortage 84, 87

teaching assistants (TAs): appointments, importance 76–7; preparation 199; service 192

technology: access 178; self-sponsored/peer-sponsored use 102; sponsor, role 105

Test Of English as a Foreign Language (TOEFL): certified teachers, shortage 84; exam scores 2; research 17–18; scores, student tracking 229

text: identification process 224; incorporation, example 54–5; rhetorical analysis 198

text types 39–41; CCSS perspective 42–3; consideration 43; expectation 42

theme-related texts, analysis 25

Title V grant, FIU application 190

tracking 9; divisions 123; usage 118

transitional writing students, people/research/media (interconnection) 202; CompoCon 204, 207–8; embedded librarians 208–9; everyday curriculum 211–12; hacked/created space 212; initiatives, integration 206–11; interactive expertise 211; local contexts 206; scholarly contexts 204–6; Socially Mediated Classroom 209–11; students, interactions/immersions/interventions, fostering 211–12; suggestions 212–13

Transitions: class opportunities 30; curricular ideologies, conflict 24–6; discussion 3–5; disruption, juxtaposition 3–4; Senior Lit class, discontinuities 29–30; students, progress 26

transitions: problems 111; support 107

translingualism 96, 139, 141, 219, 225

Trimbur, John 159, 160, 173, 191, 225

TRIO programs (U.S. Federal TRiO Programs) 119; funding 96

undocumented students (U.S. contexts) 131–3; DACA qualification requirements 132; exclusion 137; Undocumented Student Guide to College (IYJL) 138; university transfer, Dreamer assistance 133

United States: economic realities, impact 177; government legislation, impact 159; high schools, ML students (writing/social realities) 6–10; melting pot, metaphor 160; standards 37–8

Universal Design for Learning (UDL), development 191

Upward Bound (UB) 95–121; No Discount Policy 126, 128; participation trajectories, contrast 121–3; participation trajectories, redirection 125; peers, dissociation 125–6; peers, positive impact 125; pre-college outreach programs, potentials/limitations 118–19

WRITE Institute: genre discourse, skills discourse BA precedence 31–2; participation 26; writing curriculum, usage 25

writing: ability, language minority student perspectives 181; activities, percentages 70; CCSS, impact/specifics 39–42; challenge, imbalance 54–5; curricula, discontinuities 21; developmental trajectory, mind (habits) 42–4; difficulty 7–8; discourses 24; experts 106; feedback, absence (consistency) 55; first-year writing (Hispanic-serving university) 189; in-school writing, importance 57; instruction/assessment, CCSS implications 36; instruction, non-English-related general education classes (struggles) 52–3; neutral/universal perspective 17–18, 23–4; perspective 49; process, ML student familiarity (teacher assumption) 29–30; remedial writing course, usage 106; samples, usage 103; social purposes 70; social support 72–3; specialists, L2/rhetoric specialists (foreground collaboration) 199; sponsors, absence 113; student outcomes 41–2; success, example 112; text types 39–41; workshops, classmate valuation (problems) 124; writing-related support 74

writing-across-the-curriculum collaboration, construction 59

Writing and Reading Alignment Team (WRAT), creation 232

writing-in-the-disciplines (WID) approach 159

writing program administrator (WPA): activist stances, encouragement 230; examination 170; impact 183; interaction 199; time, investment 185

written accent, concept 195–6

ESL & Applied Linguistics Professional Series

Eli Hinkel, Series Editor

Ortmeier-Hooper/ Ruecker	*Linguistically Diverse Immigrant and Resident Writers: Transitions from High School to College*
Johnson/ Golombek	*Mindful L2 Teacher Education: A Sociocultural Perspective on Cultivating Teachers' Professional Development*
Hinkel	*Teaching English Grammar to Speakers of Other Languages*
McKay/Brown	*Teaching and Assessing EIL in Local Contexts Around the World*
Dörnyei/Henry/ Muir	*Motivational Currents in Language Learning: Frameworks for Focused Interventions*
Jones/Richards, Eds.	*Creativity in Language Teaching: Perspectives from Research and Practice*
Evans/Anderson/ Eggington, Eds.	*ESL Readers and Writers in Higher Education: Understanding Challenges, Providing Support*
Hinkel	*Effective Curriculum for Teaching L2 Writing: Principles and Techniques*
Farrell	*Promoting Teacher Reflection in Second-Language Education: A Framework for TESOL Professionals*
Nunan/Richards	*Language Learning Beyond the Classroom*
Christison/Murray	*What English Language Teachers Need to Know Volume III: Designing Curriculum*
Turner	*Using Statistics in Small-scale Language Education Research: Focus on Non-parametric Data*
Hong/Pawan	*The Pedagogy and Practice of Western-trained Chinese English Language Teachers: Foreign Education, Chinese Meanings*
Lantolf/Poehner	*Sociocultural Theory and the Pedagogical Imperative in L2 Education: Vygotskian Praxis and the Research/Practice Divide*
Brown	*Pronunciation and Phonetics: A Practical Guide for English Language Teachers*
Birch	*English Grammar Pedagogy: A Global Perspective*
Liu	*Describing and Explaining Grammar and Vocabulary in ELT: Key Theories and Effective Practices*
deOliviera/Silva, Eds.	*L2 Writing in Secondary Classrooms: Student Experiences, Academic Issues, and Teacher Education*
Andrade/Evans	*Principles and Practices for Response in Second Language Writing: Developing Self-Regulated Learners*
Sayer	*Ambiguities and Tensions in English Language Teaching: Portraits of EFL Teachers as Legitimate Speakers*
Alsagoff/McKay/ Hu/Renandya, Eds.	*Principles and Practices of Teaching English as an International Language*
Kumaravadivelu	*Language Teacher Education for A Global Society: A Modular Model for Knowing, Analyzing, Recognizing, Doing, and Seeing*
Vandergrift/Goh	*Teaching and Learning Second Language Listening: Metacognition in Action*
LoCastro	*Pragmatics for Language Educators: A Sociolinguistic Perspective*
Nelson	*Intelligibility in World Englishes: Theory and Practice Around the World*

Visit www.routledge.com/education for additional information on titles in the ESL & Applied Linguistics Professional Series

LINGUISTICALLY DIVERSE IMMIGRANT AND RESIDENT WRITERS

This cutting-edge collection focuses on the important transitions of multilingual students as they move from secondary to postsecondary education. Co-edited by two established scholars in this area, the book combines scholarly rigor with a compassionate focus on a growing but often invisible student population in U.S. education.

Dana Ferris, University of California-Davis, USA

Spotlighting the challenges and realities faced by linguistically diverse immigrant and resident students in U.S. secondary schools and in their transitions from high school to community colleges and universities, this book looks at programs, interventions, and other factors that help or hinder them as they make this move. Chapters from teachers and scholars working in a variety of contexts build rich understandings of how high school literacy contexts, policies such as the proposed DREAM Act and the Common Core State Standards, bridge programs like Upward Bound, and curricula redesign in first-year college composition courses designed to recognize increasing linguistic diversity of student populations affect the success of this growing population of students as they move from high school into higher education.

Christina Ortmeier-Hooper is an Associate Professor of English at the University of New Hampshire, USA.

Todd Ruecker is an Assistant Professor of English at the University of New Mexico, USA.